Perfect Pitch
A LIFE STORY

Perfect Pitch

A LIFE STORY

NICOLAS SLONIMSKY

Oxford   New York
OXFORD UNIVERSITY PRESS
1988

Oxford University Press, Walton Street, Oxford OX2 6DP
Oxford   New York   Toronto
Delhi   Bombay   Calcutta   Madras   Karachi
Petaling Jaya   Singapore   Hong Kong   Tokyo
Nairobi   Dar es Salaam   Cape Town
Melbourne   Auckland
and associated companies in
Beirut   Berlin   Ibadan   Nicosia

Oxford is a trade mark of Oxford University Press

Published in the United States
by Oxford University Press (USA)

British Library Cataloguing in Publication Data
Slonimsky, Nicolas
Perfect pitch: a life story.
1. Slonimsky, Nicolas   2. Musicians —
Biography
I. Title
780'.92'4   ML410.S5993/
ISBN 0-19-315155-3

Library of Congress Cataloging in Publication Data
Slonimsky, Nicolas, 1894–   1996
Perfect pitch.
1. Slonimsky, Nicolas, 1894–   . 2. Musicians—
United States—Biography. 3. Lexicographers—United
States—Biography.   I. Title.
ML423.S57A3   1988   780'.92'4 [B]   87-11107
ISBN 0-19-315155-3

Set by Computerised Typesetting Services, Finchley, London N12 8LY
Printed in the United States of America

My memory unfurls
    its lengthy scroll before me —
I shudder, and I curse, but I do not
    efface the wistful lines

(Pushkin)

There is a luxury in self-dispraise

(Wordsworth)

Entbehren sollst du, sollst entbehren!

(Goethe)

CONTENTS

LIST OF ILLUSTRATIONS

CHAPTER 1

ST PETERSBURG

When I was six years old my mother told me I was a genius.

This revelation came as no surprise to me. Even at that tender age I was aware that my family was a hotbed for geniuses, on both my maternal and paternal sides. Among them were revolutionary poets, literary critics, translators, economists, mathematicians, chess masters, inventors of useless artificial languages, speculative philosophers, and Hebrew scholars. My peculiar genius, however, was to express itself in music.

My mother wanted me to be a boy, and her wish was my command even in obstetrical matters. She was eager to alternate the sexes of her children. The oldest of her children, my brother Alexander, was born in 1881, followed by my sister Julia in 1884. After that there was a succession of stillborn babies, including 'three Frenchies', as my mother described them, a set of triplets miscarried during her stay in France. In order to bring me forth unfragmented, my mother had to stay in bed for a year. The increased term of gestation was my mother's poetic licence for dramatic effect, and she never tired of reminding me what sacrifices she had made for my sake.

So precocious was I that even before I was born and before my gender was determined I was named 'Newtonchik', a diminutive Newton. A circumstantial account of my birth is recorded in my elder brother's diary, miraculously preserved across the threshold of the century. Here are the minutes (all dates are in the old style Russian calendar):

14 April 1894: the entire family is in a state of feverish expectation. Our Newton is to arrive during the night. Aunt Lisa came at 10 o'clock; Aunt Liuba came at 11 o'clock. Mother had ten labour contractions.

15 April: Joy!! In the morning I was awakened by mother's moans. I heard the voices of the doctor and Aunt Liuba. Suddenly mother cried out in a most agonized voice, followed by a great commotion in the bedroom. Aunt Liuba whispered: 'A boy, a boy!!!' I jumped from my bed like a madman. It was 5 o'clock in the morning. I hurried to wake up my sister. At 5.15 we were summoned by Aunt Liuba to have our first look at Newtonchik, who was lying on the couch in the living room all swathed in blankets, with his little fists in his mouth.

16 April: He sleeps, then screams.

17 April: Today we had the honour of giving Newtonchik a bath. I poured the water and my sister held the towel. We were allowed to repeat the ritual for several days.
18 April: He begins to smile.

There are no further entries in my brother's diary until 24 October 1894; on that date I was already named Kolyenka, a diminutive of my given name, Nikolai. Alexander writes: 'Kolyenka sits in my room while I study my Latin syntax (*cum inversum & iterativum*). He's trying to grab the book, but his nurse Olga won't let him. He says Bah, gah, mah, nah!'

Following the Russian literary tradition of celebrating the arrival of a new child in rhymed verse, my brother wrote an ode entitled simply, 'To a Babe'.

> When at my daily leisure hours
> I sit with you, my angel dear,
> I feel new strength, I feel new powers
> And joyful freedom from all fear.
>
> I wish for you not only pleasure
> Not only happiness of soul,
> For happiness is but a measure
> Of a more lofty human goal.
>
> I wish that you would gain new wisdom
> I wish that you would find true love
> I wish that you would conquer evil
> And end your days in feasts of joy!

On my sixty-eighth birthday in 1962, when I was already a father and twice a grandfather, Alexander wrote to me in Boston from Moscow:

In a little corner of my brain there is still preserved the image of a little boy who about sixty-six years ago demanded that I stand on a chair to get the *luna* [Russian word for moon] for him. *Kolia nyet pau*, he would say, the last word being baby talk for drop. Where is located the imprint of this scene among the molecules of my brain, since my entire body has changed a number of times since then? Could the central control room in which all these impressions are integrated into a distinct image be what we call the soul? When the famous biologist Pavlov was congratulated by his colleagues for having liquidated the meaningless concept of an immaterial soul, he replied, 'Let us not talk about things we cannot understand'. But if even Pavlov himself implicitly accepted the possibility of the existence of an entity commonly called the soul, then why should I not believe that, since nothing disappears without leaving a trace, then something must survive within an incorporeal soul?

The births of my brothers Vladimir in 1895 and Michael in 1897 were recorded but briefly in Alexander's diary. In 1897 Alexander buried in the garden of our summer *dacha* a box containing a message to posterity to be dug up after a certain number of years. In this message he set down the year of his own death as 1945. He wrote in 1962: 'Seventeen years have elapsed since the appointed date of my death, but I still continue to burden this planet with my presence. We are situated in two different hemispheres, I in Russia, you in America, but our mutual psychology is remarkably alike.'

Alexander died in 1964. I, too, survived the projection of my death date; on the back of a photograph taken in 1910 I marked the years of my life as 1894-1967.

In a 1941 letter my mother offered her own account of my birth. In her detailed recital of my arrival, she wrote in the present tense and third person singular, as if she were the narrator of the event rather than its central participant:

All of a sudden, a piercing scream is heard: the maid rushes out of the bedroom, crying, 'They slaughtered the poor woman!' Your brother and your sister try to enter the bedroom, but are not allowed to come in. Then suddenly there is another cry: it sounds like a little kitten or a puppy. The door opens, Aunt Liuba comes out and announces triumphantly, 'You have a little brother!' 'New-tonchik?' 'Yes, either Newton or God's fool. Time will tell.' But all that your brother and sister can see is a little red face sticking out from a bundle of quickly arranged swaddling clothes. They are cautioned not to make loud noises, and are promised as a reward to be allowed to help bathe the baby. Father tries to help too, testing the temperature of the water, but he is pushed away by Aunt Liuba who is in command. Quite contrary to his usual meek disposition, your father demands attention. 'Too much water,' he cautions, 'You will drown our New-tonchik.' Your brother and sister are now allowed to approach the bed on which the tiny red body is being powdered and dressed in a doll-like shirt covering the front of the body with the back remaining exposed. They are fascinated by the novel experience; on previous occasions they never had a chance to see their little brothers; the doctor always carried them away in his satchel, like broken dolls. They admire Newtonchik. 'What a beautiful little baby, what pretty little eyes!' Suddenly, Newtonchik's face wrinkles up and he lets go a fearful cry; it seems incredible that such a tiny creature could make such a loud sound. 'Give him to me, he's hungry,' mother says. Newtonchik is placed at mother's breast, and after several attempts manages to latch his little mouth on the nipple; he will not let go until he is completely satisfied with mother's nourishing milk. Thus, to the supreme joy of the Slonimsky family, took place the entrance into life of the future genius of music.

A studio photograph taken of me in my mother's arms a few weeks after my birth shows a great physical resemblance between my mother, then 37 years old, and myself when I was 37. Once out of swaddling clothes, I grew fast. Under Alexander's solicitous ministrations, I learned the Russian alphabet almost as soon as I could talk. I became familiar with the world of books, and I proudly identified my father's publications, among them the fine edition of his *Fundamental Problems of Politics* published in St Petersburg in 1889, with a Latin epigraph from Seneca and a dedication to my mother. As I grew I became passionately interested in the philosophical problem of individual existence. The question how I became a separate individual bothered me. The word 'individual' stems from Latin and means 'indivisible'. It is the equivalent of the Greek word 'atom'. But if I was but an atom among quadrillion quintillions of other atoms making up the material universe, how could I be sure that I was me?

It was discovered early in my life that I possessed the precious gift of perfect pitch, which enabled me to name immediately and without fail any note played on the piano or other musical instrument. My maternal aunt, Isabelle Vengerova, later to become a famous piano teacher, took me under her wing, and on 6 November 1900, according to the old Russian calendar, gave me my first piano lesson.

I was exhibited to admiring relatives and friends for whose pleasure I rendered the popular tune, 'Little Bird, What did you do? I drank vodka, So did you.' Pretty soon it was discovered that I was not only a piano genius but also a wizard in memorizing meaningless numbers and calendar dates. (I recall distinctly my distress in the year 1900 when I realized that the insistence of the Russian church on making it a leap year by intercalating the extra day 29 February had increased the discrepancy between the civilized Western and the backward Julian calendars, adhered to in uncultured Russia, from twelve to thirteen days.)

I have a lovely theory about perfect (or absolute) pitch. My contention, based on numerous observations and experiments, is that perfect pitch is an innate capacity, which cannot be cultivated. Musical children who have it possess an immediate appreciation of pitch. I knew that E-flat was E-flat when struck on the piano when I was a small child, and I knew that it was as different from E-natural as red is from pink. Indeed, Isaac Newton drew his spectrum of colours analogously to the musical scale. Singers can often name a note correctly by the tension of their vocal chords necessary to produce a certain note, but this is a secondary or oblique perception of pitch.

When Newton was asked whether he believed in God he said, 'hypotheses non fingo'. As a mere Newtonchik, I felt free to fictionalize (past participle of *fingere* is *fictus* in Latin) any hypothesis that came into my head. Ruminating about noumenal matters, I postulated the existence of a subliminal unit of intellect (which I should like to term Intellectum), a module of organized vacuum which possesses neither mass nor energy but is capable of operating incorporeally in a putative zero dimension and governing such immensely significant intellectual units as mathematics and music. That such faculties have local centres in the brain does not change their inherent immateriality. The mystery lies in the working hypothesis that incorporeal essences can be transmitted by heredity into new bodies and souls.

George Bernard Shaw, who was not given to religious beliefs, speculated in a fanciful paragraph in the preface to his play *Back to Methusalah*, that 'a pianist may be born with a specific pianistic aptitude which he can bring out as soon as he can physically control his hands'. He advanced the bold assumption that 'acquirements can be assimilated and scored as congenital qualifications'. It is not an idle corollary that a specific intellectual or musical disposition can be similarly embedded in a non-dimensional space.

The possession of absolute pitch attests a musical predisposition. However, the lack of it does not exclude musical talent, or even genius. Neither Wagner nor Tchaikovsky had absolute pitch, while a legion of mediocre composers possessed ·it to the highest degree. In our family, only my Aunt Isabelle Vengerova, my younger brother, and myself had it. My aunt, who often played the piano in our house, discovered this precious faculty in us when we were very young. Since I was the older, and also a much more aggressive boy than Vladimir, my ability to name notes on the piano was revealed quite early, and became a prize exhibit for all comers. I enjoyed such demonstrations, indeed they were the formative elements of the egocentricity that plagued me throughout my young years.

I learned the notes according to the syllabic notation common in all Latin countries and in Russia: Do Re Me Fa Sol La Si Do. I experienced some discomfort at modes that could not be classified as major or minor. When Aunt Isabelle let me play a piece by Grieg in E minor, lacking in the mandatory leading tone D-sharp, I felt that something was wrong. I felt uncomfortable that the imitation of the subject in the fugue in C minor from the first book of Bach's *Well-tempered Clavier* dropped a fifth rather than the fourth as in the exposition.

When I was 14 my aunt decided to enrol me in her class at the St Petersburg Conservatory. I was led into the admission room and looked in awe at the director, the famous composer Glazunov, whose corporeal immensity (he weighed over 300 lbs) matched the contrapuntal solidity of his music. Maxmillian Steinberg, professor of theory and orchestration and son-in-law of Rimsky-Korsakov, played two notes together. I named them. Interested, he played the second inversion of the dominant-seventh chord, in the key of C. I felt like a lark ascending, and, without a moment's hesitation, named all the notes. Then Steinberg tried a diminished-seventh chord: C, E-flat, F-sharp, and A. I rattled off the notes with complete assurance. At that point Steinberg went over to Glazunov and whispered in his ear. (I did not have to be told what it was, and my ego swelled in my adolescent breast.) Glazunov sat at the piano and played a dissonant, but easily resolvable chord, F, C, B-flat, E, A, in this order, from bass to treble. It was a very Russian chord, beloved of Tchaikovsky, Rimsky-Korsakov, and Glazunov himself. Glazunov was visibly impressed when I named all the notes without fail. Aunt Isabelle, who was present, said nothing, but her face radiated family pride. To be accepted in her class, I had to play a few well-learned piano pieces by Schumann, a Chopin prelude, and *Melody in F* by Anton Rubinstein.

Half a century later I received from the archivist of the Leningrad Conservatory the transcript of the minutes of my entrance examinations, with notations by Glazunov: 'Despite his youthful years, the boy has already achieved a certain perfection in his playing, along with an attractive and powerful touch at the keyboard.' At the next examination Glazunov expanded on his first impression: 'An excellent musical virtuoso talent. His playing is full of elegance and taste.' And he put down grade 5 (the highest in the Russian school system) and, in parenthesis, '(talent)'. This '5 (talent)' was whispered about by my mother for the benefit of any newcomer, so that I developed a morbid aversion to the phrase.

Was I ever a wunderkind? My mother assured me that I was, and she did her best to protect my delicate fingers from the roughness and toughness of the outside world. When she took me to kindergarten, she made a speech to the boys in the class (schools in Russia were not co-educational): 'My son is a pianist,' she warned the class, 'and you must be careful not to hurt his hands. You must not play rough games with him.' The consequence of such admonitions was predictable. The very next day I was beaten up.

As a small child I was deeply jealous of competitors. No one could possibly match my talents, my mother assured me, and no one should try. I was, therefore, shocked when a Spanish boy pianist named Pepito Arriola gave a recital in St Petersburg in a programme of pieces I regarded as my speciality, including Schumann's *Scenes From Childhood*. His picture appeared in the papers, an honour I had not yet achieved. He was chubby in a healthy Spanish way: I was skinny in a neurotic Russian way. He wore a crown of curly hair; I could never grow a curvilinear chevelure. He was dressed in short velvet pants of cerulean blue; I had to be content with a plain cotton brand. But above all, he was Spanish! Being Spanish was the height of heart's desire for Russian boys and girls.

Half a century later James Francis Cooke, editor of *Étude* magazine to which I contributed an article on child prodigies, asked me if I knew the name of the Spanish pianist José Arriola, known as 'Pepito'. Pepito Arriola! That magic name! The boy in short velvet pants with curly hair! Cooke was trying to raise funds for Arriola, who was very ill, living in poverty in Barcelona. Would I help by word or deed? Of course I would. The only reference work in which I could find Arriola's name was a Spanish music dictionary, published in 1931. (I have written repeatedly to Spanish lexicographers to find out whether Pepito is still alive, but no one seems to know.)

When I was young, my very old maternal grandmother used to tell me about a marvellous Jewish boy violinist named Roman Friedman who played for the Czar. (All Jewish violinists seem to have played for the Czar, even though he headed the most anti-Semitic government before Hitler.) So wonderful was little Roman that he was taken across the ocean to America where he became a famous violinist. 'Practise hard, and perhaps you, too, will become famous and go to America,' my grandmother used to say with a sigh.

In 1932 I conducted a pair of concerts with the Los Angeles Philharmonic. My programme included *En Saga* by Sibelius, which had a passage for a quartet of solo violins. One of the four violinists, a middle-aged baldish man named Roman, played uncomfortably out of tune. Not wishing to offend him by singling him out as a dissonant member in four-part harmony, I let it go. He came to see me afterwards, and, speaking Russian, told me that he had once played at my grandmother's house in Minsk. 'I have since dropped my last name,' he remarked, 'and adopted my first name Roman as my legal identity.' Roman! He was the 'great violinist' who played for the Czar, became famous, and went to America.

In a way, Russian Marxism is intertwined with my family history, for it was my father who published, in 1890, the first book on Karl Marx in the Russian language, entitled *The Economic Doctrine of Karl Marx*. The book was soon translated into German, indicative of its importance in political and sociological circles. Lenin, who was 20 years old at the time of its original publication, must have read it. My cousin, the Polish poet Antoni Slonimski, remarked, half facetiously, that my family was directly responsible for the Bolshevik upheaval, for it was from my father's book that Lenin became acquainted with Marx's doctrine of a proletarian revolution. Lenin's own writings do not support this entertaining notion. In his political pamphlet, published in the underground Russian press in 1894, under a sarcastic title, 'Who Are These Friends of the People, and How Do They Fight Against the Social Democrats', Lenin has some nasty words to say about my father: 'Mr Slonimsky clearly, and unambiguously, formulates his standpoint as an ordinary liberal, utterly incapable of understanding contemporary bourgeois society. His propaganda in favour of small peasant ownership reveals the entire reactionary utopianism of his outlook.'

Tolstoy read my father's book too, and made extensive comments on the margin of his copy, which was lent to my father after Tolstoy's death. I tried, unsuccessfully, to find out whether a copy of my father's book on Marx was kept in Lenin's personal library; it is not included even in the most complete Soviet bibliographies on Marx, undoubtedly because of my father's unorthodox view on Marx's economic theories. But the German translation of the book is duly listed in old German reference works.

My father was the foreign affairs editor for the Russian liberal monthly *The Messenger of Europe* (the very title of the magazine expressed its Western orientation). Besides his comments on foreign affairs, he also wrote on general social problems. When he published an article on suicide, I was disappointed that he failed to mention in it some suicides among my own friends.

My mother always pictured my father as an unworldly intellectual who read Tacitus in the original Latin before going to bed, so that his mind was far away from the daily concerns of domestic life. (His signed and dated copy of Tacitus is still a cherished keepsake for me, even though I read Latin with difficulty.) She liked to compare my father with Simeon Stylites, the medieval monk who spent most of his life sitting atop a column, surveying the bustling life below with philosophical equanimity.

I remember my father as an idealist. His own human fault was his tardiness in delivering to the printer his monthly magazine articles, written in a fine calligraphic hand. He often worked all night long to meet the deadline. 'I will probably be late even for my own funeral,' he once remarked. He died in January 1918, just before the publication of the last issue of *The Messenger of Europe*, which was swept away by the Revolution. This last issue carried a black-bordered obituary, beginning with the words, 'To all who hold Russian culture dear, the name of Leonid Slonimsky will remain forever memorable.'

My father never took part in any overt activities during the revolutionary turmoil of the year 1905. Even so, the dark cloud of reaction that hovered over Russia in those years touched him with its ominous shadow. The Czarist censorship took umbrage at my father's edition of the Czar's own Constitution, which the government nullified shortly after its promulgation in 1905 by inserting a number of carefully worded codicils. A frightening scene stands out in my memory: three husky Russian policemen, with faces resembling bare buttocks, invading our apartment in search of subversive books. Without saying a word, one of them pulled out from the bookshelf a dozen copies of my father's edition of the Constitution and threw them in a burlap sack which he had brought along. This act alone was enough to make a revolutionary out of a boy of 11 like myself with my almost religious respect of public print.

I have another vivid memory: During the 'liberal' years in Russia which followed the abortive revolution of 1905, my father undertook the publication of a political encyclopaedia. Only a single volume was ever published. The next volume was to include an article on the Russian Prime Minister, Count Witte. One morning a uniformed messenger appeared in our apartment bearing a letter from the Prime Minister himself, in which he asked my father to grant him an interview in order to discuss the contents of the future article on him. My brothers and I were greatly impressed by this unusual token of official appreciation of my father's work, but my father declined the suggestion.

Much esteemed Sergei Yulievich [he wrote in a letter which he handed to the messenger], I am greatly honoured by your desire to hold a colloquy and to exchange views regarding your policies. I fear, however, that such a meeting might create the impression of a preliminary arrangement as to the content of the article, so that I would appear as your semi-official spokesman. I must, therefore, respectfully decline the invitation.

While I knew little about my father's youth and education, except that he graduated in law from the University of Kiev, I certainly knew a lot about my mother's early years. To be sure, her autobiographical effusions were coloured by a desire to present herself in the best possible light: first as an idealistic young woman in the 1870s, then as a loyal wife after her marriage in 1880, and finally as a devoted mother who sacrificed the pleasures of life for her children. From objective sources and from her voluminous correspondence, it appears that as a young woman she indeed entertained radical beliefs. The outward indication of her radicalism was that she wore her hair short, which was regarded as a sign of 'nihilism'. She enrolled in the newly opened college for women in St Petersburg in the class of medicine, and managed to pass her examination in anatomy (for years to come she used to recite the Latin names for parts of the brain); but when a cadaver was brought in for scrutiny, she promptly fainted. This episode marked the end of her career as a medical student, and it was also in all probability the first instance of her epilepsy, the *grand mal* from which she suffered all her life.

In her student years my mother lodged with a room-mate in a modest room in St Petersburg. One day, when she arrived at her residence from the railroad station in a horse-driven carriage, she generously gave *na chai* (a curious Russian locution, meaning literally 'for tea') to the coachman for helping her unload her baggage, but the man still hesitated to leave. 'What are you waiting for?' she asked. 'If I may speak up,' the coachman said, 'would your ladyship let me have a few more copecks for a drink of vodka?' The mention of the intoxicating beverage made it impossible for my mother to comply with his request, for she was firmly convinced that alcohol was the devil's brew. Her landlady intervened, and sternly ordered the man away, but my mother would not abandon the argument without solving its moral problem. 'Isn't that house across the street where Dostoyevsky lives? I will ask him what to do,' my mother declared. 'Who is he, a priest?' the landlady inquired. 'Much more than a priest. He is a saint who can judge good and evil. What he declares is our moral law.'

Dostoyevsky's house was indeed on Basin Street, where my mother had her lodgings. She ran over and found Dostoyevsky's name on the door of an apartment which had its entrance from the backyard. She pulled the cord of the doorbell; a woman wearing a plain blouse opened the door. 'I want to see Fyodor Mikhailovich,' my mother said. The woman called out: 'There is a young lady to see you.' A voice answered: 'Let her in.' Dostoyevsky was working at a table, holding a metal pen in his right hand. My mother recognized him at once from his photographs, but she was taken aback by his shabby attire — an old discoloured pea-jacket, and trousers with grease spots on them. She was also surprised by the shoddy appearance of the room itself, which was small, with a low ceiling. The furniture consisted of a writing desk and a couch with two pillows covered by pieces of motley fabric. Dostoyevsky always lived on the brink of poverty. 'What is it that you wish to speak to me about?' Dostoyevsky asked. After my mother had overcome her initial embarrassment, she related to him her dilemma with the coachman. Dostoyevsky said: 'Your action was correct, but, before making any judgement, I want to know what you do for a living.' My mother explained that she was a medical student. 'All right,' Dostoyevsky continued. 'Now consider the following situation: If you, as a medical doctor, were to call on a patient who was to pay you a certain fee, would you ask for an additional payment?' 'Of course not,' my mother replied. 'Then why do you consider it proper to give a tip to a simple peasant? Do you regard him as inferior to you? Undoubtedly he felt your condescension; plain people are conscious of the inequality, and they resent it. This is the core of your problem.'

I was born thirteen years after Dostoyevsky died, but in the spring of 1917, by an extraordinary chance, I spent an evening with his widow. I had dinner at the house of the parents of one of my female piano pupils. An energetic middle-aged woman, lively and talkative, was also a guest. She kept referring to one Fyodor Mikhailovich, and after a while I ventured to

ask who he was. She replied, with a smile, 'My husband, Dostoyevsky!'
The name struck me with an electric force, and I pressed her for stories
about Dostoyevsky, which she was perfectly willing to relate. When it
came time to depart, we went out together; she hailed a horse-driven
carriage, while I took a streetcar to my place on Grand Greenery Street,
across the branch of the Neva River, and kept rehearsing in my mind our
conversation during dinner. She died a couple of months later, and I
wrote a page of reminiscences of our meeting for an afternoon Petrograd
newspaper.

In her photographs of the 1870s and early 1880s, my mother appears as
a rather attractive woman without a trace of the nervous condition that
made almost her entire life a series of 'scandales'. Her photographs of
1894, with me as a babe in arms, shows her figure as slender, but in
subsequent years she put on weight until she almost lost the power of
locomotion. She had difficulties going up the stairs in our apartment and
my two younger brothers and I regularly had to push her up the steps.
These extraordinary actions appeared normal to an unreasoning child,
and I was surprised to learn that none of my classmates had to push their
mothers up stairs. My mother's periodic epileptic fits provoked by minor
domestic altercations were a frightening sight; her body became rigid, her
face was distorted by hideous convulsions, while her muscular strength
increased prodigiously so that it required the help of several people to
move her. Sometimes a whole bucket of water was poured on her without
effect. To me, this was a rehearsal of death.

My mother had an obsession about people stealing things. Whenever
she missed an object, an alarm clock or a piece of silverware, she turned
upon the servants, and instituted a search of their miserable belongings,
not excluding even our sainted nurse Olga. To my younger brothers and
me, these scenes, accompanied by my mother's virtuoso display of shouting invectives and by the weeping of the accused, remain among the most
horrible memories of my childhood.

One day a young medical doctor, versed in the modern ways of sexual
psychology, put a blunt question to my mother: What did she do to
enlighten her growing sons about sex? 'Sex!' she exclaimed in horror. 'My
dear fellow, this is a literary family!'

It seems strange that my mother, who had attended medical classes and
actually learned a lot about bones and muscles, should have believed in
folk medicine. As a child I overheard her admonish my sister to be careful
not to take a bath in a tub in a hotel room that had been previously
occupied by a gentleman, because such an action might make her
pregnant.

As for the younger children, myself and my two brothers, my mother preferred to adopt the stork's theory of procreation, citing as her authorities the fanciful illustrations in children's books, depicting long-legged and stout-beaked birds delivering babies wrapped in swaddling clothes down chimneys. I was puzzled, however, at the age of 4 or 5, as to how the recipient of a baby delivery by aviary transport can be determined in a household where there are several women. My mother explained that a baby is brought only to a married couple, and that in my case there was no difficulty in deciding that she was the one to receive me.

But then something happened that I could not figure out. My nurse Olga began gaining weight visibly around the stomach and then had to go to the hospital. A week later she returned with a little baby, and the bulge around her stomach was gone. She was not married, so why did the stork bring her a baby? The question was unresolved until a gent, wearing a cap and a workman's jacket, appeared in the kitchen and asked to see the baby. My mother was extremely shocked by this apparition, but allowed the baby, Margarita, to stay with us. Alas, the little girl died when she was about 7 or 8. Olga bought some tinsel and paper flowers to put on her dress in the coffin, and she cried a great deal. My brother Michael described the child's death in one of his novels, even retaining the name Margarita. During the famine of 1918, which decimated the population of Petrograd, Olga proved to be the saviour of the remnants of our family by bringing food into the city from the country where she had moved. Later she joined Michael's family, and became the nurse of my nephew Sergei. I saw her in 1935 when I visited Russia. It was an emotional reunion, for in my subconscious she remained the symbol of protection from danger. Even now, whenever I sink into the deepest recesses of a nightmare, I cry out, not for my mother, but for Olga.

As I grew, I found so many contradictions in the stork theory that I began to search for a more rational explanation. We used to spend summers on a farm in the country where there were lots of animals. A sow brought forth a litter of piglets, but there were no storks around to bring them down. Besides according to my mother's mythology, storks served only people. There was also a female cat which grew very fat, but suddenly lost weight and simultaneously began carrying around four blind kittens, hiding them in dark corners. I never saw storks around to perform their obstetrical missions. It did not take me long to conclude that babies, human and animal, came out of the stomachs of their mothers. But how could they breathe there? And how did they eat? It was all very confusing.

Apart from my mother's home-made mythology, a lot of confusing information about the origin of life came to me from the Bible. Mary's words to Elizabeth, 'And the child stirred within my belly,' baffled me. I could not imagine little Jesus actually playing inside Mary. Needless to say, I had never seen a naked woman, but exposed female forms appeared to me in my dreams. I felt that there was something ineffably delectable in bodily contact with girls.

One summer day in 1908 I was romping with our governess, and she playfully threw herself down on the couch, giggling and squirming. I went after her and found myself on top of her. Then something monstrous happened in my body; an excrescence protruded from it, forming a protuberance, expanding into a promontory. Bewildered by this deformation, I jumped off the couch; the governess gave me a quizzical look. Did she notice that I had become a dragon? There are horrors that one does not talk about, sins that no act of contrition could expiate. Should I go on living with the consciousness of something inexpressibly hideous? Or should I kill my sin by destroying my own sinful body?

I decided to write to Tolstoy, who was the ultimate arbiter of moral values in literary circles of the times.

Greatly esteemed and revered Lev Nikolayevich [I would begin]. Something unspeakably horrible has happened to me of which I can judge neither cause nor effect. I was playing around with my governess and unintentionally I came in contact with her body. I know that bodies are sinful. I am not allowed to read your great novel *The Kreutzer Sonata*, but my older brother tells me that it deals with a violinist who played Beethoven with a woman pianist. Carried away by the tempestuous finale, he put his violin aside and fell into her arms. I play the piano myself, but the *Kreutzer Sonata* is too hard for me. Anyway, if it were within my technical means I would still not play it with a person of the opposite gender knowing to what dreadful consequences Beethoven's music can lead. But even without Beethoven's sinful enticement, I am already guilty of carnal contact with a governess. Should I kill myself? Please, let me have the benefit of your great soul, and tell me what to do. I am 14 years old.

I knew Tolstoy's address: His Luminosity (the proper honourific for titled men) Count Lev Nikolayevich Tolstoy, Yasnaya Polyana, Government of Tula. A stamp out of town cost only 4 copecks, and I had a fairly good stamp collection. Would it not be absolutely breathtaking if I received an answer! I would get my name and my picture in the newspaper, with a caption, 'Lev Tolstoy Answers Letter From Young Schoolboy Contemplating Suicide.' Even my mother would be proud of it! But would I dare disclose the true reason for intending to kill myself? I was not even sure that what happened to me was technically a sin, and I had no idea it was connected with that dreadful Russian monosyllable *pol*, which means 'sex'.

I never posted that letter. I never even wrote it, except in my imagination. Tolstoy died two years later. The papers said that he died in a railroad station; he decided to leave his home after receiving a letter from a student reproaching him for leading a life full of luxury while urging others to imitate the simple life of working men. What if I had been in correspondence with Tolstoy and what if he had asked me whether he should leave his home and die, and I would have written to him not to, and he would have remained in Yasnaya Polyana! My imagination ran wild, and in it I played the role of a hero saving the most valuable life in the whole world.

To supplement my father's meagre earnings, my mother borrowed money and in 1909 acquired a small movie theatre, called 'Sympathy', conveniently located on the corner of our block in St Petersburg. Her business prospered, and she would bring home a sackful of silver change each day the theatre was open for business. It was in her theatre that I received my second taste of adumbrative sex. I used to help count receipts, sitting in close proximity to the cashier, a girl of 15 whose name I remember to this day: Katia Ivanova. One day she absented herself for a few minutes, and when she came back I felt (oh, ecstasy ineffable!) her moist lips touch the nape of my neck. To say that I was transfixed with untold delight would be using ordinary language to express the state of heavenly bliss. I did not dare to tell Katia Ivanova how much I enjoyed that kiss, but, after she sat down next to me, I took her deliciously exposed left forearm in my hand, and began to play the mouth harmonica on it, sliding back and forth with my lips from the warm inside of the palm of her hand to the mysterious hollow of the inside of her elbow.

Back home I wrote down an emotional account of Katia's kiss in my diary. I put it down on my table with my schoolbooks. By the week's end everyone in the family, except my father, was reading it. Her reading done, my mother asked me whether I knew anything about syphilis. I was startled by this question. Yes, I knew that a German professor named Ehrlich discovered a cure for syphilis, called 'Salvarsan'. It was all over the newspapers. 'Well,' my mother continued, 'if you let Katia kiss you again, you will get syphilis and your brain will become soft like jelly.' Katia was promptly fired from her employment as movie cashier in my mother's cinema. A few day's later the telephone rang. 'Kolya?' a girl's voice asked. 'This is Katia.' I said nothing and hung up in fear. I learned some time afterwards that Katia had been seduced by the movie electrician. His name was Valerian Leontievich.

The concealment of the facts of life was not the only concern in my mother's educational programme. There was a deeper secret, of direct relevance to our family. We were racially Jewish, but were baptized at birth to safeguard us from the humiliation that persons of Jewish faith had to suffer in Czarist Russia. I grew up in the belief that Jews were an extinct race, like the Midians and Sumerians about whom my high school history book said, 'Midians and Sumerians were ancient races about whom nothing is known,' a sentence that became a byword of educational nonsense among Russian intellectuals.

Family legend has it that I asked the poet Nikolai Minsky (who was first married to my cousin, and later to my Aunt Zinaïda) whether there were any Jews still living. 'I wish I could see a real Jew,' I was supposed to have said, to which he replied amiably, 'Just look in the mirror.' I took it as a joke. The real traumatic discovery came only when I was 15 years old. My Aunt Isabelle was about to leave for her summer trip to Vienna, to join her second cousin, Leo van Jung, a pianist who was also her first lover. She showed me her passport, and I was surprised to see that her first name in it was given as Irene, with 'Isabelle' in parentheses. I had never heard anyone calling her Irene. 'Irene is my Christian name,' she explained matter-of-factly, 'and Isabelle is my Jewish name.' This puzzled me, and I asked her again what she meant by 'Jewish'. 'But I am Jewish,' she said, puzzled in turn by my question. 'You mean to say that you were never told that you were Jewish?' I felt the artificial world constructed by my mother begin to collapse. Was I then at one with my classmate Berkowitz who made a conspicuous exit before class in religion? Was I an alien to Russia, to Russian literature, to Russian music? I remembered that boys in the street used to call me *zhid*, an insulting word for a Jew, and would pull out a handkerchief and make a corner of it stand out in the form of a pig's ear to mock Jews who were forbidden to eat pork. But I always liked pork chops, so how could this animal pantomime apply to me?

I knew that my father's family came from Poland, and my mother's from the Ukraine, so that when my classmates asked me whether I was Jewish I could truthfully say that I was half-Polish and half-Ukrainian. The final blow came when I looked up my father's biography in the Russian encyclopaedia and found a cross reference, 'son of the preceding'. The preceding was Haim Selig Slonimsky, who was described as an eminent Hebrew scholar and scientist. So it was true; I was Jewish.

I worked up enough courage to ask my mother point-blank whether she too was Jewish. She became furious. 'It is not true!' she cried. 'I am a Ukrainian, and your father is a Russian Pole.' She dispatched an indignant letter to Aunt Isabelle, accusing her of interfering with the education of her children. 'There are families who have hereditary syphilis,' she wrote, 'but no outsider has the moral right to tell innocent children that their blood is tainted by syphilitic infection. It is the same with Jewish blood.' And she hurled a dreadful charge at Aunt Isabelle: 'You destroyed your own child when you became pregnant at 16. What right have you to destroy the children of others?'

Still determined to deny our Jewish origin, clinging to her crosses and icons for protection, my mother concocted a fantastic story to account for the name Slonimsky. My remote ancestors, she told me and my younger brothers, were the rulers of the town Slonim in Poland, but they were overthrown after a revolution in the Middle Ages. Nikolai Minsky, the poet, who happened to be present as my mother recited her version of the 'Fall of the House of Slonimsky', interrupted rather rudely. 'This was not a revolution,' he said. 'It was a pogrom!'

Apparently, my younger brother Michael, the future Soviet novelist, was even more painfully affected than I by the revelation of our Jewish origin, as shown by his conversation with the Russian *émigré* writer, Roman Gul:

Michael Slonimsky confided in me that he was not aware until he was 12 years old that he was Jewish [Gul wrote]. I remember this conversation very well, because his story seemed almost incredible to me: 'We were fed all kinds of fables to the effect that we were *echt* Russian, with our ancestry going back almost to the founders of the Russian state, and we believed it. But when I was about 12 years old, my aunt, my mother's sister, came to visit us in St Petersburg. I had never met her before, but I noticed that she was characteristically Jewish. [That must have been my Aunt Maria whom indeed we had never met previously.] When I said something about our family being of a pure Russian stock, she began to laugh uproariously and informed me, rather caustically, that we were Jews, only that we were baptized. For me it was the most terrible shock of my whole life.' Those were Michael's exact words.

It took me several years to reconcile myself to my false condition between Russian consciousness and Jewish origin. I could no longer wear a golden cross around my neck without a sense of dissimulation, and I removed the icon of my patron saint St Nicholas, which faced me from the bed board, every night before I went to sleep. Could I still believe in God, any kind of God? My brother Alexander consoled me by explaining that God was merely a poetic myth, and that Pushkin did not believe in God either.

The legal status of Jewish musicians in Russia was paradoxical. More than half of the St Petersburg Conservatory students were Jewish. Technically, their presence in the capital was illegal. But Russian aristocrats, and even members of the Imperial Family, were music lovers. It was an open secret that the Grand Duchess Elena sheltered young Jewish musicians in her own palace to protect them from police harassment. Glazunov, director of the St Petersburg Conservatory, was a great admirer of Jews; he used to remark about some non-Jewish Conservatory students that their playing was 'disappointingly Christian'.

There was a quota for Jewish students in Russian high schools and universities, carefully adjusted to the percentage of Jews in the population. Those among Czarist officials who liked to profess liberal views, especially in their contact with foreigners, contended that the Jewish quota was scrupulously fair. The Jews were so much more clever than the ethnic Russians, they argued, that, had they been given equal status, they would have swamped schools, universities, sciences, and arts, leaving the inferior ethnic Russians far behind, with no equal opportunities for advancement. The Jewish quota system often led to ludicrous situations. Since Jews constituted $3\frac{1}{2}$ per cent of the total population of Czarist Russia, they were given proportional representation in schools and universities. Sometimes, when there were not enough Christian boys in a class to make it possible for a rich Jewish family to enrol their offspring, Jewish parents would pay tuition for a supernumerary Christian to make up the required quota.

Shortly after the birth of my older brother Alexander in 1881, my parents decided to adopt the Greek Orthodox faith, the official religion of Russia. Like most members of the Russian intelligentsia, they were agnostics, and had no particular loyalty to any religion; to persist in the Jewish faith was to condemn their children to uncomfortable discrimination. And so it came to pass that I was baptized with all the due solemnity of the Greek Orthodox ritual.

My godfather was the great Christian philosopher Vladimir Solovyov. He was well known among the Russian intelligentsia not only as a liberal Christian philosopher (he appealed to Czar Alexander III not to hang the assassins of his father), but also as a brilliant modernistic poet. So venerated was Solovyov among religious Russians that, when I told one of them that I was Solovyov's godson, he suddenly touched me on the shoulder with his index finger. 'I wanted to touch Godhead,' he said. Solovyov was unhappy that I was not named after him, even though he personally dipped me into the baptismal font. This default was corrected when my younger brother, also christened by Solovyov, was named Vladimir.

Why was I given the name Nicolai (Nicolas is the French spelling which I eventually adopted) in the first place? Could it be that my mother, eager to proclaim her Russian loyalty, named me after Nicholas II, who was the Czarevich at the time I was born? (There was always a sentimental regard for the person of Czarevich in old Russian society, even among Russian liberals.) And why was my older brother named Alexander? He was born in May 1881, shortly after the assassination of Alexander II, known as the Czar Liberator, for he emancipated the serfs. Was my mother moved by sympathy for the Imperial Family after that regicide, and was there any sentimental connection with her naming her first-born after the 'martyred

Czar', or after his reigning son Alexander III, who was to prove himself the most reactionary of all the Czars? Perish the thought! It never occurred to me to ask my mother to clarify my suspicions.

Religious instruction received great emphasis in old Russian schools; attending church services was compulsory. The classes opened with a prayer: 'Save, O Lord, your people and give blessings to their welfare. Grant victory to our most august Czar and Emperor over his adversaries . . .' The prayer was recited in old Slavonic, the church language in which Greek Orthodox services were conducted. As in the Catholic Church, we had to go to confession, but so deficient was I in cardinal sins that I was hard put to find anything worth confessing. True, I was vain, but vanity was not regarded as a sin by the Russian church, unless it led to conspicuous self-aggrandizement. However, I could confess to prevarications. I once told my father that I had lost a three-copeck copper piece he had given me, while in reality I had used it to buy rum-filled chocolate candy; it was pleasingly intoxicating, reminding me of the eucharist at Easter when we were given a taste of wine.

Transubstantiation was hard for me to swallow, figuratively speaking. Standing in line at eucharist, I was beset by the problem of the wine being the blood and the bread being the flesh of Jesus. With so many little boys in our school, was there enough flesh and blood in poor Jesus to provide salvation for us all? I finally popped the question to Father Aggeyev. He explained that if Jesus could multiply loaves and fishes to feed the multitude he could do equally well with his own flesh and blood. Still, the idea of drinking blood, however abundant, repelled me. And in my obligatory readings from the scriptures I recoiled from the cruelties of Jehovah. In my illustrated book on the Bible there was a picture of a Hebrew soldier holding a Philistine child by the leg and smashing him against the wall. The text, in a mixture of modern Russian and old Slavonic, recounted to its Christian readers that the Lord ordered His chosen people utterly to smite the Philistines, men, women, and children. The Lord also smote and slew those Hebrews who spared Philistine female children with the purpose of letting them grow to be concubines. Then there was that bald prophet who was mocked by small children and who appealed to Jehovah for help; the Lord harkened to his plea; forthwith, two she-bears came out of the woods and devoured forty-two children. I thought that the punishment was out of proportion to the offence.

*   *   *

Despite all my determination to succeed, I failed to receive the coveted gold medal at my graduation from high school, and had to be content with the silver. In this failure I disgraced the family tradition, for both Alexander and Julia were gold medallists. My sister was only 14 when she graduated from high school, and she had to undergo fierce competition for the prime gold medal with her rival, a sickly girl named Ryzhova. As Alexander recalled the scene, the school board was in session until late at night while the contestants, accompanied by their mothers, kept vigil in the hall awaiting the final verdict. It culminated in a triumph for Julia, who won by a single point, for she had 12 (the highest grade in girls' school) in French, while Ryzhova received only 11. Ryzhova broke down, shouting: 'Damned kike! Damned kike!' The epithet must have been a shock to both my mother and my sister, who took such pains to assert their Christian faith.

After her triumph as prime gold medal holder in high school, Julia entered the Women's College. She selected mathematics as her major course. I remember with what deference I, as a small boy, looked at her notebooks filled with the mysterious symbols for integrals resembling the F-holes in the violin. Simultaneously Julia enrolled in the school of drama and dance. She never became a professional dancer, but she made some headway as a dramatic actress. Among her roles were Ophelia in *Hamlet*, and Nora in Ibsen's drama *A Doll's House*. She never transcended her own self; it was always Julia pretending to be Ophelia or Nora. Still she had several seasons in a travelling theatre troupe, filling engagements as far as Baku and Irkutsk. Her dual pursuits were honoured in the names of our two kittens, a grey one called Integral, and a tawny one, Melpomene. In the meantime, Julia turned to journalism, which was to remain her principal vocation.

My failure to match the honours received by Alexander and Julia did not deter me from preening at the final examination. I possessed a sort of *cacoethes loquendi*, an incontinence of speech. My hobby in high school was Latin. At the final examination students had to translate an ode by Horace. My name being in the latter part of the alphabet, I was called to the panel towards the end of the examination. I was given a copy of the textbook and was told to read and translate Ode No. 13. I looked at the opening lines, ostentatiously closed the book and began to recite the ode from memory: 'Tu ne quaesieris, scire nefas, quem tibi quem mihi finem di dederint . . .' Assuming a professorial tone of voice, I proceeded to translate it into Russian: 'You should not quest, for it is sinful, which end the gods will vouchsafe to you, and which to me . . .' I also offered some scholarly comments on the reference in the text to 'Babylonian numbers', which were an abomination to the Romans. And while thus performing for the benefit of the board I never missed an occasion to cast peripheral glances at my examiners. Were they properly impressed? They were, and their visible amazement fully repaid me for the trouble of memorizing Horace.

Among other wasteful things I did in high school was to commit to memory the entire text of Pushkin's *Eugene Onegin*, including the unfinished stanzas relating to the travels of Pushkin's Byronic hero. Since the entire poem was constructed in a series of fourteen-line sonnets, all in iambic tetrameter, I could guide myself by the regular succession of masculine and feminine rhymes to pinpoint the exact position of the lines. I held regular contests with my brother's university colleague, an eminent Pushkinist. He beat me easily, and in addition he could supply historical commentary to Pushkin's topical references. To confuse him I found a line that was duplicated in another chapter, and therefore was difficult to identify, 'Ostanovilasia ona'. I can still recite a chapter or two of the poem, but it would take some effort for me to match my record of seventy-five years ago.

My eagerness to amaze manifested itself particularly in music, which, after all, was my central pursuit. While a student at the St Petersburg Conservatory, I learned to astound audiences by playing Chopin's *Black-key Étude* with an orange, rolling it in the treble with the right hand while the basic harmony was supplied by the left hand using bare fingers. Another trick was to produce a reasonable facsimile of the difficult violin passages in the *Tannhäuser Overture* with the aid of a hairbrush glissando. I developed a technique of playing with my back to the keyboard which I called 'retrodigital tergiversation'. I could also run off Chopin's *Minute Waltz* (minus the repeats) in 43 seconds, a world record, as far as I could ascertain.

I liked to impress my willing audiences with these facile tricks, but a gnawing thought began to intrude on my clowning: I produced not a single tangible accomplishment, while my supposedly less-gifted contemporaries had already advanced into the world arena. One received a certificate of membership from the French Astronomical Society signed by its illustrious president, Camille Flammarion; another composed a song that was sung by a famous singer. Not in my wildest imagination could I then foresee the future when I, too, would have achieved merit, when I would have established myself not only as a reputable musician but also as the author of several books written in a language of which I had as yet no knowledge whatsoever, published in a legendary land on the other side of the globe. But when it all happened, I was a failed wunderkind, deprived of my self-sustaining vanity, my posturing in front of friendly mirrors, my savouring the printed encomiums which once sent me into ecstasy. Even an honorary doctoral degree, which was the ultimate fantasy in my self-centred adolescence, lost its patina of glory when, no longer a wunderkind, I finally received it.

CHAPTER 2

MY GRANDFATHER INVENTED THE TELEGRAPH

The intellectual history of my family illustrates the pervasive presence of purely abstract faculties, independent of cultural or national environment. My father's family stemmed from Poland; my first cousin Antoni was an eminent Polish poet. My two surviving brothers were novelists in Russia; my sister wrote literary criticism for Russian *émigré* publications in Paris and New York. As for myself, I evolved as a writer on music in America. On my mother's side, intellectual achievements were exemplified by my uncle Semyon Vengerov, an eminent literary critic, and my aunt Zinaïda Vengerova, a notable translator and writer on foreign literature. Musical talent resided in my illustrious aunt, Isabelle Vengerova, who became a legendary figure of piano pedagogy in America.

My mother used to talk endlessly of the 'genius' of the Slonimskys, so that eventually I developed an aversion to the very word. But she also said that the quality of genius often combines with a lack of simple humanity, and she told me some horrendous tales about my paternal ancestors, with an obvious heuristic suggestion that whatever inhumanity was lurking in my psyche was a heritage of my father's family. Of these tales, the most repulsive was the one she retailed about my paternal great-grandfather, Abraham Jacob Stern. His daughter fell in love with an impecunious Hebrew student, and my great-grandfather was adamantly set against her marrying him. He was also critical of her lack of tidiness around the house, and of her failure to wash her clothes properly. When the suitor came to dinner, Stern put his daughter's dirty socks in the soup tureen; they surfaced after the soup had been served and consumed, much to the dismay of the young suitor, who never came to the house again. Abraham Stern's daughter eventually married my paternal grandfather, Haim Selig Slonimsky, to whose genes I am supposed to owe most of my eccentric traits. If my paternal great-grandfather had not been such an insufferable curmudgeon, had not put his daughter's unwashed socks into the soup tureen, and had let her marry her suitor to be fruitful and multiply, would I have been only three-quarters me?

In the history of Jewish culture Abraham Stern was a significant figure.

He was born in 1760. (It fills me with chronological awe to contemplate that only three generations separate me from the middle of the eighteenth century.) Around 1810 Stern invented an adding machine, a wonderful contraption which elicited an invitation to demonstrate his arithmetical prowess to Czar Alexander I, an extraordinary honour for a Jew. A court adjutant proposed a mathematical problem. The Czar, who himself dabbled in science, dipped his quill pen into ink and began his calculations on a large sheet of paper. No sooner had he reached his preliminary arithmetical operation, however, than my great-grandfather announced the solution. The Czar looked at him quizzically. 'The machine is good,' he said, 'but the Jew is bad.' It was indeed a serious breach of etiquette to outsmart the sovereign. There is a lifesize portrait of Abraham Stern in the municipal museum of Poznań. During my trip to Poland in 1963 I spent some time gazing at my great-grandfather's luxuriantly bewhiskered visage, wondering whether I really had an eighth of his genes in my bodily frame.

My mother's attitude towards members of my father's family was ambiguous. On the one hand they were geniuses, on the other hand they were mean. 'Psja krev,' my mother used to say, the only phrase she knew in the Polish language, and which means 'cur's blood'.

On 25 August 1952, walking home from the Boston Public Library, I picked up an early afternoon edition of the *Boston Traveler*, as was my daily custom. The front page was uninviting. Turning to the letters column, I was startled to read:

Personal Post Card. Joseph Stalin, Kremlin: Dear Joe: You say Muscovite Z.Y.Slonimsky invented the telegraph a dozen years before Americans thought of it. That makes you the champ. After all, you invented Slonimsky.

The letter was signed, 'Boston Common'. Stalin invented Slonimsky! Then he must also have invented the genetic content of one-quarter of me, for Z.Y.Slonimsky, known to the world of Jewish scholarship as Haim Selig Slonimsky, was my paternal grandfather. A swarm of childhood memories invaded my brain. For long as I could remember, my mother had told me amazing tales about my grandfather, who was a genius, but an impractical one. 'Don't follow in his footsteps,' she cautioned. Inevitably, I did exactly that, stepping right into the mudprints of his galoshes. As an example of my grandfather's lack of practical sense, my mother said that he had invented the electric telegraph, but never patented it. He was satisfied with the act of his invention; after completing his paper he said to his wife, 'Sarah, I have just invented the telegraph. Now let us see how long it will take them to invent it.'

Years passed, and the news arrived from America of the first successful demonstration of the new and amazing means of electric communication. 'Fetch me that old paper of mine,' my grandfather commanded his wife, and, brushing off the dust of a decade, he set out to compare his finds with the American dispatch. 'Good for them!' he exclaimed upon examination. 'They got everything exactly right!' He then proceeded to throw away his manuscript. Now the ancient tale that my mother had recited for my enlightenment had achieved legitimacy by the claims of the Russian government itself!

I traced the original publication of the story to an Associated Press dispatch published in the Paris edition of the *New York Herald Tribune* of 23 August 1952, under the caption, 'Moscow Claims Telegraph Credit'. The article narrowed the claim to the specific development of a multiple system of telegraphic communication, and quoted as a source an article by two Soviet military engineers, Lt-Cols. Gorodnichin and Shlyapobersky, published in the Red Army paper *Krasnaya Zvezda* (*The Red Star*) of 19 August 1952. I obtained a copy of this issue; the article, entitled 'Glorious Pages in the History of National Science and Technology', reflected the Soviet tendency of the time to claim priority for Russia for all kinds of inventions, from incandescent light to aeroplanes. The section referring to my grandfather's invention read in part:

During our work in the Central State Historical Archives in Leningrad, we discovered a letter written by Z. Y. Slonimsky, dated April 15, 1858, addressed to the Directorate of the Russian Ministry of Transportation. The author of the letter was an eminent Russian scientist who received a prize of the Russian Academy of Sciences in 1854 for his invention of an adding machine based on an original mathematical system devised by him. In this letter he revealed a thorough understanding of processes that take place in duplex telegraph, and for the first time proposed a method to obviate certain difficulties of simultaneous transmission of messages over a single wire. In 1859 he published a separate brochure containing a detailed description of his method. Comparing Slonimsky's proposal with similar devices developed by the American scientists Stirnes in 1871 and Edison in 1874, it appears that neither of the two Americans introduced any innovations. Thus the examination of historical evidence leads to the conclusion that our fatherland holds the priority on the duplex system of electric telegraphy made public by the Russian scientist Z.Y.Slonimsky 12 years before Stirnes and 15 years before Edison.

The image of my grandfather as an impractical genius was borne out to some extent by his biography published in the Russian encyclopaedia of 1900, while he was still living (he died in 1904 at the age of 94):

The mathematical gifts and inventive power with which Slonimsky astounded both theoretical and practical scientists in his youth were not exploited by him in full, partly because of the unfavourable living conditions of Russian Jews and partly because of Slonimsky's own intellectual idiosyncrasies. Once he had found the solution of a specific problem, he was in no hurry to publish it, so that it frequently happened that his ideas were duplicated much later by a foreign scientist and were thus credited to the West.

Among the fables recounted by my mother was an episode involving a solar eclipse in my grandfather's native town of Bialystok. A German astronomical expedition was set up there for the eclipse. The villagers looked with apprehension mixed with curiosity at the shiny telescopes, and my grandfather, then a boy of tender years, also watched the proceedings. A German astronomer was moved to speak to him (the Yiddish-speaking natives could understand elementary German fairly well). 'The sun will be gradually blotted out, and the day will become as dark as night,' he explained. 'But you do not have to be afraid. The sun will shine again after awhile.' My grandfather listened to the lecture attentively and then said, in passable school German: 'I know all that. What I can't comprehend, however, is how you expect to make any worthwhile observations of the corona without a double diffraction lens.' The German was startled. 'Where did you learn all this?' he asked. 'Why, every street boy in the village knows such elementary stuff,' my grandfather replied. The German then filed a dispatch to the Berlin Academy of Sciences, in which he declared that Bialystok was in all probability the most civilized community in the world, and advanced a theory that the extraordinary scientific knowledge of its largely illiterate population was due to the preservation through the centuries of secret rabbinical doctrines dealing with celestial phenomena.

I undertook some research to ascertain whether there was in fact a total eclipse of the sun in the vicinity of Bialystok during my grandfather's boyhood. Sure enough, the classical *Canon der Finsternisse* by T. von Oppolzer listed a total solar eclipse in the region of Bialystok on 7 September 1820, when my grandfather was 10 years old. But a diligent search for the German report on my grandfather in the voluminous bulletins of the Berlin Academy of Sciences for 1820 and subsequent years was fruitless.

If the eclipse saga lacked documentary corroboration, the claim that my grandfather had invented a meridian is beyond dispute. The Slonimsky Meridian is identified by name on the world map published as an illustration in the entry on the Meridian Date in the *Jewish Encyclopaedia*. The Slonimsky Meridian did not replace Greenwich in world usage, but it was nice to have a personal meridian in the family. My grandfather's preoccupation with the meridian and the longitude in general was not an idle whim. He was deeply engaged in the problem of the proper celebration of the Sabbath now that the rotundity of the earth was finally accepted as a fact by biblical scholars. My grandfather's problem concerned two hypothetical Jews watching the setting sun on two adjacent islands in the Pacific separated by the International Dateline, so that it was Friday for the Jew on the island west of the International Dateline, but still Thursday for the Jew to the east of it. When should the hypothetical Jews celebrate the Sabbath, which begins, according to Jewish law, at sundown on Friday?

My grandfather provided the definitive solution to this problem in his address to the local Rabbinate, under the title 'What Sabbath Shall the Jewish Traveller in the Far East Observe?' In it, he made concessions to the civil authorities of the lands which a wandering Jew visited, without sacrificing the basic belief in the centrality of Jerusalem and the division of the globe into two equal parts with the International Dateline in the longitude 145 degrees 13′ 25″ west of Greenwich, the Slonimsky Meridian.

Slonimsky is not a common name in Russia or elsewhere. It was astounding, therefore, that, when I enrolled in the Fourth Municipal High School in St Petersburg in 1907, there was in my class another Slonimsky whose first name was also Nicolas, and who was definitely unrelated to any branch of my family. As a result, I had to be listed in the school register as Nicolas II Slonimsky. Since the name of the reigning emperor of Russia was Nicolas II, I became the butt of jokes about my being the Czar. I lost track of my namesake after graduation.

My two paternal uncles were both professional men. Wanda Landowska, the famous harpsichord player, knew them in Warsaw. She related to me some amusing stories about Uncle Stanislaw, a doctor of medicine who was more famous as a raconteur than as a medical man. He caused discomfort to his patients by telling them that medicine was but an experimental science, and that the best he could do was to make sure that the pills and potions he prescribed would cause no harm: they were placebos calculated to make them feel good through sheer faith in their curative power. After listening to his reasoned discourse, a patient would go to another doctor.

My other paternal uncle, Josef, was a language teacher. His grand design was to publish a series of manuals for visitors to Poland who might like to learn Polish, Russian, German, or any other language spoken in Poland. Uncle Josef even invented a language of his own, which he called 'Universal Romanic Language', etymologically derived from Latin, Spanish, and Italian. There is a copy of his manual *Linguo romane universale* at the New York Public Library, a slim brochure containing elementary rules of grammar and syntax. Here is, *à titre documentaire*, a little story in Romanic from this booklet, which hardly needs a translation: 'Un viagiator irlandese qui describen lagos delectables di Killerney, comunicen d'un echo remarcable in istes locos, qual in replico al sue questio, "Quam valean vos, Pat?" instantem responden, "Optimen, gracia!".' But for an accident of fate, Romanic could have achieved a universal acceptance vouchsafed for many years to Esperanto, which was also invented by a Polish Jew, named Zamenhof. There is a whole library of publications in Esperanto, while poor Uncle Josef had to limit himself to just a few samples in Romanic.

Uncle Josef excelled in Talmudic humour. A young Polish boy came to him to take some lessons in Spanish, for he planned to emigrate to Brazil. Uncle Josef took him on, and the boy made excellent progress. Just before embarking on his long journey, he came to say goodbye to Uncle Josef. After he was gone, Uncle Josef turned to his wife and said, 'Will he be surprised when he finds that they speak Portuguese and not Spanish in Brazil!'

The most notable representative of the Polish branch of my family was Antoni Slonimski, son of Stanislaw. The Polish spelling of my family name is Słonimski, with a slant across the letter 'l' which makes it a liquid semi-vowel, and is pronounced Swonimski. Poland is the only European country whose inhabitants have no trouble in pronouncing my name. When I landed at Warsaw Airport in December 1962, on my way from Russia, the customs officer asked me whether I was related to Antoni. 'He is my first cousin,' I proudly replied. The officer passed my luggage without opening it.

After the Nazi invasion of Poland, Antoni went to London. He returned to Warsaw after the war, and made uneasy peace with the new Communist regime. Gomulka, the prime minister of Communist Poland, was Antoni's friend from pre-Revolutionary days, and he welcomed him without ceremony. As a good party man, Gomulka pressed Antoni for information on anti-Communist Polish groups in London. Did Antoni return to Poland with a particular mission on behalf of the London Poles? Antoni's reply was typical. 'Friend Gomulka,' he said to the prime minister, 'I cannot stand physical torture, so please don't waste your time calling your star chamber men. Just list my crimes, and I will sign a confession.' Gomulka was deeply offended by Antoni's remark, and their friendly relationship ceased. Yet no reprisals were taken against Antoni. He and his wife were allowed to keep their Warsaw apartment and he was permitted to publish his *feuilletons* in a literary Warsaw weekly. The Polish State Publishing House put out a magnificent two-volume edition of

Antoni's old poems. But by way of an exquisite turn of the screw, the edition was never put on sale. When I was in Warsaw, I tried my luck and asked for a book by Antoni at a large Warsaw bookstore. Great was my surprise when the clerk handed me a copy of the Polish translation of a novel by my brother Michael. 'This is not our Słonimski,' she said, 'but [and she lowered the tone of her voice] I have an old book by Antoni Słonimski in case you are interested.' I certainly was, and carried off my treasure. Antoni was quite amused when I showed him the book. 'Where on earth did you get it?' he asked. 'It has been out of print for years!'

Contrariness was Antoni's irrepressible mental trait. In the year of the Sputnik, when the Soviets were expected to be the first to land a man on the moon, Antoni published a poem in which he passionately pleaded that the moon should be left to poets. The poem was described in the Soviet Press as a reactionary publication designed to undermine the public faith in the Soviet space programme.

Antoni's unstable honeymoon with the Communist Polish regime came to an end when in one of his *feuilletons* he sang his praises of children's hour on the Polish State Radio, particularly the one broadcast daily at 7 o'clock in the evening: how skilfully the fairy tales blended truth with fiction, what originality of inventive power, Antoni exclaimed. The point, overlooked by the editor, was that the hour specified in Antoni's *feuilleton* was set for a daily news broadcast of the Polish government. Antoni's piece produced a sensation at Warsaw sidewalk cafés, and the issue of *Wiadomosti literacki* in which it was published became a collector's item. But Antoni's further *feuilletons* were abruptly cancelled, and he had to resort to the Soviet method of *samisdat* (self-publishing) to make his writings known.

Antoni died in 1976 as a result of an idiotic automobile accident near Warsaw; he never learned to drive and entrusted his transportation to a woman who ran the car into a telegraph post.

I owe it to Dr Neil Rosenstein of Elizabeth, New Jersey, a genealogist by avocation, to have traced my ancestry on the maternal side all the way to my great-great-great-great-great-great-great-great-great-great-great-great-great-grandfather Beneviste, a strange name for a Jew, explained by the fact that he was a member of the Spanish Jewish community. He was expelled from Spain during a general pogrom organized by Queen Isabel in the same year that she sent Columbus to discover the western route to the Orient. His progeny surfaced in Central Europe. Of this line, the most fascinating of my ancestors was the Maharal of Prague, who flourished from 1525 to 1609 and who was the creator of the original Jewish robot, the legendary Golem. Maharal begat Bezalel who died in 1600; Bezalel begat the spouse of Zechariah known as 'The Prophet'. Zechariah begat Aryey Leib, known as 'The Tall', who was Chief Rabbi of Cracow (d.1671). Leib begat Zechariah Mendel (d.1706) who begat Simeon Zemel who begat Eliezer Lipman who begat Pesel, the wife of Jehiel Michael Epstein (d.1812). Epstein took his name from a small German town in which he hid from unfriendly regimes. He procreated Simeon Zemel Epstein (d.1854), who settled in Warsaw and became known as a Talmudic scholar. Simeon Zemel Epstein generated Judah Epstein (d.1879). My grandmother, Pauline Wengeroff (or Vengerova), née Epstein, was his daughter.

The prevalence of literature and abstruse scholarship in both the maternal and paternal branches of my family is appalling. The card catalogue of the Library of Congress is full of Slonimskys, in various spellings, and has quite a spate of Vengerovs and Vengerovas, sometimes spelled Wengeroff. Jewish women were not ordinarily given to literary pursuits, but my grandmother, Pauline Wengeroff, published a book that acquired a certain renown among Jews, *Memoiren einer Grossmutter*, published in two volumes, in the German language, in 1913 and 1919. One sentence stands out as a silent reproach to the author's descendants: 'Da kam die dritte Generation die weder Gott noch den Teufel fürchtete.' The third generation, that 'feared neither God nor the devil', was my generation, which abandoned the Jewish faith for the sake of convenience. Yet my grandmother seemed to condone her daughter's (i.e. my mother's) decision to baptize her children, so as to spare them the abiding fear that was part of her own life in Minsk. She was a privileged Jew; her husband, my maternal grandfather, Afanasiy Vengerov, was a successful contractor for taverns and real estate in Konotop, a small *schtetl* populated to the brim by Jews; later he established himself as a banker in Minsk. He was well regarded even by the Czarist authorities who favoured prosperous Jews whom they could trust in financial transactions, and my grandfather Vengerov was certainly loyal to the sovereign. When Alexander II was assassinated in 1881, he genuinely grieved, for, apart from his aversion to any shedding of blood, he had hoped that the 'Czar Liberator', as the slain ruler was described by official Russian historians, would follow the liberation of Russian serfs in 1861 by the liberation of Jews from the senseless restrictions in their residential areas. In an extraordinary gesture, the municipal council of the city of Minsk included my grandfather in a delegation to go to St Petersburg and deposit a basket of flowers on the tomb of the martyred Czar.

In her memoirs, my grandmother describes this period:

Pogrom was the newest word . . . The Jews of Kiev, Romny, Konotop and other towns were the first to experience these horrors; they were the first to be assailed by the savage local mobs. A fear reigned in Minsk. One could see Jews hurry furtively through the streets, looking over their shoulders for potential dangers. They were always on guard, and were ready to offer desperate resistance. An explosion could come any time. Jewish housewives who came to my house told me about the rudeness of the peasants who brought their produce to the Minsk market twice a week. These people openly predicted that an assault on Jews would come soon. My husband heard similar warnings in his bank, and the children in their school. The hatred of the Jews increased with each passing day. Even little street urchins became so bold as to throw stones at the windows of the houses of respected Jewish families in Minsk and to shout imprecations at them. One day there was a loud knock at the door of our house which was on the street level. Our maid opened the door and was surprised to see a young boy, who, without bothering to take off his cap, impudently asked the name of the owners. When the maid gave him our Russian-sounding name, he flew into a rage and screamed: 'Pack of Jews! And they have a Russian name!' and he fled from the house . . . The Jews of Minsk prepared for resistance, and their houses became military redoubts. Some collected canes and sticks, others mixed sand and tobacco to throw the mixture in the eyes of pogrom makers. Eight-year-old children took part in these defence measures. One such young hero tried to calm his mother, telling her not to be afraid, for he had a knife in readiness to fight back. And indeed he had a little knife in his pocket, which he had bought for ten copecks. In our house we no longer felt safe. The Russian servants who had been in our employ for several years suddenly became hostile and rude, so that we had to protect ourselves even from our own hired help. At night, after the servants retired, I gathered all knives and hammers from the kitchen and put them in a closet in my bedroom. For further protection, I built a barricade of benches, chairs, and other pieces of furniture in front of the entrance door. Of course, I could not hope that such an obstacle would hold back the pogrom makers, but I rigged up a barricade every night, and dismantled it early the next morning and put everything in order, so that the servants would not notice anything wrong. There was no pogrom in Minsk after all; our town was accidentally, or perhaps not so accidentally, spared this terrible ordeal.

Recently I have discovered an American connection in my family: a Dr Ephraim Epstein, my maternal great-uncle, brother of Pauline Wengeroff, who emigrated to the United States in 1850 and settled in Ohio where he became a teacher of classical languages. In 1905 he published an article in an American medical journal entitled *Why Do I Live So Long*. He also recounted that he reached the age of puberty very early in life and married his first cousin in his seventeenth year. In 1849 he determined to go to the United States. He landed in New York early in 1850 'after a perilous voyage by sea in a damaged sailing vessel where-in we preserved our lives in a 9-week struggle with waves, hunger and thirst'.

Despite Ephraim Epstein's Jewish orthodox upbringing, he decided to study Christian theology and enrolled in Andover, Massachusetts, Theological Seminary, graduating in 1856. He also studied medicine. I was greatly impressed by my great-uncle's mention of the fact that his father and grandfather, both of whom he knew, 'lived within a year or two of one hundred years'. I had known already that my grandfather and my great-grandfather on the male line lived very long, and now comes an encouraging testimony that my maternal ancestors lived even longer! Ephraim adds that both his father and grandfather were 'tall, stout, and portly, had many children, used alcohol and tobacco moderately and drank much tea'.

I never expected to hear anything more about my only known American relative Epstein. It was therefore quite a surprise when, around Christmas 1985, I received a letter from one Howard Burke, who said he was a grandson of Ephraim Epstein and lived in Wyoming where he maintained a successful furniture factory. He was half Jewish; his father was an Irishman. Most beguilingly, his stationery bore the designation 'Retired Philanthropist'. He must be my only relative, no matter how remote, who made good in business.

Among the literary luminaries in my family, the name Zinaïda Vengerova, my mother's younger sister, daughter of Pauline Epstein Wengeroff, is respectfully remembered in Russia for her excellent translations from foreign languages. She lived many years in London where she became a translator of several British authors, among them George Bernard Shaw (whom she fondly remembered as a tall man with a flowing red beard) and H. G. Wells. Late in life, Aunt Zinaïda married the poet Nikolai Minsky, a distant cousin whose real name was Wilenkin. (The pseudonym Minsky was taken from the name of his native town Minsk, a common practice among literary men in Russia.) He was a well-known poet in a romantic and symbolist vein. Rachmaninoff and other composers had set some of his poems to music.

In his youth, Minsky joined various revolutionary groups, not very subversive, but dangerous enough to set the Czarist secret police after him. He usually managed to elude arrest, and went to Paris. Returning to Russia, he then made a niche for himself in history as co-editor with Lenin of the weekly periodical *Iskra* (*The Spark*) which was published for a couple of years in the wake of liberal reforms following the abortive revolution of 1905. Lenin used Minsky for purely practical purposes, because Minsky had already secured a permit to publish, while Lenin was too deeply involved in revolutionary activities to be allowed to publish. When the political situation eased up somewhat, Lenin haughtily dismissed Minsky from his editorial post. 'Get rid of the poet,' he ordered. But the Bolshevik government gave Minsky a life pension for his revolutionary poem, with its fiery opening stanza,

Proletarians of all nations
Unite!
Barricade your stations
And fight!

Minsky died of cancer in Paris in 1938; Aunt Zinaïda joined Aunt Isabelle in New York, where she died in 1941.

The most famous among my mother's relatives was her brother, my uncle Semyon Afanasievich Vengerov, professor of Russian literature and editor of collected works of Pushkin, Shakespeare, Schiller, and other classics published in profusely illustrated editions. His most significant contribution, however, was a critical biographic dictionary of Russian writers, which was never published but remained in the state of 'cartothèque', consisting of tens of thousands of 'fiches', or filing cards, containing information on Russian writers, including personal communications from such giants as Tolstoy and Turgenev. Students to this day make a pilgrimage to the Vengerov 'carthothèque' for their research work.

The honour in which Uncle Semyon's name is held among Russian intellectuals is indicated by its passing mention in Vladimir Nabokov's novella *Ada*, in which his name is spelled in full, but the dates of his life are deliberately altered, making him a nonagenarian at his death. As often in his writings, Nabokov manipulates his army of intellectual Poltergeister bent on pointless mischief in order to confuse and mislead the innocent reader with malice aforethought. But who except me and and a handful of specialists in Russian literary criticism would penetrate the murky intent of this futile mystification?

The intellectual armamentarium of my family also included a chess gene; its principal carrier was Semyon Alapin, my mother's second cousin. His name is known to chess players all over the world through the so-called Slav Opening (even though Alapin was a Jew, not a Slav). Ironically, it has been immortalized in one of the most celebrated games in chess history which Alapin lost to the international grandmaster Nimzowitch who sacrificed a knight in order to entrap Alapin in an inextricable bind. A checkmate threatened in all directions, and Alapin resigned. Every time I replay this game, I feel offended in my family pride. Alapin also made himself famous in the chess annals by inventing a logarithmic calculus of chess in which each position on the chessboard could be rated as to its winning chances. When in one of his games he arrived at the high position rated by the number 7, he declared himself a winner. Unfortunately his opponent checkmated him on the next move; Alapin's logarithmic calculus proved to be faulty.

The theatrical field was represented in the family by Alexander Tairov, whose real name was Kornblatt. My earliest recollection of him was a feeling of acute envy when he casually engaged in a long kissing bout with a plump red-haired girl at a party at Uncle Semyon's apartment. Tairov's mother was my mother's first cousin. Tairov was the founder of the Chamber Theatre in Moscow which inaugurated a 'constructivist' principle of staging, with actors going up and down ladders to symbolize their changing emotional states. After a brief flurry of success in the avant-garde circles in Moscow, Tairov's theatre was shut down by the Soviet authorities as a formalistic perversion of stagecraft.

A weird exception among members of our supposedly intellectual family was my unfortunate nephew Dmitri, or to use the Russian diminutive, Mitia, the son of my unhappy sister Julia. He tormented her by proclaiming his various diseases, mental, physical, and sexual. Once she asked me to take him to a dermatologist because he said he was getting bald. I responded by saying that indeed he was rapidly getting bald under his bushy hair, but the gross humour of this remark missed her. During his life Mitia only once held a paying job, as a Western Union messenger for a few months in the 1940s. What saved him from total delinquency was the U.S. Army which drafted him. He was quickly discharged as a psychoneurotic, with a life pension of $100 a month which kept him alive in Paris where he eventually settled.

Although he never made a thorough study of history, Mitia apparently accumulated a wealth of unrelated data which he could retrieve at will. I have known people who have an extraordinary memory for dates and events, important and unimportant, but I have never encountered another person who could work out historical or personal events in reverse, beginning with a given month and day, as Mitia seemed to be able to do.

Thus, in a letter dated 2 May 1971, Mitia informed me that Berlin fell to the Russians exactly twenty-six years before; on the same day and month in 1960, Mitia told me, California executed Caryl Chessman. The fall of Berlin is, of course, a historical event of great importance and it is not surprising that he could identify it. But the execution of Chessman was not a matter of cosmic import. Mitia was living in Paris at that time and, even assuming that he had read about it in the French papers, how could he summon the date from the dark recesses of his brain eleven years after the fact?

In a letter dated 11 May 1971 (Mitia would write to me two or even three times a week), he told me that on that day in 1745 an important battle was fought in the vicinity of Fontenoy, in which the French won a decisive victory over the combined forces of English, Dutch, and Austrian armies in the course of the war of the Austrian succession. His information was always accurate.

The floods of letters unleashed on me was nothing in comparison with the inundation of which my brother Alexander was a victim in Moscow. Mitia wrote to him in Russian, somewhat quaint in its usage but remarkably idiomatic for one who had never lived in Russia. Alexander wrote to me in 1959:

Mitia sends me bagful upon bagful, Leviathan upon Leviathan of letters, with their size increasing astronomically. The latest packet contained 364 pages of note paper! These manuscripts arrive in torn envelopes which are tied together with a piece of string in our own post office in Moscow, usually marked, 'Received in damaged condition'. I number them systematically. No letter is shorter than 100 pages. I have now reached Letter no. 40, and I have still about 500 pages to go. Mitia tells me that he writes these letters in the Paris sidewalk cafés where he is known as 'écrivain', and he is often asked who his publisher is. He never disabuses his well-wishers of this notion. He even signs his letters 'Graphomaniac'.

My sister Julia was deeply distressed about Mitia's inability to organize his sex life. She even tried to arrange an assignation for him with a woman she knew. Mitia promptly kept the appointment but failed miserably, and the woman threw him out of her apartment.

Julia told me once, with total conviction, that it would be better to have syphilis than to remain a virgin. She knew whereof she spoke. She was married to a Russian actor, one Peter Sazonov, a son of deaf-mute parents. Whether this parentage had anything to do with his particular deficiency is not clear, but he was completely impotent; the best he could do was to bestow on my sister an occasional kiss, whereupon all power went out of him. Incredibly, Julia seemed to be unaware of the mechanism of human reproduction, and after twelve years of marriage she decided to consult a gynaecologist to find out why she could not have a child. The doctor examined her and exclaimed in astonishment: 'You are a goddam virgin!' He promptly proposed personally to put an end to this state of affairs and she fled in horror.

At the age of 36, Julia met a real man, a Russian painter Nicolai Milliotti, who gallantly offered his expert services to end her humiliating condition. He warned Julia, however, that though he was willing to give her a child, he would not assume any financial responsibility; he was an *homme du monde*, he explained, and women loved him; his service for Julia was to be an act of charity. The fruit of that benefaction was the unfortunate Mitia, who was born in emigration in Bulgaria in 1921.

The demon of genetics is capricious. Laying out its molecular solitaire, it plays tricks with a human deck of cards, which contains a number of jokers that have a chameleonic ability to dissemble. Some are aborted; others masquerade as picture cards. In this blind game my unfortunate nephew Mitia was a sterile joker. On the other hand, Sergei Slonimsky, son of my brother Michael, has been endowed with the best of our family chromosomes. His father was a writer, but Sergei turned towards music. In our family, musical inclinations have followed a knight's move in chess: Aunt Isabelle handed over her gift for music to me; Sergei followed a knight's move from me. My aunt became one of the most celebrated piano teachers of her time; I veered in the direction of speculative music theory; Sergei has established himself as one of the finest Soviet composers. I saw him first during my Russian visit in 1935 when he was a small child; then as an aspiring young composer when I went to Russia in 1962; and as an acknowledged master of Soviet music in 1985. Although separated by half the globe and active in two different cultures, we maintain a cordial and affectionate relationship.

CHAPTER 3

JOYLESS YOUTH, JOYFUL REVOLUTION

By the time I graduated from high school in 1912 I realized that I was no longer a wunderkind. The world was not waiting with bated breath to be conquered by my genius. Plainly, I failed to attract attention, and my thoughts turned to renouncing life. My problem differed from Hamlet's: I was interested mainly in making a lasting impression on the world at large, or at the least on my family, whereas Hamlet was moved by the spirit of vengeance and was condemning himself for his weakness of will.

Suicides were very much in vogue in St Petersburg early in the century; there was a romantic aura attached to the act. A classmate of mine, a young writer named Sergei Ostrogorsky, shot himself; he left a will bequeathing the royalties from his literary publications to talented poor writers (his collected works consisted of a slim volume of poetry). The name of Ostrogorsky sank into total oblivion; a mention by my brother Michael in a short paragraph in his autobiography is perhaps the only reference to him in print. But it was the next suicide that plunged me into a flurry of excitement, that of another classmate of mine named Zhuravlev. He was not a close friend, and I am at a loss now, some seventy years after the event, to account for my horror and desolation at his death. Perhaps it was the manner in which I learned of it that shook my already unstable equilibrium: a friend of the family deemed it suitable to make a special visit and to announce dramatically, 'Zhuravlev hanged himself!' The unwelcome messenger proceeded to describe in morbid details how Zhuravlev fashioned a noose with his belt and hanged himself in the clothes closet.

I hesitated for days before I decided to follow Zhuravlev's example. I selected the bathroom as the scene of action; it was more spacious than the closet, and provided more room to move about. I used a piece of string from a Christmas package to make a noose. I attached it to a hook in the ceiling, but it gave way at once under my weight, and I collapsed ingloriously on the wet floor of the bathroom. In his memoirs my brother Michael gives a circumstantial account of my pseudo-suicide. He tells of a 'suicide club' formed at the Fourth Classical High School in St Petersburg, which we attended.

Three of the club members made a pact to kill themselves on an appointed day and hour. One of them carried out his intention successfully; another confessed the plot to his parents, and the third was saved by me personally when I took him off the noose in the bathroom where he had locked himself. I became so provoked at his senseless act that I violently slapped him on the face. I was 13 years old at the time, he was 16. Last year, already at an advanced age, reminiscing of the remote past, he thanked me for rescuing him and explained that the motive for his attempt at suicide was to attract attention to himself.

I was the third would-be suicide in Michael's account of the trio of self-killers. I did reminisce with him concerning this episode during our last meeting in Leningrad in 1962, and I did say that in all probability my motive was to attract attention. But there was no suicide club in our school such as described by Michael, and the two suicides that did occur took place long after my class had already graduated. The difference between our ages, three years, was reported correctly in Michael's account, but my pseudo-suicide took place in 1913, when I was 19, and Michael was 16. In the context of his story Michael represents himself, at 13, as a mature Bolshevik who slapped me on the face in a symbolic gesture of disgust. He writes: 'My horror at seeing a member of one of the local decadent groups suspended under a ceiling alienated me for all time from the society in which such acts could occur.' He never mentioned my name, or his relationship to me, in recounting this episode.

On 27 December 1925 Michael was called upon, in his capacity as Chairman of the Leningrad Writers' Union, to take down a real hanging suicide, the poet Sergei Esenin, who hanged himself in a Leningrad hotel, L'Angleterre, leaving a poem written in his own blood. The poet of the people, as he was hailed in 1918 when I met him at the house of Merezhkovsky, became a self-proclaimed 'hooligan' (a word adopted by the Russians to describe a riotous person), and left a drunken trail, with the barefoot pseudo-Grecian American dancer Isadora Duncan, who became one of his three wives (another was Tolstoy's granddaughter). Years later Shostakovich became for some reason morbidly interested in seeing the exact room in which Esenin hanged himself and asked several people in the know to show it to him.

It is a rueful commentary on the fate of four of Russia's greatest poets that they should have died a violent death. Pushkin was shot in a duel in 1837. His killer, a Frenchman, was deported and became a senator of the Second Empire. He was interviewed by a Russian 'Pushkinist' in Paris many years after the event, and was asked how he could raise his hand against a great poet. 'But I, too, was an important man of aristocracy', he replied. Pushkin's younger contemporary, Lermontov, was killed in a duel with a fellow officer. The officer lived to see the time when his children and grandchildren were assigned in school to commit to memory the verses by the poet who had perished at his hands. Vladimir Maya- kovsky reproached Esenin in a poignant poem for depriving Russian literature of his native talent, but five years later Mayakovsky shot himself in consequence of an unfortunate love affair.

Would Pushkin have exposed himself to a stranger's bullet had he known that his verses would be enshrined as the greatest achievement in Russian poetry? It was Pushkin's own fault in precipitating this fatal encounter; he was incensed to the highest degree by an anonymous letter from a fictional Society of Cuckolds electing him to an honorary member- ship; indeed, his wife had the reputation of a flirt; a rumour had it in St Petersburg that even the Emperor Nicholas I himself was not insensible to her charms. (She remarried shortly after Pushkin's death.) Pushkin suspected a French attaché of the Netherlands Embassy in St Petersburg of being the author of the offensive note, and Pushkin wrote him a scurrilous letter abounding in choice French invectives (French was the natural language of the educated circles in old St Petersburg). Would Lermontov have provoked a duel had he foreseen his elevation to the highest rank of the Russian poetic pantheon next to Pushkin? Would Esenin have hanged himself had he known that he would become an idol of a generation yet unborn, that a Soviet cruiser would be named after him? Would Mayakovsky have shot himself if he had had an inkling that he would become the poet laureate of the Revolutionary era, that Moscow streets, squares, and subway stations would be named after him?

I had a pseudo-posthumous satisfaction of having my fraudulent pen- dency immortalized in a short story by the Russian poetess Zinaïda Gippius; in it I was described as a young mystic eager to explore the unknown state of non-existence; she must have heard about my case from mutual acquaintances in St Petersburg. It was much later that I met Zinaïda Gippius, but I never asked her whether she really based her novella on my experience.

In order to justify the attention which was shown to me, I had to continue voicing my feeling of unworthiness and my desire for self-liquidation. A family council was held, and it was decided to send me abroad for psychic treatment. My destination was the charming village of Ahrweiler, deep in the Rhineland valley. My mother accompanied me on my journey; I was not trusted to travel unescorted. In Ahrweiler I was placed in an institu- tion for mentally disturbed individuals and was kept under constant surveillance by a burly Swabian; I was not allowed to handle any sharp utensils. Even though I was 19 years old I did not have to shave, so the problem of supplying me with a razor did not arise.

I spent much of my time writing lengthy letters addressed to a classmate of Zhuravlev, in which I reproached the deceased for 'stealing death' from me. What I did not know was that my entire correspondence was forwarded by the directors of the institution in which I was confined to my parents, and that my mother read my letters in council with a psychiatrist to determine the gravity of my condition. Not a single rational person in this gathering of Russian intellectuals and psychologists ever suggested that I was merely indulging in a morbid streak of self-advertising. And not one person in Ahrweiler asked me whether I had a desire to be with a woman. Yet retrospectively it seems certain that a decent arrangement for an assignation would have instantly cured me of my distractions. In the meantime I was busily studying German; my overwhelming desire was to enrol in the University of Bonn, a town near the place of my confinement, which I visited several times (invariably accompanied by a guardian), and which I came to love. I bought a pocket edition of Schopenhauer; I absorbed enough of it to form a certain spiritual kinship with his pessimistic *Weltanschauung*.

At Ahrweiler I had access to an upright piano, and I used my free time (all my time there was free) to play a piano reduction of *Die Walküre*, relishing the acrid Wagnerian harmonies still new to me. A staff psychologist, passing by, asked me, 'Was haben Sie daran?' I told him. 'Wagner,' he sighed. 'Had you succeeded in your intention to kill yourself you would have never been able to play this beautiful music.'

I read Nietzsche, too, and ruminated on his savage injunction: 'If one stumbles at the edge of the precipice, push him down!' I was aware of the fact that Nietzsche ended his life as a mindless human wreck. Another modern ruminator who captivated my imagination was Otto Weininger, the author of a volume dealing with sex. Incapable of controlling his sexual desire, he shot himself to death at the age of 23. I certainly had a suitable gallery of intellectual models to guide me on the road to psychological self-destruction. I indulged in what Germans call *Grübeleien*, a word difficult to translate, connoting aimless broodings focused on oneself, with the outside world serving only as a resonance box for unbridled egoism.

In February 1914 I was released from Ahrweiler. The doctors found that my physical body could henceforth be put once more in trust of my troubled mind. I revisited Ahrweiler in 1963, trying to recall my experience there fifty years before, and made an appointment with the director of the sanitarium (the old director had died long before). I was anxious to find out why I had to undergo psychiatric treatment in the first place, and whether I was ever abnormal, even in the narrow technical sense. But the director refused to let me see my dossier.

I was back in Russia in the spring of 1914, and resumed my studies in physics, astronomy, and mathematics at the St Petersburg University. I also took private composition lessons with Professor Kalafati who, a generation earlier, had been the first teacher of Stravinsky. He said Stravinsky had had great difficulties in mastering elementary harmony, and for that reason never took a regular conservatory course, never passed an examination, and never received a degree. Kalafati's teaching method was curious. Without saying a word, he would write on the blackboard a few bars in four-part harmony, then take a second look at what he had written and say in a soft voice, barely touched by an ancestral Greek accent, 'You can also do it like this,' and he would write another example.

I followed Kalafati's precepts with great care, avoiding at all costs the forbidden consecutive fifths, the great taboo of Russian composition teachers. I remember my horror when, after having composed a song to the words of my Uncle Minsky, and going over it in my mind, I suddenly realized that a pair of consecutive fifths had crept through into my otherwise placid harmonic setting. But I took heart when Kalafati told me that it was all right to use consecutive fifths in the treble over an organ point in the bass. Encouraged, I composed a prelude in which I intro-duced four consecutive fifths hovering high over a deep double organ point in the bass. I brought the piece to Kalafati who said the fifths were permissible under the circumstances. He complimented me on my style, so laudably Rimsky-Korsakovian, so properly Kalafatian, and showed my piece to other students as a model worth following. Eventually I published my prelude as Opus 1. My publisher said it was the most beautiful piece of music he had ever heard. Shortly afterwards he went out of business.

I was 20 years old, and it was about time for me to get some gainful employment, so I put an advertisement in a newspaper seeking a summer position as a resident tutor of music, mathematics, literature, and any other academic subject. An offer soon came from a family which owned an estate near the town of Kursk, south of Moscow. I had never been to Moscow and never travelled south, so I was delighted at the prospect. The conditions were excellent: room and board and 50 roubles a month. I was to teach three girls: Natasha, the daughter of the family, aged 15; Tania, a summer guest, aged 16, and Lily, another guest, aged 19. Three girls! Would there be one who would kiss me in the nape of my neck?

I was met at the railroad station in Kursk by a family attendant, and taken in a horse-drawn carriage to a prosperous country estate. The head of the family was a Russian army officer; the mother was an amiable housewife. There was a German governess. My duties as a tutor were arranged according to a strict regimen. I was to give separate lessons to each of the three girls in the morning; then an opulent lunch was served, with food and dairy produce from the countryside. A couple of hours in the afternoon were devoted to lessons in Russian literature and mathematics. In the evening I exhibited my artistry at the piano. A rumour spread around that a great artist resided in the neighbourhood, and people solicited invitations to attend my performances.

My memory of that remote summer of 1914, the last before wars and revolution destroyed the world I knew, retains a night in the garden spent talking to Tania, the guest of the family. I never touched her, she never touched me; ours was an amorous feast of verbal intimacy. She was frail, had brown hair and tiny eyes. In the morning it was discovered that our respective beds had not been slept in. There was a great deal of whispering and commotion around the house. That same day, Tania was taken to the railroad station and told not to come back. No reprisals were taken against me. 'Er hätte mit Lily angefangen,' the governess explained by way of exoneration of my role in the affair. Indeed, if I had had my choice, I would have 'angefangen' with Lily; my remembrance of her is that of apple-fresh, milk-white face with wide-open round eyes; the stroboscopic lights of my recollection reconstruct a scene of romping with her in the grass, rich in unintended but delectable digital contacts.

What irony! It was neither Tania nor Lily with whom I came closest to an *amitié amoureuse*, but with Natasha, the daughter of the strict owners of the estate. We often held hands riding in a horse-drawn *telega* in the country. That August I asked her to travel with me to Kiev to watch the total eclipse of the sun, which was observable only as an unexciting partial solar occultation at our summer residence. We would have returned by train on the same day, so no moral issue was to be raised, but it was not to be. I overheard a lengthy conversation between her and her mother, but they spoke in English, a language I did not understand. The decision was in the negative. In the meantime, Russia declared war against Germany and Austria; the government distributed leaflets reassuring the populace that the darkening of the sun was not a sinister omen presaging disaster but a natural phenomenon, which would have taken place even in the time of peace; a safe return of the sun was guaranteed by the Czar. I recalled Borodin's opera *Prince Igor*, in which the eclipse plunged Igor's army into disarray. So I went to Kiev alone; alas, clouds obscured the sky during the eclipse.

I maintained my *amitié amoureuse* with Natasha for several weeks after that romantic summer of 1914. I called her 'alouette' and sometimes a penguin, for there was indeed something enchantingly birdlike in the shape of her lips and her eyes. She called me 'a little chickadee', for indeed at that time I appeared rather emaciated. Her family dispersed during the war, but they maintained their spacious apartment in St

Petersburg, where I stayed for a few nights after my return from the country. Natasha had just turned 16, and we spent an evening in a wild kissing bout. After my emigration we continued to correspond; she became rather friendly with the Russian writer Alexei Remisoff, whom I later got to know in Paris. In 1931, when she learned from him that I was about to be married, she handed over to him my various memorabilia which had remained in her possession. Remisoff returned these materials to me in Paris. There was a fleeting reference to Natasha in one of my brother Michael's letters to me. He said Natasha came to see him and told him she would remember me for ever.

In 1915 I was befriended by the poetess Zinaïda Gippius and her husband, the poet and novelist Dmitri Merezhkovsky. Both belonged to the group of Symbolists, to whom the passing events of everyday life were but fleeting symbols of eternal verities. My Uncle Minsky summarized the Symbolist yearnings in one of his best-known poems: 'I yearn for something other than the living earth, I dream of something vague and strange beyond my mind's eye . . .' Minsky even originated a system of philosophy which he called 'meonism', from the Greek word 'meon', non-being (Minsky knew his Greek; he translated the *Iliad* into Russian). Meonism was a mystic belief in the unbelievable.

In the year that I met her, Zinaïda Gippius organized in St Petersburg a series of weekly meetings of 'young poets and non-poets'. I qualified by dint of being young, though a non-poet. During one of these meetings she introduced us to a newcomer, a genuine peasant poet, with long, blond hair, whose very name, Sergei Esenin, was redolent of the Russian birch trees. He made his way to St Petersburg from Central Russia on foot as an itinerant book vendor, a profession that fascinated city poets; and he still wore the *lapti*, peasant shoewear made of birchtree bark. He read his poems in a resonant voice, without affectation; his verses rhymed, in contrast with the free verse that polluted the modern school (Zinaïda Gippius was an exception to this wretched dislocation; her verses also rhymed). How different were Esenin's Russian trochaic tetrameters from the anxiety-riddled urban poetry of St Petersburg!

As a non-poet, I had to perform various chores that did not require plenary inspiration. I was appointed secretary of the Religious Philosophical Society of St Petersburg founded by the Merezhkovskys and their associate Dmitri Filosofov (a fitting name!), at which home-grown philosophers divagated on mystical phenomena. I contributed occasional essays and reviews to the monthly publication *The Voice of Life*, founded by the Merezhkovskys. I gloried in my proximity to famous people. My ego stirred prodigiously when Zinaïda Gippius asked me to write a 'marseillaise' for her play, *The Green Ring*. The plot of the play concerned a group of young men and women, some of whom were poets, and others who were not. They assembled periodically to discuss the problems of life. In the last act they unfurled a tricolor banner, green, white, and red, symbolic of youth, faith, and revolutionary fervour. I asked what country's flag had such colours. Filosofov looked at me quizzically, and said, 'Bulgaria'.

I felt humiliated; I should have understood that the flag was a symbol. Anyway, I did write a 'marseillaise' for *The Green Ring*, and it was duly sung at the production of the play by the Moscow Art Theatre Studio.

Years later, crossing the Atlantic on the *SS Majestic*, I happened to find myself on the same boat, and in the same class (tourist), with the troupe of the Moscow Art Theatre Studio. Their fabled director Stanislavsky was with them. I introduced myself as the composer of the 'hymn' of *The Green Ring*, and they sang it for me. I used the tune in my album of *Minitudes* published in New York in 1979, sixty-four years after its composition. I named it 'A National Anthem in Search of a Country'.

For a number of years Merezhkovsky, Zinaïda Gippius, and Filosofov shared the same apartment in St Petersburg, in a happy *ménage à trois*. Ugly rumours had it that Gippius was anatomically incapable of having sexual relations with men; alternatively, she was described as a modern Messalina, an immoral person who regarded intercourse as of no more consequence than a drink of absinthe. What was not generally known about the third member of the trio, Filosofov, was that he was a first cousin of the notorious pederast Serge Diaghilev, and also his lover. Gippius was determined to 'save' him from this homosexual abyss. She wrote in her diary: 'I have pity for Filosofov who dwells in outer darkness. If he remains with Diaghilev he will perish utterly. We must do what we can to rescue him.'

In the summer of 1905 Filosofov joined the Merezhkovskys in their *dacha* near Pskov, about midway between St Petersburg and Moscow. It was there that Gippius made an overt assault on Filosofov's virginity; she entered his room at dawn, but he turned her away. She refused to admit defeat, however, and eventually succeeded in seducing her reluctant guest. Filosofov was seized with horror at his sin. In a remarkable letter which he wrote to Gippius shortly after his fall he expressed his feelings:

Zina! I may be wrong but the memory of our intimacy is physically abhorrent to me. This repugnance goes far beyond a mere morality. It is something physical. In my previous intimacies I experienced a sense of sin; I felt ashamed of my carnal delinquencies. With you it is quite different. I yearn for you spiritually, but your flesh is loathsome to me.

Gippius answered Filosofov's letter immediately with a missive of thirty-two pages, in which she delved deeply into the philosophical and religious aspects of his fall from grace. His aversion to her body was an antithesis of her love for him, she argued; her love for him was 'noumenal' and transcendental, but so was his opposition to her. Unless a synthesis of this antithesis was effected, the result would be a mutual defeat. To assuage Filosofov's consciousness of sin, Gippius advanced the blasphemous notion that a sensual element exists even in one's relationship to God. Her love for Filosofov, she wrote, was sacred and must not be equated with lust. Carnal lust, devoid of the mutual coition of souls, is cold and naked, but spiritual sensuality is benign. 'In my relationship with you,' she wrote, 'I feel the presence of Christ. My love is blessed by His divinity. I am convinced of it, because even before I began loving you, my feelings toward you were open to Christ; my love was sanctified by Him.'

Filosofov was horrified by this 'exploration of one's spiritual intestines'. She was both a saint and a demon, he warned her. She could never know whether the spirit guiding her feelings was God's or Satan's.

Merezhkovsky must have been fully aware of the extraordinary relationship that existed between his wife and Filosofov, but was not apparently perturbed by it. He was probably ascetic by nature, or perhaps totally asexual.

Zinaïda Gippius was obsessed with the necessity of the Revolution. She used to say: 'We must kill the bloody Nicholas,' as if regicide would solve all the problems of political oppression or social injustices in Russia. I, too, was animated by the idea of a revolution that, I hoped, would solve my own psychological problem. When the Revolution finally came in February 1917, I rushed to share my joy with Zinaïda Gippius. She wrote in her diary: 'Nicolas Slonimsky, a student, came to see us, full of joy of the Revolution. He even forgot all about his egocentrism.'

It was in the house of Merezhkovsky and Gippius that, on the first day of the Revolution, the 'good' Revolution of February 1917, I met Alexander Kerensky, a man of magnetic personality who even in private was given to oratorical diction as if addressing a public political meeting. Zinaïda Gippius admired his revolutionary zeal and his great power of speech, but her admiration changed to disdain and even hatred when Kerensky failed to take strong measures against the growing Bolshevik menace. To the Merezhkovskys, Bolshevism was the satanic perversion of the sanctity of the Revolution, with Lenin as its Antichrist. Gippius wrote a poem damning Kerensky as a poseur and a coward. Its wrath is lost in translation, but here is a quatrain:

> Of cursed memory, a fool,
> No hero, nor a monster in a rage,
> A false Pierrot, a schoolboy with a drool,
> A third-rate actor on the summer stage.

In January 1918 the Constituent Assembly, elected by universal suffrage, the first in Russian history, was summarily disbanded by Lenin. Zinaïda Gippius published an impassioned poem about the 'dream of the century' slaughtered by brute force. She never wavered in her detestation of the Soviet rule.

My brother Michael recalls in his memoirs that Merezhkovsky approached him repeatedly for financial assistance at the time when Michael was a close associate of Maxim Gorky in the affairs of the Literary Fund. 'He spat on my soul,' Michael said about Merezhkovsky. The Merezhkovskys went to Paris in 1920, and remained there during the Nazi occupation. Merezhkovsky blackened his once honoured name by making propaganda broadcasts to Russia for the Nazis. He died shortly after the end of the war and thus escaped the possible charge of collaboration.

Our family, once so compact and so cohesive, began to dissolve under the impact of war and revolution. The mystical conviction that we were protected by the beneficent 'Slonimsky providence' that my mother fostered in us, was challenged by inexorable events. My younger brother Vladimir was dying of tuberculosis. He was sent to Davos, Switzerland, in the hope of a cure. Then the war erupted, and my mother decided to bring him home. Heroically, she travelled by the only route that remained open during the war, through Stockholm, London, and Paris. In London she was met by Aunt Zinaïda (who worked in England as a translator), then crossed the English Channel in a boat without lights, in constant danger of lurking German submarines. She arrived safely in Paris, and then went by train to Zürich and Davos, the tubercular centre of the world, with the air so pure that it was supposed to arrest, if not kill, the rapidly proliferating bacilli.

The Swiss doctors offered little hope for Vladimir; he probably would have been beyond help even if penicillin had been discovered forty years earlier. Most tragically, his mind, once so sharp, so incisive, gave way to dementia praecox. His return trip to Russia tested my mother's heroism, and she managed to bring Vladimir back to Petrograd alive. Just before dying he asked for a bottle of oxygen; his last words were: 'My apperception has completed changed.' I was amazed at his use of this precise psychological term. He died on 12 January 1916.

January was a cruel month for our family. My father died in Petrograd on 10 January 1918. He was not quite 68 years old, but he suffered from a number of debilitating ailments, the most tragic of which was the gradual loss of eyesight due to the increasing opacity of the eyeball. The immediate cause of his death was a mechanical one, a constriction of the intestines. A resident German doctor was hastily summoned but arrived too late. He consoled us all by saying that blood poisoning had set in and the case was inoperable.

My mother survived him by twenty-six years (she died in New York, also in January). After my father's death only she and myself remained in our old Petrograd apartment on Grand Greenery Street. Both my brothers were away. Julia was in Yalta. My mother made our loss all the more painful by constantly asking me if I would not have preferred to see her dead instead of my father, insisting on my giving her an honest answer to this monstrous question.

There were ominous signs of disruption of the social fabric during the years of war. One day in 1915 all silver coins suddenly disappeared from circulation, no doubt in consequence of Gresham's law, according to which bad money drives out good (the silver content of the familiar pieces of 10, 15, 20, 25, and 50 copecks was worth more than their nominal value). Copper coins of 1, 2, 3, and 5 copecks soon followed into the maw of Gresham's paradox. The Czarist government, caught unaware, placed in circulation postage stamps of small denominations to serve in lieu of change.

The absurd war was continuing. I was of draft age, and the time came when I had to present myself before the draft board. Did I have any physical ailments? 'Yes,' I said, 'constipation.' 'You will be cured of it very quickly the moment you get under fire,' the presiding officer told me. And so it came to pass that I became a member of the Russian Imperial Army. With conscripts like me, how could Germany fail to win its war? I never had to learn how to shoot. I was assigned to the music section of the Preobrazhensky regiment, a famous old regiment founded by Peter the Great.

In the summer of 1916 I followed the regiment to Rostov, in the delta of the Don River. There I played the piano with the regiment orchestra, and even appeared as soloist in the first movement of Rachmaninoff's Second Piano Concerto. Returning to Petrograd (it was renamed from St Petersburg to remove the stigma of its Germanic sound) in the winter, I found myself a privileged person as a soldier called upon to defend my native land against the alien invader. Among these privileges was a free ride in the electric streetcars. But the military authorities set down an unenforceable regulation, that no more than six soldiers were to ride in a single car; if another soldier boarded it, the military police arrested all seven, even though the original six were innocent of any violation of the rule. This was eminently unfair and resulted in frequent clashes between soldiers and the military police. To put an end to disorder, detachments of the regular army were called in, but soldiers refused to act against their comrades.

Losing control, the military authorities ordered the most loyal Imperial regiment, the Preobrazhensky, to subdue the disobedient army recruits. This was my own regiment, and I found myself in the absurd situation of being called upon to defend the gradually disintegrating Czarist order. But the Preobrazhensky regiment also refused to intervene, and suddenly the authorities were powerless. In a rapidly deteriorating situation, the Duma which exercised power as a nominal Russian parliament, however undemocratically elected, sent its representatives to the Czar to advise him to abdicate. The Czar complied with astonishing meekness, and relinquished his power to a provisional government formed by members of the Duma. And this was the autocratic ruler who so stubbornly withstood a much more violent revolutionary outbreak in 1905! Had the Czarina been with him at the scene, history might have taken a different course. She firmly believed that the Emperor was divinely anointed and that the source of his power was God.

The leader of the party of Constitutional Monarchy, Miliukov, vainly tried to save the throne by the Czar's abdication in favour of his brother, Grand Duke Michael; however, the latter declared that he would assume the crown only if the people of Russia would express preference for a monarchy in a freely held referendum. The rushing tide of revolutionary events swept away any monarchical compromises. The 'bloodless revolution', as it was called, continued on its predestined course, and the sense of newly won freedom was exhilarating. 'We no longer have to have an official permit to hold the sessions of our Religious Philosophical Society,' Zinaïda Gippius solemnly remarked to me. Inevitably, there were abuses of freedom. The yellow press printed stories under such titles as 'Rasputin and the Czarina', with gaudy illustrations showing the Empress of all the Russias in passionate embrace with the Siberian muzhik. But the Imperial family continued to dwell peacefully in their palace in the Petrograd suburb, still named Tsarskoye Selo, the Czar's village. (It was not until the Soviet Revolution that it was renamed Detskoye Selo, a Children's Village, and later still Pushkin, for it was in that Imperial resort that Pushkin went to school.) Concerned about the safety of the Imperial family, Kerensky arranged for their transportation to a seemingly safe provincial town in the Urals. He could not have foreseen that he was unwittingly signing their death warrant. There were rumours that King George V of England expressed willingness to send a British cruiser to take his first cousin Nicholas II and his family to England, but the plan was deemed politically unwise by the British, since they still hoped that the Russians would remain in the war. I attended as many political meetings as I could, and absorbed with peculiar delight the revolutionary rhetorics so lavishly dispensed by Trotsky and Zinoviev. When food became very scarce, Zinoviev screamed: 'We will let the bourgeoisie have just as little bread as possible so that they will not forget its taste!' I remember the merry *chastushka*, a street ballade: 'Pey ty shampanskoye, kurochku zhuy, Den tvoy poslednyi prihodit, burzhuy!' ('Drink your champagne and guzzle your wine! This is your last day, you bourgeois swine!')

We had a friend, a rich Jew named Samuil Poliakov, who owned a mansion on the fashionable Quai des Anglais in Petrograd. During his frequent travels abroad he had collected a cellar of fine French wines, some of it dating back to the Second Empire. When, after the Bolshevik seizure of power, the Soviets ordered the destruction of all intoxicating beverages, accusing the anonymous bourgeoisie of planning to drown the Revolution in alcohol, he decided to obey the order. The alternative would have been to risk the sacking of his house, the destruction of his library, and the confiscation of his collection of valuable paintings. He called the 'anti-alcohol' squad. The honest Bolsheviks poured vintage wine into the sink; not one of them was tempted to appropriate a single bottle, but they yielded to the owner's tearful entreaty to let him have just a few bottles for his own use. He treated me to this wine the next time I was at his house for dinner.

All revolutions devour their children, and the Russian revolution was no exception. Lucky were the great revolutionary leaders who died before the beast went on its rampage. Plekhanov was one of those fortunate men. He opposed Lenin at the London Congress of the Russian Social Democratic Party of 1903, but Lenin obtained plurality (the name Bolshevik is derived from the comparative degree 'bolshe', which means 'more' in Russian). Plekhanov lived in exile during the Czarist rule but returned to Russia after the Revolution. When he died in May 1918, Lenin, Zinoviev, and Trotsky (the latter had joined Lenin's Bolsheviks) were conspicuously absent from his funeral. There was, of course, no religious ceremony; Plekhanov, although born into Russian Orthodoxy, was an atheist, but eulogy was offered by socialists who cherished his memory. It so happened that I was asked to play a funeral march at the service; Plekhanov lay in state in an open coffin, according to the ancient Russian ritual; I studied intently the conformations of his face, trying to form a rational theory about the interdependence between men of great ideas and blind historical events. I played not the Chopin funeral march, which had become a musical cliché at European funerals, but the slow movement from Beethoven's Sonata No. 12, Op. 26, entitled 'Marcia funebre sulla morte d'un Eroe'. It was never ascertained who was the hero whose death was mourned by Beethoven in this music; to me Plekhanov was such a hero.

On the day of the the the Bolshevik Revolution, 25 October 1917 (according to the Old Russian calendar), I was on my way from Moscow to Petrograd. I travelled by night train; upon arrival, the only sign that anything was changed was that Petrograd was unusually quiet. Soldiers patrolled the streets; some carried red flags. I asked one of them what was going on, and he answered rather disdainfully, 'The Soviets have taken over'. I took a streetcar in the direction of the section of the town across the Neva River where we lived at the time. I picked up an afternoon paper representing the moderate faction of the Russian Social Democratic Party, which had been regarded before the Revolution as the extreme radical wing. The revolutionary tide towards the left was so rapid that the former left soon found itself occupying the extreme right.

A sailor riding in the same streetcar asked me why I was reading this counter-revolutionary newspaper. 'How can you read this rag which works for the Jew Kerensky?' he asked. 'As a Russian sailor, I am for Trotsky, the true defender of our native land and our revolution!' I did not take the trouble of informing him that it was Trotsky who was a Jew, and that Kerensky was a pure Russian from the Volga. After all, the sailor carried a bayonet.

In February 1918 I happened to pass by a field in a Petrograd suburb, where a group of ragtag peasants and workingmen was being harangued by an unprepossessing but intense man wearing glasses, with shocks of black hair tossed by the wind. I stopped and stood beside him. It was Trotsky. The war was finished, he screamed, but the Germans had set conditions for a peace treaty that would dismember Russia and destroy the Revolution. There was no alternative, therefore, but to declare an immediate peace without signing a treaty. Pending negotiations with the Germans, he proposed to organize the remnants of the old army as a new military force consisting of workers and peasants, the Red Army. I was witnessing an historic event; the ragtag company constituted the nucleus of the future Red Army, which under Trotsky's leadership confounded and defeated several groups organized by Russia's former allies sworn to 'strangle the Bolshevik revolution in its cradle', in the elegant phrase of Winston Churchill.

Revolutions are full of contradictions. While the Bolsheviks were promising the destruction of the old world in the Russian version of the Internationale, the Czar's brother Grand Duke Michael and his family still continued to live in luxury at their palace in Gatchina, a suburb of Petrograd. Through some extraordinary circumstances, months after the Soviet Revolution, I was engaged as piano teacher of Grand Duke

Michael's son and daughter. I was to give them weekly lessons at 10 roubles a lesson, a fairly respectable fee in the early spring of 1918. Every week a troika was sent to fetch me with the well-fed horses figuratively breathing fire, driven by an Imperial coachman wearing a fur coat right out of some nineteenth-century picture postcard.

I was met at the Palace by the Grand Duke's morganatic wife who introduced me to my prospective pupils, a girl 14 years old and a boy about 10. But I found to my dismay that the boy, like most children of the Imperial family, could speak only English, a language with which I was unfamiliar, and so it was decided that he would not study with me; the girl, however, spoke Russian, and there was no obstacle in communicating with her. I gave her the usual repertoire which I myself had learned from Aunt Isabelle: some Mozart, Beethoven, Schumann, and Chopin. After the morning lesson I was served a sumptuous lunch on Imperial china still decorated with the double-headed eagle of the Romanov dynasty. The sugar bowl was trimmed with gold; spoons, forks, and knives were of sterling silver. I usually saw the Grand Duke after lunch; he seemed to be an easy-going person who spoke Russian and British English with equal fluency; he could play the guitar and liked to sing popular gypsy songs. Our ethnic and social backgrounds could not have been more different, but my Imperial employers never let me feel that I was their social inferior. While waiting for lunch (which was served to me separately from the family) I looked at the framed pictures of the Czars on the walls. There was one of Nicholas II, signed in English, which said, as far as I could make out the unfamiliar words, 'To my dear brother Michael, from Nicky'. Next to it was the stern-visaged bearded Czar Alexander III, father of Nicholas II and of Grand Duke Michael.

The Czar and his family were executed in July 1918, and I was at a loss to know how to express my condolences to his brother, but by that time my employment had come to an end, and I never saw the Grand Duke again. His fate remains unknown to this date.

Petrograd deteriorated rapidly; in the summer of 1918 it was a city of death. Whole families died of starvation; a slight illness was fatal because of lack of medicaments. A silent image lingers in my memory: an elderly Russian lady, wearing a Victorian dress, stands on a corner on Nevsky Prospect, accompanied by a little pedigree dog standing on its hind legs, silently begging for food. Some compassionate souls threw a crust of bread to the animal; it seemed that its mistress would have welcomed a piece, too. Soon dogs, and even before them cats, vanished from the streets of Petrograd. They were eaten by their owners.

Horse flesh became a delicacy. At the time when family dinners could still be served, someone with a misguided sense of humour would announce, 'Milady, the horses are ready!' Another memory: a horse, or rather an emaciated form of it, dragging a sled on the snow-covered street of Petrograd, stumbled, collapsed, and died. Forthwith, men and women wielding long kitchen knives rushed out of neighbouring courtyards and proceeded to carve the fallen animal for food.

So precious did food become for sheer survival in Petrograd that the music critic Boris de Schloezer, brother-in-law of Skriabin, sold his Bechstein grand piano for 12 lb. of black bread, and was envied for his deal.

Alexander Glazunov, director of the Petrograd Conservatory, was a man of imposing corpulence; he liked good food and he drank liquor to excess. When I saw him again in 1918, he looked like a skeleton covered with loosely hanging clothes; he must have lost half of his weight.

Food hallucinations became common. Once I opened the empty cupboard and saw a loaf of white bread on it. I reached for it, but my fingers groped in vain along the empty shelf. The phantom apparition was a play of light and shadow.

It was during that terrible summer of 1918 that I received an excited telephone call from Zinaïda Gippius. Cleaning her kitchen shelves, she had found a round piece of pie that must have been there for several years. It was somewhat rat-riddled, she said, but it could be heated and made edible. She invited me to come over and partake of this rare delicacy. The Merezhkovskys had some sugar and tea left, too, from antediluvian times, and Zinaïda Gippius served a real old-fashioned tea with that precious pie. I tried to chase away the thought that rats had been there before me.

CHAPTER 4

EXODUS

In the autumn of 1918 I decided to leave Russia. My immediate destination was Kiev, the capital of the Ukraine. I applied to the Foreign
Department of the Commissariat of Internal Affairs of the Russian Soviet
Republic for a passport to travel abroad, and in August 1918 obtained the
precious document which read as follows: 'The bearer, citizen of the
Russian Soviet Federal Republic Nikolai Leonidovich Slonimsky, born
on April 15 (27), 1894, in St Petersburg, 24 years of age, departs for the
purpose or organizing concerts in the Ukraine, via Chernigov and Orsha,
and will remain there for three months, whereupon he will return to
Petrograd.' It was a long time, seventeen years to be exact, before I
actually revisited Petrograd, by then renamed Leningrad.

On the way to the railroad station I bought some sandwiches of bread
made of straw husks with slices of vobla, a herring-like fish. It was the
main food item for citizens of Petrograd for several weeks, after a load of
frozen vobla was found in an abandoned freight train. Because of very
cold weather it was well preserved, and so represented no threat to health.
I paid 75 copecks each for a couple of vobla sandwiches.

One of the most disruptive clauses of the separate peace treaty the
Soviet government signed with Germany in Brest-Litovsk in March 1918
was the formation of an independent Ukrainian Republic. Headed by a
former Czarist General, one Skoropadsky (a prophetic name as history
proved, meaning 'quickly falling' in Russian), the Ukrainian state existed
only by the grace of the German occupation army. Thus it was a German
commandant at the railroad station on the border of the Ukraine who put
an all-important stamp on my passport, adding in Gothic script, 'Eine
Persone darf nach Kiew hinreisen' — one person is allowed to proceed to
Kiev.

My family had friends in Kiev, among them the Jewish industrialist
Daniel Balachovsky, who owned the only skyscraper in the city, an edifice
fully six storeys high, boasting a hand-operated elevator. Once in Kiev, I
was lodged in Balachovsky's house. Balachovsky was a friend of Skriabin,
and had arranged several concerts for him in Kiev. After Skriabin's death

in 1915, his widow Tatiana, and her three children Ariadna, Julian, and Marina moved to Kiev and took over several rooms in his house. Soon they were joined by Boris de Schloezer, Tatiana's brother. Julian inherited his father's genius. He was barely 10 years old when he wrote piano pieces very much in the manner of Skriabin's last opus numbers. In Kiev he took private lessons with Glière, director of the Kiev Conservatory. A tragedy cut short his young life. In June 1919 he went on a school picnic to an island on the Dnieper River. The children and the woman in charge returned late in the evening without Julian; they could not find him after dark. A search party was sent out and I joined it. Nearly seventy years have passed since that night, but the pitiful scene is etched indelibly in my memory. We found Julian's body in a bay where there was a sudden drop in the shallow water. A fisherman attached a rope to Julian's neck and towed him in to shore; his body looked like a long slender fish, his feet making a tiny whirlpool in the water.

Julian's funeral was held with a full Russian Orthodox ritual, and Glière delivered a eulogy. The added tragedy was that Julian's mother was in Moscow when he drowned, and there was no way of letting her known, for the telegraph service was not working. She arrived unexpectedly, and it was left to her brother, Boris, to break the news. He kept saying in an anguished voice: 'Mais non! Mais non!' Was he trying to delay the tragic news by this futile denial? Tatiana returned to Moscow, where she died a couple of years later. Schloezer made his way to the Crimea, and eventually to Paris. Ariadna Skriabin lost her life during the Nazi occupation of France; she was active as a courier in the Resistance. Marina also went to France, and remained there.

In Kiev I obtained employment at 12 roubles an hour in Ukrainian currency as a piano accompanist in the vocal department of the Kiev Conservatory. I also profited by Glière's presence and took composition lessons from him. The voice department was headed by the famous tenor Nikolai Figner, a friend of Tchaikovsky, who sang the leading part in the première of Tchaikovsky's opera *The Queen of Spades*. It was a thrill for me to accompany him in the dramatic aria, 'What is our life? A game!' I knew every interlude and recitative of the opera by heart. I was still in the employment of the Kiev Conservatory when Figner died; I remember vividly the sight of his body shrunken in death.

Civil war raged in and around Kiev. Between 1918 and 1920 the city changed hands seventeen times, and one had to be very careful in adjusting to the constantly changing rules of conduct and ideologies. I developed a degree of virtuosity in handling the various documents, those suitable for the Bolsheviks, for the White Army, and for some Ukrainian nationalist groups. The one faction with which I was unable to cope was the band of Ukrainian anarchists, known as the Green Army, which fought both the Red Army and the White Army, and whose political slogan was classical in its simplicity, 'Kill the Jews! Save our souls!' The Green Army utilized a rather simple test to ferret out Jews by asking those suspected to say 'kukuruza', which meant corn. Suspects who failed to roll the 'r' the way the Russians and Ukrainians did were put to the sword. Boris de Schloezer, who briefly fell into their hands, was subjected to this test because the Green Army men thought he looked Jewish. He was not Jewish; in any case he passed the 'kukuruza' test because he could roll the r's *à la française.*

Ironically, precedent for this mortal trial can be found in the Bible, in the Book of Judges:

And the Gileadites took the passages of Jordan before the Ephraimites; and it was so, that when those Ephraimites which had escaped said, Let me go over; that the men of Gilead said they unto him, Art thou an Ephraimite? If he said, Nay; then said they unto him, Say now Shibboleth; and he said Sibboleth; for he could not frame to pronounce it right. Then they took him, and slew him at the passages of Jordan; and there fell at that time of the Ephraimites forty and two thousand.

After the defeat of Germany in November 1918, and the subsequent fall of Skoropadsky, Kiev was captured by the bands of the Ukrainian nationalist Petlyura who made his triumphant entry into Kiev on 6 December 1918. He immediately ordered shop owners to change their Russian signs to Ukrainian, under penalty of arrest and imprisonment. Citizens of Kiev sharpened their wits by creating words for terms that did not exist in Ukrainian: photography became mug-painting, automobiles were self-pushers, and typewriters were finger-pokers. Petlyura's hold on Kiev was militarily weak. One day we found ourselves conquered by an extraterritorial army wearing strange uniforms and speaking a language of Slav origin which was neither Russian nor Ukrainian. The invaders turned out to be Polish soldiers who boarded an empty train and simply rode it for a couple of hundred miles east to Kiev. The Poles had no reason to remain in Kiev, and soon took the same train back to Poland.

After this strange interlude, the Bolsheviks moved in; they occupied Kiev in February 1919, and began looking around for suitable lodgings. The Balachovsky skyscraper was an obvious objective. One day a detachment of Soviet military came to the house and brusquely ordered all of us to get out. The looked strangely unwarlike; the commanding officer carried a tennis racquet, and his appearance suggested a leisurely vacation rather than combat. They also seemed willing to engage in dialectical debate about the right of private citizens to remain neutral in a civil war. I pointed out that our house was the residence of artists and intellectuals, and that the Soviet government was always in favour of arts and sciences. The Bolsheviks countered by observing that, intellectual or not, the skyscraper was obviously capitalist property, which belonged to the people. To gain time, I decided on a bold move. I dispatched a telegram addressed to Lenin, Chairman of the Council of People's Commissars: 'While Moscow is erecting a monument to the great composer Skriabin, his family is being evicted from their apartment in Kiev by the Soviet military forces. I appeal to you for protection.' I signed 'Secretary General of the Skriabin Society', which was a group we founded *ad hoc* for just such eventualities. The tennis-playing Bolsheviks never showed up again.

The Balachovsky skyscraper became a guest house for an extraordinarily varied group of people during that memorable winter of 1918 – 19. Politically, they ranged from former royalty to left-wing socialists and terrorists. For a brief while the morganatic wife (by now in all probability the widow) of Grand Duke Michael stayed there with her daughter (my former piano pupil) and her English-speaking son. Among the guests was also the former minister of justice of the provisional government, Pereverzev, who in July 1917 had ordered the arrest of Lenin. There was a member of the Jewish Bund who personally hanged the double agent Gapon, the revolutionary priest who had led demonstrators to the Winter Palace during the abortive revolution of 1905 while at the same time serving as an informer for the Czarist secret police. And there was a member of the Constituent Assembly, so brutally dissolved by Lenin.

There were also pianists, violinists, and singers whom the wealthy host had patronized during better and calmer days. Glière was a constant visitor. The remarkable young pianist Alexander Dubiansky shattered the peace of the house with his tempestuous rendition of Szymanowski's piano sonata. When the White Army took over in 1919, Dubiansky was arrested on suspicion of being a Communist, and spent a few days in jail. I went to visit him and passed him a newspaper in which I underlined individual letters that spelled the name of a person whom I suspected of informing on him and warned him to be careful in what he said. As cryptography goes, it was a rather elementary code, and I even told Dubiansky to follow the underlined letters right in front of the prison guard without arousing suspicion. Alas, in April 1920 Dubiansky shot himself because of an unrequited passion for a married woman; he was barely 20 years old. A great pianist perished in him; Russian critics compared him with Anton Rubinstein in his technical virtuosity and the poetry of his interpretation; his thundering octave passages in the bass register were especially impressive. He used to demonstrate the power of his little finger by striking my forehead with it, and it actually hurt.

Among the motley crew of politicians and artists who lodged in Balachovsky's skyscraper was the great Russian philosopher Lev Shestov, brother of Balachovsky's wife. In the midst of the Civil War he continued to write his philosophical essays, which combined positivism with a tantalizing glance into indeterminacy; one of his extraordinary insights was a speculation that it is theoretically possible that boiling water could suddenly freeze should its molecules defy the laws of probability. Shestov's real name was Schwarzmann; his family owned small factories in Kiev and elsewhere. The Bolsheviks burned down a Schwarzmann shop; Shestov philosophically watched its destruction from the top floor of Balachovsky's skyscraper. From the Bolshevik standpoint he was an unliquidated capitalist, a social position no less dangerous under Soviet rule than being a Jew in a region occupied by the White Army, which in due course entered Kiev.

The generals of the White Army equated Bolsheviks with Jews. Trotsky, the commander-in-chief of the Red Army, was the Jew Bronstein, whose goal was to kill Russians; the Russians therefore had every right to retaliate by killing Jews. Squads of White Army soldiers, led by uniformed officers, methodically canvassed Jewish homes in Kiev; they rang doorbells and inquired politely whether the tenants were Jews before embarking on their murderous exploits. They shot down entire families, not sparing even small children. During the three days of the Kiev pogrom, local newspapers were covered with black-rimmed announcements reporting the deaths of whole families. The following was typical: 'Relatives and friends announce with great sorrow the sudden deaths of Sam, Ruth, Heidi, Sonia, David, Daniel, and Mark Rosenstein.'

Unable to protect themselves by force of arms, the Jews of Kiev devised a method of defence almost biblical in its inventive simplicity. They gathered in the courtyards of their houses, armed with pots and pans, and organized a concert of noise, beating the utensils with spoons in weird counterpoint; the large iron pans were as resonant as gongs, while silverware provided sonorous tintinnabulations in the treble. Amazingly, this impromptu charivari scared away the cowardly pogrom-makers who, after all, had no formal orders to do their killing and could not expect the regular White Army to send help.

My passport listed my religion as Greek Orthodox, but White Army men, like Hitler a generation after them, judged Jews by their ethnic extraction and their cast of countenance, rather than by their religious affiliation. It was deemed wise for me to move out of the conspicuous Balachovsky mansion, and I found shelter in a small cottage owned by the Shestov family in a Kiev suburb.

Shestov was married to a Gentile woman, and their two daughters,

Tatiana and Natalie, were fair-headed and very Russian-looking; they were entrusted to ward off the beasts in case of confrontation.

Still I was not completely out of danger. One morning a mounted Cossack rode by the cottage and shouted, 'Any Jews here?' Tatiana Shestov came out and assured him that there were none. Visibly impressed by her Russian blonde looks, the Cossack explained almost apologetically, 'I don't mean any harm, Madam, just looking for some Jews to kill.'

Anti-Semitic literature is full and abundant, but it would be hard to find a piece matching in savagery the one that appeared in a Kiev newspaper under the signature of Shulgin, a former member of the Czarist parliament, the Duma. It was entitled 'Three Days of Horror', and it advanced the notion that the Jews of Kiev had received their just reward for their war against Russia, pointing out with an almost scholarly precision that the majority of the membership of the Council of People's Commissars were Jews. How ironic it was that these Jewish members of the Bolshevik party were to perish in Stalin's grand purge a couple of decades later! Had Shulgin lived to witness Stalin's grand design, he probably would have welcomed him as a liberator, as did his monarchist colleague in the Duma Markov who went over to the Bolsheviks after the Second World War, appearing in public at a congress of the Communist Party as a full-fledged delegate. He explained his change of heart by a belated realization that Stalin was a true guardian of Russia's national interests.

Towards the end of the White Army occupation of the Ukraine, my mother made her way to Kiev and joined me in Balachovsky's hospitable skyscraper. With her shrewd instinct of self-preservation, she brought with her a suitcase full of pre-war goods, old laces, satin fabrics, fine linens, and other things that had become rarities in the revolutionary times. She exchanged these treasures for food, which was plentiful in the Ukrainian countryside.

Egocentric as always, my mother was resentful at my spending most of my time with the Shestovs rather than with her. She put forward a psychological gambit. She would not in any way interfere with my life if I were to escort her to Yalta where I could hand her over to the care of my sister Julia. There was no way of getting to Yalta directly south from Kiev, for the intermediate territory was occupied by the roving Green Army bands, and we had to proceed east and then south through Novorossiysk. In October 1919 my mother obtained, through her own efforts, permission for both of us to proceed to the city of Kharkov, about 300 miles east from Kiev, in a sanitary train. Our journey took twelve days. Sometimes the train would stop for hours, but these stopovers were welcome, because peasant women would rush to the train offering incredible delicacies, eggs, white bread, butter, fresh milk, and tasty home-made cutlets, in exchange for manufactured products, particularly lingerie and coloured ribbons. My mother seemed to have an inexhaustible supply of these, so that we never had to go hungry during our long journey. She shared food generously with other passengers. The car still bore the ancient description: 24 men, 6 horses. Actually there were thirty-two humans in our car, but then there were no horses.

The train chugged along making occasional stops for no ascertainable reason. Then suddenly the locomotive engine seemed to breathe its last in a desperate puff of black smoke. We had just reached a small railroad station. I looked at the sign: Putivl! The town of Prince Igor, from which he had marched forth to fight the invading Polovtsy; I could almost hear the exotic sounds of the Polovtzian Dances from Borodin's opera. But the Putivl railroad station was deserted; there were no soldiers of the White, Red, or Green Army in sight. I quickly went over my collection of protective documents. Which of these was I to produce if a soldier appeared out of nowhere? A mistake would have been fatal under the circumstances. But all was quiet at this historic landmark. The engineer got out and made a tour of the train announcing to the passengers that he had no more fuel left, and that, if we were to continue our journey, we would have to get out and gather firewood in the surrounding forest. We complied dutifully, and after the engine received its necessary portion of woody nutrition, it came back to life, and the train pushed hesitantly ahead.

At the Kharkov railroad station we were told that we would have to wait a couple of days for a train that would take us to our next point of destination, Novorossiysk, on the east coast of the Black Sea, from where we could board a boat to Yalta. We spent the next two days and three nights sleeping on seats and benches in the waiting room. But food vendors circulated regularly, and we were able to eat.

With a determination prompted by necessity, I persuaded the station master to authorize my mother and me to purchase the exclusive *Platzkarten* which guaranteed a seat on the train. Being in the zone occupied by the White Army, I flashed an impressively worded certification from the Pan-Russian National Centre of Kiev stating that I was a special emissary of the Centre to the township of Yalta, and requesting officials to lend me all possible assistance. My tenure of office as a member of the staff of the State Opera of Kiev, issued by the all-Ukrainian Division of Fine Arts, was another supportive document. The station master yielded to my importunities, and issued the precious tickets, which I paid for with the Ukrainian money my mother had gathered from the sale of her goods.

The train ride from Kharkov to Novorossiysk proceeded in a surprisingly orderly way. The conductor collected our *Platzkarten*. My mother had a comfortable seat on the lower bench. I occupied a berth on the third level (Russian sleeping cars had three levels). From my high perch I observed a bearded orthodox Jew and his ample-bosomed spouse; they also had *Platzkarten*. A group of White Army officers came in and cast a disdainful look at the Jewish couple. 'Look at them!' one of them growled. 'The way those kikes behave you would imagine the whole train belongs to them.' Then he went over to the seats occupied by the Jews and ordered them to surrender their *Platzkarten*. They obeyed instantly. Another officer said, 'Let me take the woman!' The bearded Jew became agitated. 'Please, do not take my wife away,' he begged. 'We are getting off at the next stop. If you want our money and jewellery, just ask. We are only too glad to do a favour to patriotic Russian officers.' The White Army men paid no attention to the poor man's entreaties, and dragged the woman out unceremoniously with them. The conductor came in to check on the *Platzkarten*, now in the possession of the officers; he looked scared and said nothing about the validity of the tickets. Hours passed. It was dark when the woman returned to her seat, her blouse torn, her hair rumpled, her eyes moist with tears. Her husband rose and led her to the back of the car. The officers soon got off the train, but the Jewish couple no longer dared to assert the claim to their *Platzkarten*.

I was apprehensive for my mother who still occupied the seat guaranteed by her ticket. She had her small golden cross conspicuously displayed on a necklace, and she nervously touched it once in a while. I was out of sight of the marauding officers on my perch on the third level. We arrived at Novorossiysk without further trouble. Getting off at the railroad station I was amazed at the sight of palm trees that lined the broad avenues of this subtropical resort town. I had never seen palm trees before except in a botanical garden. I made arrangements for the boat trip to the Crimea. There were no cabins, of course, but we could stay on the deck, breathing the fresh air of the sea, and spending nights under the star-studded sky. The North Star was quite low on the horizon in these latitudes, and some unfamiliar southern constellations emerged at the horizon. Food was served, and in a matter of four or five days we arrived at Yalta. We had not been able to notify Julia of our coming, because the telegraph services were practically non-existent, but Yalta was full of familiar faces from Petrograd and Kiev. We had no difficulty in finding a place to stay, and we located Julia the next day.

I established contacts with several singers whom I had used to accompany in Kiev, and who providentially turned up in Yalta. Many of them were Jews, but the White Army authorities in the Crimea were less anti-Semitic than their Kiev colleagues, possibly because there were few indigenous Jews in the Crimean peninsula. Several musicians of my acquaintance found gainful employment in a dilapidated shack which bore the imposing name of Conservatory of Yalta; soon I joined its faculty. The mild Yalta climate made it unnecessary for me to be concerned about clothes and footwear. My wearing apparel had deteriorated to the point of dissolution; I had only a single shirt left, and even that one had a lengthwise tear in the back. I laundered it by tying a string through the hole and lowering it down the whirlpool in a watermill, which cleaned it more thoroughly than a professional laundryman, and it dried in seconds under the warm Crimean sun. My socks lacked heels, and my only pair of shoes had no soles, so that when it rained outside it also rained in my feet. A wild rumour spread around that a shipment of socks was discovered in a forgotten warehouse — not complete socks, however, but just the heels. I rushed to the warehouse, and got several heels of durable fabric of pre-war manufacture. I covered the central holes in my shoes with some strong cardboard, and my newly acquired impermeable sock heels made me quite comfortable even when it rained.

In Yalta I received an education in the basic laws of economics. Only those people who possessed manual skill or could provide entertainment had a chance of survival. Poets, philosophers, mathematicians, and professors had to learn a useful trade or perish. Some of them adapted themselves very quickly as janitors, streetsweepers, porters, and shoe-shiners. It was a source of amazement to me that in Yalta, which was the last outpost of a defeated army, there were so many men who wanted to have their shoes shined; the trade was flourishing. Former professors and assorted intellectuals even developed a certain pride in their lowly jobs. A mathematics graduate got a job as a janitor in a municipal men's room, and he evinced great pride in his maintenance of the toilets. He pointed out how carefully he cut up the local newspaper into geometrically uniform squares (he was a mathematician after all) and how accurately hooked them on the nail within easy reach of a person occupying a toilet. (There was, of course, no toilet tissue in Russia during the Civil War.) He was shrewd enough politically to make sure that the newspapers thus employed did not carry a picture of General Denikin, commander in chief of the remnant of the White Army, or his successor General Wrangel, or Admiral Kolchak, supreme commander of all anti-Soviet forces, for a conspicuous display of the visage of such a respected personality hung on a hook near the toilet bowl could be judged as a deliberate affront at the dignity of the Army.

The dying beast is the most savage. The fateful word 'Evacuation' was already heard quite openly in Yalta, when the local commandant, General Slashchev, decided to make a show of force. He put out large posters proclaiming that all able-bodied men between the ages of 17 and 60 not in possession of their draft cards would be shot at sight, adding, 'I take the sin upon my soul.' He also ordered immediate execution of everyone suspected of Communist sympathies, and he carried out his threats with theatrical flair. The beautiful beach of Yalta presented a strange sight during that early spring of 1920. A row of improvised gallows made out of telegraph poles lined the road paralleling the beach, with bodies of young men and women grotesquely swinging in the breeze, carrying signs 'RED' on their breasts. Arkady Averchenko, one of the best-known humorists in pre-revolutionary Russia, and an ardent anti-Bolshevik, published in a Yalta newspaper a piece of grim gallows humour in the form of an allegory. In it he described himself as taking a leisurely walk along a broad alley lined by beautiful cypress trees on a windless day; suddenly he realized that the tree branches were bodies of men and women. Averchenko's reputation saved him from being penalized for his boldness. By that time General Slashchev, drenched in alcohol and besotted with cocaine, was removed from his post. Remarkably enough, after the inevitable end, he went over to the Soviets, flew to Moscow, and declared himself a socialist. The Bolsheviks made whatever use they could of him, and then shot him just the same.

Throughout the changing fortunes of the armies fighting in the Civil War I adopted one firm rule: passive resistance to authority. It worked well, but the situation in Yalta became critical for me at the age of 25, and thus subject to all the dire penalties threatened by the murderous Slashchev. I reported my predicament to Lev Sibiriakov, a former operatic bass of the Imperial Opera, whom I accompanied at various local concerts in Yalta, and who, although a Jew (his real name was Spivak), had powerful connections in the highest echelons of the White Army. As I was recounting my problem to him, he suddenly burst into hysterics. 'Merciful God!' he cried. 'Why, oh why Sibiriakov,' (he was in the habit of addressing himself in the third person singular), 'why, in addition to all his miseries should he have his accompanist shot before his eyes?' His litany sounded like an aria from a Verdi opera. 'Go away!' he screamed. 'You are a ghost, a corpse, a cadaver!' Then, suddenly changing the tone of his voice, he lamented, 'And where will I find another accompanist now?'

After my failure to enlist Sibiriakov's assistance, I found unexpected help from Julia. As a contributor to a monarchist paper in Yalta, Julia was in good standing with the civil authorities of the White Army. Despite her uncommon intelligence, she had become an earnest believer in the divinity of the Russian monarchy. In one of her articles, describing a historic confrontation between Kerensky as head of the provisional Government and the ex-Czar, she made a rather extraordinary statement: 'Kerensky represented the power of the state, whereas the Emperor was deprived of all his rights. Yet it was clear that Kerensky was nothing but a petty lawyer enjoying a brief period of dominance while the Emperor was invested in the glorious light of a divinely anointed monarch.'

During the brief Bolshevik interlude in Yalta in 1918, Julia had interceded with the cultural department of the Red Army in favour of a Czarist general who was under the threat of arrest. Now the general held an important post in the White Army. Julia gained admittance to him in his office, and told him bluntly: 'A year ago I saved you from the Bolsheviks. Now I ask you to save my brother from your people.' The General listened to Julia's plea with sympathetic attention. When informed that I was my mother's sole support in Yalta, he asked Julia whether I ever applied for exemption as the only son. Well, I was not the only son; I had two brothers in Petrograd, but Julia was careful not to disclose this information. The General jotted down a few words on a piece of paper, put an official rubber stamp on it, and handed the document to Julia. I was to present myself at the local draft board for action. All went off without a hitch. I received the all-important certificate of exemption from military service, and thus became immune to arrest and execution. Sibiriakov was beside himself with joy when I told him about the happy solution of my problem. 'Will you play for me again?' he asked anxiously. Rich Jews fleeing south from Petrograd, Moscow, and Kiev to escape the Bolsheviks were in double jeopardy, as capitalists in the Soviet-occupied territory, and as Jews under the White Army rule. But both the Bolsheviks and White generals were careful not to touch foreign nationals. Counting on this protection, a group of enterprising individuals opened a Brazilian consulate in Kiev, supposedly accredited from Rio de Janeiro, and proceeded blithely to issue Brazilian passports authorizing the bearer to travel abroad. One might have thought that the authorities, both Bolshevik and anti-Bolshevik, would have realized that the spontaneous generation and remarkable proliferation of so many Brazilians in the Ukraine was artificially contrived, but a proper bribe in the right place quickly allayed such a suspicion.

Less exotic but just as effective was the activity of the Latvian consulate that opened in Yalta early in 1920 during the dying days of the White Army rule. It was amazing to observe how many Latvians walked the streets of Yalta during the worst period of General Slashchev's murderous spree, protected against arrest by the newly issued passports attesting to their citizenship of the independent Republic of Latvia.

Chances are that neither the Brazilian nor the Latvian governments were aware of the fraud perpetrated in their names, but there were nations that openly traded citizenship rights to stateless persons. A number of Russian *émigrés* obtained passports legally issued by the government of Honduras which held the promise of the most coveted prize of all, a visa to the United States. All the applicants had to do was to make out a cheque for US$100 payable directly to the President of the Republic of Honduras, and a freshly minted passport would be in their hands in a matter of days. Another curiosity was citizenship of the Republic of Haiti, which was openly peddled in Paris in the 1920s. Several Russian violinists and pianists made their way to the United States on Haitian passports, and were shocked to discover under questioning by the immigration authorities that Haiti was a Negro republic. They need not have resorted to such subterfuges; artists of whatever quality were exempt from the US quota.

After obtaining a protective document from the military authorities of the White Army at Yalta, I made a determined effort to get out of the Crimea, out of Russia, whether White, Red, or Green. My destination was Paris, which had become a centre of Russian emigration; the only way to Europe was through Constantinople, which was then occupied by the British. I obtained passage on a small boat sailing under the Turkish flag. It was crowded to capacity; my 'stateroom' was the middle step on the stairway leading from the deck to the engine room. To assure my squatting rights, I placed on the middle step of the stairway my well-worn suitcase containing my worldly belongings, a copy of *Les Dieux ont soif* by Anatole France, a Russian translation of *Elements of Psychology* by William James, and some more books and music. I also had in my possession a worn-out fur coat, which was not needed in sub-tropical latitudes. The weather over the Black Sea was clement; a slight west wind wafted gently. I slept semi-recumbent on the stairway but felt no discomfort. In the morning I could get some tea and a Russian pretzel; for lunch the passengers had hard-boiled eggs.

Russian currency of any political faction was no longer valid, and I wondered what would happen to me on my arrival in Constantinople. I made several acquaintances on the boat who were amply supplied with French francs and English pounds. They encouraged me about my chances for survival in the outside world; there was a considerable demand for musicians to play in restaurants and cinemas.

It took us ten days to cross the Black Sea from Yalta to Constantinople, a trip that would normally require not more than two. Flocks of birds over the ship heralded the imminent landing. Arising from a refreshing sleep, I beheld an extraordinary sight: dozens of small boats laden with fruit, bread, packaged sausages, and large chunks of cheese, with boatmen peddling their wares in French, English, and occasionally Russian, offering tempting treats for a few pennies in Turkish or English money. Alas, I had no valid currency, and had to be satisfied with a purely visual feast. Several of my newly acquired boat friends bought baskets of fruit, cheese, and sandwiches, and some of them shared these tasty products with me.

Another unforgettable sight: black smoke from the stacks of numerous small steamers on the Bosporus, so invigorating to see after the undernourished sickly puffs emitted by the Russian engines. It took half a day for the passengers and refugees to disembark. We were all taken to a large reception hall, presided over by officials in shiny uniforms, Turkish, French, and English. This time I had no fear of displaying all my documents, including my Soviet passport. I was in a free world, and the word freedom assumed a literal meaning for me.

An interpreter asked each Russian refugee about his or her skills. 'Poet,' declared one proudly, raising his arm. 'Left,' the official ordered. 'Painter,' declared another. 'Housepainter?' 'No,' the other replied. 'A modern art painter.' 'Left,' came the command. 'Journalist!' another refugee announced. 'Can you write in French or English?' he was asked. He replied in the negative. 'Left!'

Then it was my turn. 'Pianist,' I said. 'Pianist? You play the piano? Can you read music?' the interrogator asked almost incredulously. Regaining my feeling of pride at my accomplishments and delighted at the opportunity of declaring my genius to the world, I said, 'I am a professional pianist. And I can read music, even difficult music.' I was about to mention what Glazunov said at the St Petersburg Conservatory about my playing, but was cut short by the official. 'Right!' he instructed. A few more people who could play the trumpet or had some manual skills joined me on the right, but the majority ended up on the left side. The scene suggested the Last Judgment, with sheep led to the right and goats to the left. I was a sheep qualified to enter Heaven.

Once out in the new world, I was overcome by sensual impressions, visual, auditory, olfactory. Carriages rode by at full speed, drawn by horses the like of which I had not seen for an eternity, black, white, grey horses, well-fed, strong, muscular horses. Even the smell of their excrement bespoke animal vigour. A solitary automobile passed by at a slow pace, belching petrol fumes that exuded energy. I had 25 Turkish piastres in coins in my pocket, a gift of one of my moneyed boat acquaintances, and I stopped by a stand overhung with delicious-looking pretzels. The vendor looked at me and said, 'Iki buchuk gurush!' I held up my index finger to indicate that I wanted only one pretzel, and handed him a

10-piastres coin. He returned seven and a half piastres; the Turkish words 'iki buchuk gurush' must have meant two and a half piastres. The pretzel was most nutritious and I relished its goodness.

My only contact in Constantinople was at Hotel Parthenon, where one of my Russian acquaintances who had arrived on an earlier boat had a room. It was in Galata, the lower part of the city on the waterfront. I wandered along the Golden Horn, a channel between Galata and the Asiatic half of the city which was then called Stamboul (now the entire city is called Stamboul, or Istanbul), but had no way of locating the address. I caught the attention of a cosmopolitan-looking young man with a moustache and asked him in French where Hotel Parthenon was. 'Parthenon?' he said with an unexpected display of animation, 'Parthenon! Kala!' He took me by the hand and after a short walk led me to a ramshackle cottage on the waterfront. I figured out by derivation from such words as calligraphy that 'Kala' meant 'good' in Greek; Greek was the second language in Constantinople. 'Parthenon?' I asked him again. He shook his head and said, 'Kala! Ne!' I was utterly confused, for I did not know that the sign of the affirmative in the Near East was a shake of the head from right to left and that 'Ne', which I took to be the negative, meant the positive in Greek. And the place where my cicerone left me did not look at all like a hotel. A young girl sat astride the window sill, completely naked, cleaning her private parts with singular concentration. Abstracting herself from her occupation for a moment, she waved at me with a most friendly smile. It looked to me as if she was motioning for me to go away, but, as I found out later, this motion meant exactly the opposite and what she intended me to do was to come in closer. I approached her, and she said, 'Kala! Kala! Una lira! Una lira!' I was bewildered. I tried to tell her in French that I did not want a room, but that I wanted to know if my friends were staying at the hotel. She must have misunderstood me, for she said in French, 'Cinquante piastres'. It was only then that it dawned on me that I was in the wrong place. 'Parthena' in Greek means a girl, for the Parthenon was the temple of the goddess Athena Parthenos on the Acropolis. When I said 'Parthenon' to the kindly Greek who conducted me to this place, he apparently thought that I was in need of a woman. But even had I been tempted by the young 'parthena' in the window, I did not have 50 piastres to pay for her services.

Constantinople was full of Russian musicians, who gradually monopolized the music business there. In no time at all I found a job to accompany a couple of Russian dancers in a dance studio. The fee was 50 piastres an hour, a fantastic sum of money for which I could get twenty pretzels. A piano arrangement of Tchaikovsky's *Nutcracker Suite* was placed on the rack. Could I read that at sight? 'I know the music by heart,' I said in a weak effort to show my superiority, but the dancers paid no attention. I acquitted myself brilliantly and was hired to accompany the same dancers every day. At the end of the first rehearsal I pocketed my 50 piastres, adding them to whatever remained from my initial purse of 25 piastres, and in a state of high elation took a walk to the central part of the town. I passed by a restaurant of the Alliance Française, and boldly entered the dining room. French was spoken there, much to my relief. Unbelievably, a complete dinner cost only 60 piastres, and it included a glass of red wine. A large basket filled with fresh French white bread was conspicuously placed on the counter with a sign over it, 'Pain à volonté' ('Bread at will')! I took a couple of slices, sat at a table and had a meal served by a French waitress. No tips were required or accepted, which was fortunate for me, for I had barely enough money to pay for the meal. The menu consisted of soupe à l'oignon, a couple of delicious meat cutlets with mashed potatoes, a cup of coffee, and a tart. I do not believe that I had ever enjoyed a meal as much as I did that one at the Alliance Française; it gave me an almost aesthetic satisfaction. The French bread alone was a work of art.

The first few nights in Constantinople I slept in a flophouse at 10 piastres a night. But soon my fortune took a turn for the better. I got a job playing in a Russian restaurant, in a trio, with a violinist and a cellist. The emolument was stupendous: 5 Turkish liras an evening plus a real Russian dinner with borsht, magnificent Russian cutlets, and blancmange for dessert. For playing overtime after a late dinner, we got tips. I recall one glorious day when we finished our stint with 14 Turkish liras each for working from 6 o'clock to 3 o'clock in the morning.

I moved to a nice house with a Greek family on 37 Rue Bairam. There was a large printed sign on the front door, 'Ici demeure une honnête famille', to forewarn passers-by that it was not a house of prostitution; most other houses on Rue Bairam were private brothels. I found out later that the Greek woman who owned our house was a former madam. I was paying her 7 liras a week, a substantial rent. She was impressed by my making so much money, and told me that I ought to get married. She had two daughters, Nina and Alexandrine, aged 19 and 18 respectively; both were luscious Greek brunettes, but I was not going to form any dangerous attachments. Soon both of them were affianced to Greek men from Beirut, after exchanging photographs by mail.

As a pianist in restaurants and cinemas, I earned enough money to buy an elegant suit of clothes, a pair of leather shoes, several shirts, long underwear (shorts were not yet in fashion), and plenty of socks. It was a strange feeling to wear a shirt which was not torn at the back, and shoes which did not leak when it rained. I also bought real toothpaste, real soap, and brilliantine to grease my hair so as to have the parting clearly delineated. And there were gustatory delights: Swiss chocolate and Turkish rahat-lukum. But these luxuries did not make me forget about my prime goal in life: to become famous as a concert pianist, composer, and writer. I composed a *Valse Bosphore*, to celebrate the waterway on which Constantinople was situated; I took the piece to the printer, and in a week I had a hundred mimeographic copies of it. I was a published composer!

American foxtrots were extremely popular in Constantinople in 1920; I played such classics as *Dardanella* in restaurants from printed sheet music. What song could be more appropriate to play on the banks of the Bosporus, across the Sea of Marmara from the Dardanelles? I was fascinated by its syncopated melody against a rapid running bass, and decided to compose a foxtrot of my own. Just like *Dardanella*, it had a swinging syncopated melody, and it was set in the customary song form, with an introduction and a refrain. I gave it a suggestive title in Turkish, 'Yok, yok, effendi' ('No, no, milord'), supposedly a demure refusal by a Turkish girl to yield to a man's inducements. I included it under the title *Obsolete Foxtrot* in my collection of *Minitudes* published fifty-nine years later in New York.

As another offering to the exotic glories of the East, I wrote *Danse du Bairam*, purportedly mirroring the religious frenzy of the Muslim carnival. It abounded in augmented seconds, the obligatory intervals of anything oriental. The *Danse du Bairam* is probably the most shameful of my creations, but I had it published, first *in extenso*, and then in an abridged version, cutting out the most egregious orientalia. In that sterilized form I included it among my *Minitudes* under the self-exculpatory title, *Danse du Faux Orient*.

Besides celebrating the rebirth of my physical person, I became deeply involved in Constantinople in a romantic passion for a young Russian dancer who liked to be called by the name Jenny. As with most of my romances, this one had a hesitant beginning. We spent hours together, sitting on the cold marble steps of the mosque Aya-Sofia in Istanbul, holding hands, talking, and reading the Russian edition of *Elements of Psychology* by William James. We never finished the book.

Jenny entertained curious notions about romance. She thought the physical part of it was undignified, and she objected to my passionate advances. Why did I agree to her reservations? 'Si jeunesse savait. . .' If youth had known, but was I ever youthful? The second part of the famous French distych, 'Si vieillesse pouvait . . .', had no meaning to me. How could one not be able to love? The fault of youth, in my generation at least, was not a lack of knowledge, but the timidity in applying it. In the throes of my *amitié amoureuse* with Jenny, I never felt 'jeune', even though our intimacy was that of total mutual absorption. We ate out of the same plate;

we intertwined our fingers while walking; we sat cheek to cheek. I mumbled the erotic lines of Pierre Louis, set to music by Debussy: 'Tant nos membres étaient confondus que je devenais toi-même.'

There was a ritual: Jenny would collect the Turkish liras from my now lucrative income, and add a few piastres from her own earnings as a member of the corps de ballet in a travelling company; the money would then be put in a box marked 'for our children'. Through some morbid perversion, she called me by the name of a dead child, her cousin Muma. At moments which the French describe as 'transports', she would reproach me for trying to commit incest, for she was my mother, she insisted, and I was her child. She was profuse in protestations of her undying love for me, but insisted that it had nothing to do with physical passion. She was reluctant to serve as an instrument of release of my purely physiological impulses, and often said that she would not mind if I would seek relief with another woman. After a few months she went to Bulgaria where she joined a ballet troupe; I followed her there. Still, my sense of self-preservation was strong enough to break this exquisite torment.

Some years later I saw Jenny in Paris; she was living in a 'mariage blanc' with a former dancer of the Diaghilev Ballet, an avowed homosexual. It was he who wrote to me in 1963 to inform me of her death. Jenny had left instructions that a teddy bear, which I had given her in Constantinople, and which she had kept through the years as a memento of our romance, be buried with her. Her request was faithfully carried out. I sent roses to be placed on her grave.

My stay in Constantinople and Sofia was psychologically darkened by a gnawing uncertainty about the fate of my mother. After the Bolshevik occupation of the Crimea all communications between Russia and the outside world were cut off. More than a year elapsed after my mother vanished into the silent vastness of Russia before the dark curtain was lifted. Then suddenly, a letter from Aunt Zinaïda, from Riga, Latvia, reached me by a circuitous route, and from it I learned that my mother was safe in Petrograd with my two brothers, and that Aunt Isabelle was on her way to Vienna to join her lover, Leo van Jung. Isabelle survived the worst years of famine in Petrograd thanks to the food she received in payment for her concerts. Particularly rich were the rewards proffered by Soviet sailors in the port of Kronstadt, which consisted of potatoes, bread, butter, milk, even fresh meat.

Isabelle formed important connections. The Admiral of the Soviet Fleet was a former student of Uncle Semyon, who adopted the *nom de révolution* Raskolnikov, after Dostoyevsky's mystic murderer in *Crime and*

Punishment. One of Aunt Isabelle's piano students, Dimitri Tiomkin, held an important position in the Music Division of the Soviet Ministry of Culture. When Aunt Zinaïda fell desperately ill, Isabelle appealed to Tiomkin for aid; he managed to get scarce medication for her and, wonder of wonders, a horse and carriage to take her to the hospital. She survived. Tiomkin eventually went to Hollywood where he became an extremely successful film composer.

As the Russian situation stabilized, Aunt Isabelle decided to emigrate. Vienna was her second home; she had been educated there, and spoke impeccable German; as a young girl she had been kissed on the forehead by Brahms (the height of the great composer's attentions to the fair sex). She was friendly with Arthur Schnitzler; several brilliant men admired her for her plump attractiveness. Felix Satten, the future author of the celebrated children's classic *Bambi*, followed her all over Europe, but she would have none of his professions of affection; she invariably selected the worst of her men for lovers. For years she clung to Leo van Jung, despite his outrageous fickleness. A letter from her to Aunt Zinaïda dated Kiev, 1 October 1898, has been preserved in the family archives.

No letters from Leo [she wrote], so I decided not to go to Vienna right now. My feelings towards him remain the same, and if he needs me even for a minute, I will run to him. But I cannot, and I will not, return to a life of hypocrisy that darkened my relationship with him when we were together. Now my anger, my horrible, wild jealousy have disappeared, and I can think of him only with tender affection.

After the end of the Russian Civil War in 1920 Aunt Isabelle secured permission from the Soviet authorities to export her Bechstein piano, one of the best of the brand famous for its liquescent tone and its fine articulation. In Vienna, she found to her intense distress that Leo had in the meantime set up a household with one of his female pupils. Humiliated and shocked, Aunt Isabelle left Vienna and went to Berlin. Despite the economic chaos that reigned in Germany at the time, she successfully organized a class of pupils. In 1923 she received an invitation to join the faculty of the Curtis Institute of Music in Philadelphia; she left for America, and settled in New York, with weekly trips to Philadelphia.

Leo van Jung managed to escape the Nazis in 1938; he went to Riga, Latvia, then an independent republic, which had a large German-speaking colony. From Riga he wrote to Aunt Isabelle in New York asking her to help him come to America. But this time she felt she could not accept him. He died shortly before the Nazis invaded Russia and occupied Riga; his last mistress came to New York and became Aunt Isabelle's companion around the house. In the meantime, Isabelle formed another unhappy alliance with a Russian *émigré* violinist. They quarrelled violently; she accused him of philandering.

Normal postal communications were finally established with Russia; my mother wrote me voluminous letters. Still full of nervous energy and eager for action, she got a most enviable job as manager of one of the regional centres distributing food supplies, the American Relief Administration, the famous ARA organized by Herbert Hoover. Hoover's name is not greatly honoured in the United States, but it was a symbol of salvation for thousands of Russians during the dreadful famine years 1920 and 1921. As a token of gratitude to Hoover, the Soviet government donated to him a valuable collection of documents and printed periodicals covering the Russian revolutionary period. This collection, now housed at the Hoover Institute at Stanford, California, constitutes a primary source of Russian studies in America. There exists in its archives a remarkable photograph showing a large group of Russian peasants kneeling before the members of the American Relief Administration, with a pyramid of boxes of food and other necessities marked ARA in the background. In later years Soviet historians downgraded Hoover's philanthropic initiative, and his name is rarely mentioned in Soviet publications.

My mother's service for the ARA was the proudest chapter of her life. Through the years she preserved the official certificate dated 15 September 1921, and stamped 'American Relief Administration in Petrograd'. It read:

The bearer, Faina Afanasievna Slonimskaya, is charged with the administration of the American dining room located in the building of Second Public School in Petrograd on Zamyatin Street. The above person is responsible for the proper handling of American provisions and for the distribution of food on the premises. Official authorities are requested to lend to the above person such assistance as is necessary to facilitate the fulfilment of her duties.

My mother invoked her service to the Americans each time she felt that her children failed to appreciate her accomplishments. In a letter to me, she wrote:

As the appointed administrator of the American food centre and restaurant in Petrograd, I had to deal with 400 undisciplined children. I had to run from the kitchen on the third floor to the dining room on the first floor, to catch up with the elevator that carried provisions in large baskets to make sure that the waiters did not steal food. I worked from 9 o'clock in the morning to 6 o'clock in the evening. Often there was no time left for my own dinner and, risking criminal charges, I had to take food home with me. Michael was staying with me then, and naturally I shared the American food with him, heating it up with newspapers in the oven, since we had no firewood. Considering the surgical consequences of my bearing innumerable children, with my 'innards falling out', to use your Aunt Isabelle's elegant expression, I often collapsed, leaving a puddle of blood on the floor. Michael would then pick me up and put me on the bed. Even though I was completely exhausted, I still had to get up to write out a detailed account of the distribution of the food during the day.

She finally had to leave her job because of her nervous condition, which became critical when, instead of signing her official report Faina Slonimskaya, she wrote Faina Stolovaya, 'Faina Dining-room'.

CHAPTER 5

PARIS

I reached Paris in late 1921. By then the invasion of the city by Russian *émigrés* had assumed astronomical proportions. Ideologically, the Russian colony in Paris was a detritus composed of derelicts of all political factions, from the defeated generals of the White Army to bandits of the Green Army, interspersed with some genuine members of aristocracy and royalty. There were also writers of varied political colours. All these factions conducted continuous feuds among themselves. Comical scenes were enacted at Paris cafés. A Jewish journalist would engage in loud debate with another Jewish journalist about the equitable borders between autonomous parts of the future Russian Democratic Republic. The most vociferous of them, Boris Gourevitch, drew up a plan for a world government of which he himself was to be installed as a supreme spiritual mentor without portfolio. After his death in New York, he left behind a huge manuscript in Russian which expounded his ideas.

Boris Gourevitch had a brother Gregory, a talented, though erratic, pianist, who specialized in works of Liszt and Skriabin, which he played in a state of dreamy alienation, focusing his gaze on the ceiling and letting the wisps of his greying hair fall listlessly on the back of his balding head. Fond of sensational exploits, he made headlines by flying to America on the first passenger dirigible that crossed the ocean in 1922. He induced the captain of the airship to install a lightweight piano on board, and played Liszt and Skriabin on it, looking upwards towards the richly ornamented candelabras while muttering incantations.

But the general mass of Russian *émigrés* in Paris were not concerned with high politics or mystical insights. Their problem, and my own, was physical survival. Those capable of manual labour hired themselves out as bricklayers or doormen. I knew a Russian literary critic who stood in line all night to get a factory job, and had to cope with a mob of husky hungry men when the gates opened. Those who rushed in first got the few jobs available, while the others were chased away by armed guards. I was, of course, in the fortunate position of having a marketable skill as a pianist. Once I was offered a well-paying job at a reception for the Shah of Persia who was visiting in Paris, but the occasion demanded a tuxedo, which I did not own.

I also lost my chance of being hired by Chaliapin as an accompanist. I had an audition with him in a private house. He came in, looked around and said, 'I need a woman'. This was a strange introduction, but Chaliapin was known for his rough ways. At my audition Chaliapin asked me whether I could play the *Songs of Death* by Mussorgsky. I could. Chaliapin sang in his velvety bass; I played. Without finishing one song, he tried another. Then he stopped paying any attention to me and asked for a drink of vodka. I was not hired. Perhaps it was just as well, for Chaliapin was beastly to accompanists. In America his favourite pianist was Max Rabinovich, who attuned himself wonderfully to the vagaries of Chaliapin's free rhythm. Whenever Chaliapin was not in full command of his voice, however, or forgot the words, he would point his forefinger accusingly at Rabinovich as if to suggest that something was wrong with the pianist and not with himself. After a few exhibitions of this nature, Max Rabinovich quit. Chaliapin was unhappy about losing his pianist, and hired a British accompanist, very tall and very blond, who played the piano quite well but was unable to re-create the peculiarly Russian mood of the songs. After one particularly unsatisfactory concert, Chaliapin flew into a rage. 'Take these goddamn Jews away from me!' he screamed. 'Give me Rabinovich!'

Chaliapin was also notorious for his brutal behaviour towards his colleagues on the opera stage. Even the great Koussevitzky stood in awe of him. During a rehearsal of *Boris Godunov* at the Paris Opera conducted by Koussevitzky, Chaliapin suddenly stopped singing and said to him in Russian, 'Can't you count?' Thereupon he proceeded to beat time with his foot to set the right tempo. Koussevitzky became so flustered that he could not go on with the rehearsal, and after the intermission notified the management that he would not conduct the opera. Chaliapin feigned disbelief when he was told the news. 'I only asked this haemorrhoidal Jew to keep time,' he observed.

One of my most striking memories of Paris comes from a mixed Russian – French party I attended. Among those present was a very tall, middle-aged woman with a rather small head which looked like an extension of a long slender neck, continued in an elongated torso, with the whole upper body reposing rather incongruously on a disproportionately large pelvis and fat legs. I asked the hostess who the woman was. 'Why, she is Mademoiselle Eiffel,' was the reply, 'the daughter of the builder of the Eiffel Tower.' I was amazed at the genetic resemblance between the woman and the tower, but I withheld comment.

In Paris I renewed my acquaintance with the Russian bass singer

Alexander Mozzhuhin, whom I had accompanied in Kiev, and whose interpretations of Mussorgsky's songs were musically superior to Chaliapin's, if not as dramatically effective. Mozzhuhin asked me to play for him again at his Paris recital. At the intermission, an artistic-looking man with a shock of greying hair approached me. It was Serge Koussevitzky. He asked me whether I would be interested in playing for him while he practised conducting. I certainly would. He gave me his address which was in a fashionable Paris suburb, and asked me to come to lunch the following day.

At lunch I met Koussevitzky's wife Natalie. She was an imperious-looking woman who rarely spoke, and when she compressed her taciturn lips, she reminded one of an owl at her silent watch. The famous Koussevitzky publishing house, Éditions Russes, listed her as partner. In fact, this important publishing enterprise was financed by her family fortune derived from a large lumber company. It was her money that had enabled Koussevitzky to start his career as conductor in Moscow. He used to hire an entire orchestra to come to his palatial mansion for weekly rehearsals, and he practised conducting until he was ready to appear before an audience. At first he lacked the purely technical skills of conducting, but he was a superb 'animateur', as the French put it.

Koussevitzky gave me a piano arrangement of Rimsky-Korsakov's *Scheherazade* and asked me to play it. I banged out the familiar opening unisons. Koussevitzky sat down, with the full orchestral score in front of him, and proceeded to conduct, giving cues to imaginary instruments in the room. I followed his beat with great curiosity and not a little trepidation. So this was the way conductors practised. Still, I had never known a conductor who used a pianist for practising; Koussevitzky was apparently unique in this respect. But whatever he did, the very fact that he could beat time, now with the right hand, now with the left, then with both hands, turning his head towards the imagined orchestra, was to me a revelation.

While working for Koussevitzky I had plenty of time to fill other engagements, among them a stint with the Diaghilev ballet company. Despite his fame, Diaghilev was in constant financial straits. One morning before a rehearsal he came in and announced the bad news to his company: he had no money to pay either his dancers or the pianist. Would we continue to rehearse on credit? There was no choice, not for me anyway. I had plenty of time on my hands, and very little money. Eventually, Diaghilev found a new sponsor with money and paid us off.

Koussevitzky was apparently satisfied with my playing and asked me if I would care to join him for a summer in Biarritz. He planned to conduct *Le*

Sacre du printemps by Stravinsky, and had to practise to master the tricky rhythms of the score. I was but vaguely aware of the tremendous impact that the work had produced on the audience during its first performance in Paris in 1913, and accepted Koussevitzky's offer without a moment's hesitation. Koussevitzky gave me money for the train fare to Biarritz where I was to join him a few days after his own arrival. In Biarritz I rented an inexpensive furnished room, which included breakfast consisting of *café au lait* and a delicious croissant. I telephoned Koussevitzky as soon as I arrived and he told me to come to lunch. Both he and Mrs Koussevitzky were extremely cordial, and I no longer had a fear of failing the test. He gave me a four-hand piano arrangement of Stravinsky's score, and I quickly adapted myself to combining the four staves of the arrangement so as to preserve the essential harmonic and rhythmic elements of the music. It was my first experience in tackling a real modern work. What discords! A simple tune in C major was set against the same tune in C-sharp major. A B major triad was combined with a B minor triad. No wonder a French critic suggested that the title should be changed to *Le Massacre du printemps*. But I was determined to do my best to give a fair account of the music. As usual during a particularly intense challenge, I projected myself in my imagination into a higher dimension. Stravinsky's asymmetrical metres were not entirely new to me. I was familiar with compound time signatures such as 11/4 in Rimsky-Korsakov's opera *Sadko*, which constituted a stumbling block to the chorus, and sometimes to the conductor. Indeed, conservatory students devised a jingle of eleven syllables to practise this particular section of the score, with the words, most disrespectful of the great master of Russian music, 'Rimsky-Korsakov sovsyem sumasoshol' ('Rimsky-Korsakov is altogether mad'). But the changing metres of *Le Sacre du printemps* compounded the difficulties far beyond such simple arithmetical arrangements; they ran in fast rhythmic units, so that one had to follow the music not bar by bar, but beat by beat.

To my dismay, I realized that Koussevitsky was incapable of coping with these complications. When precise metrical changes occurred, as from 3/16 to 2/8, he kept slowing down the sixteenth-notes and accelerating the eighth-notes so that the distinct binary ratios dissolved into formless neutral triplets. It occurred to me that the situation could be remedied by combining adjacent bars so as to reduce the basic beat to an eighth-note; for instance, the succession of bars of 3/16, 2/8, 1/16, 4/8 could be integrated into a single bar of 4/4. To be sure, the downbeats would be dislocated at several points, but Stravinsky had numerous syncopated accents anyway, so that the basic rhythm would be preserved. In the very beginning of the most difficult segment in the score, *La Danse sacrale*, there was a sixteenth-note rest followed by a full orchestral chord on an eighth-note, with a fermata over it. The conductor was supposed to give a powerful downbeat for the sixteenth rest and expect the orchestra to come in together on the following chord. But, since that chord had an indefinite duration created by the fermata, the effect would be no different if this bar were to be written without the initial rest. The joke went around that when Stravinsky himself conducted this bar he made an audible burp on the downbeat which justified the syncopation that followed. But Koussevitzky was too delicate a person to make animal sounds to emphasize the rhythm, so a different expedient was required.

I showed Koussevitzky how all those metrical fractions could be connected up without sacrificing a single beat, but he dismissed the idea out of hand. 'We can't change Stravinsky's rhythm!' he said. Koussevitzky also had trouble in passages of 5/8 in a relatively moderate time, particularly when 5/8 was changed to 6/8, or to 9/8 as happens in Stravinsky's score. He had a tendency to stretch out the last beat in 5/8, counting 'one, two, three, four, five, uh'. This 'uh' constituted the 6th beat, reducing Stravinsky's spasmodic rhythms to the regular heartbeat. When I pointed it out to Koussevitzky, he became quite upset. It was just a 'luftpause' he said. The insertion of an 'airpause' reduced the passage to a nice waltz time, making it very comfortable to play for the violin section which bore the brunt of the syncopation, but wrecking Stravinsky's asymmetric rhythms.

Stravinsky also spent much of the summer of 1921 in Biarritz, and he came to Koussevitzky's house practically every day. At evenings we played poker for nominal stakes, but I was never allowed to lose a single sou. I took the opportunity of these leisurely evenings to talk about composers with whom I had become friendly. In particular, I tried to boost the career of a young Polish composer, Alexandre Tansman, whose manuscript scores I brought with me to Biarritz. Koussevitzky amiably agreed to consider a piece by Tansman for performance, but Stravinsky, with his usual gross humour, said, 'A person named Danceman should dance, not compose'. (In Russian, or for that matter in German, the pun comes out better: 'Tanzmann muss tanzen.') Who could foresee that Tansman would become one of Koussevitzky's favourite composers and a worshipful friend and biographer of Stravinsky? Tansman appreciated my efforts in his behalf by inscribing one of his scores to me, 'A mon accoucheur'.

The Biarritz interlude over, Koussevitzky and I returned to Paris. Rehearsals of *Le Sacre* went badly. Koussevitzky made the expected mistakes, and kept adding those obnoxious 'luftpausen'. He was sullen as we drove back to his suburban villa in a chauffered limousine. After lunch he suddenly said: 'Show me that arrangement you made in the score.' I eagerly explained to him my idea of summation of adjacent bars. He looked at the music with glazed eyes. 'I can't understand a thing you say,' he remarked. 'Sit down and put the barlines in blue pencil in the score.' I withdrew to the workroom and at the end of the afternoon had the tricky metre all nicely rebarred in long lines in blue traced from top to bottom of the huge score. 'You have a genius for mathematics,' Koussevitzky said to me after he looked over my handiwork. The mathematical genius involved required no more than the ability to add fractions, but to Koussevitzky it was high science. The parts of *Le Sacre du printemps* which Koussevitzky used in Paris and later in Boston were rebarred according to my arrangement, and Koussevitzky used it at all his performances of the work. Interestingly enough, some twenty years later Stravinsky himself published a simplified arrangement of *Danse sacrale*. Not being constrained to follow his original metrical divisions, he freely altered his syncopated textures.

In the natural course of musical events, Leonard Bernstein, the instantaneous magician of the art of conducting, was engaged as guest conductor with the Boston Symphony Orchestra, with *Le Sacre* on the programme. No sooner did he begin the *Danse sacrale* than he was confronted with my metrical rearrangement. He quickly collated the score with orchestral parts and proceeded to beat time according to my simplified Koussevitzkian version. In a note he sent me in April 1984, on the occasion of my ninetieth birthday, he recalled the occasion.

'Dear Nicolas,' he wrote. 'Every time I conduct *Le Sacre*, as I did most recently two weeks ago (and always from Koussy's own score, with your rebarring), I admire and revere and honor you as I did the very first time. Bless you, and more power to you. Lenny B.'

The gift of music is a compartmentalized faculty. A composer of genius may be a poor performer and may not even possess that talisman of precocious genius, the sense of perfect pitch. Ravel was completely helpless in spotting wrong notes in his own compositions when he conducted. Alfredo Casella told me that even Debussy let pass the most horrendous mistakes in his orchestral works, and in one instance failed to notice that the clarinet player used a clarinet in B-flat instead of one in A; one could only imagine what heterophony resulted from such an unintended transposition of a semitone.

Stravinsky had a very limited sense of pitch. I recall an embarrassing episode wherein Stravinsky conducted his *Ragtime* for eleven players, a work which calls for the Hungarian keyboard instrument, cimbalom. Since there was no cimbalom to be found in Paris, I was hired to play the part on the piano. At a rehearsal, Koussevitzky turned the pages for me (I would dearly love to have a photograph of that scene!). Towards the end of the rehearsal I noticed that the left hand of the cimbalom part was written in the treble clef, an obvious error, I thought, for the hands crossed all the time. Koussevitzky also noticed this incongruity; we both came to the conclusion that the clef in the left hand should have been a bass clef, and I blithely played on. During the intermission I pointed out this apparent error to Stravinsky. Perspiring profusely, as he always did during conducting, and wiping the sweat from his neck with a towel, he said, 'No, the treble clef in the left hand is right, because the part was written for the upper manual of the cimbalom, which sounds an octave higher.' I was perplexed. There I was, in effect transposing the piece in the double counterpoint of the 13th, right under Stravinsky's nose, and he was never the wiser for it.

Stravinsky was also a poor proof-reader. When his *Symphony of Psalms* was being engraved in Koussevitzky's publishing house, Prokofiev, who was in Paris at the time, happened to look at the proofs. He told me with obvious glee that he had found fifty-three gross errors on the very first page of Stravinsky's score. 'You will not find such errors in my music!' he boasted. It so happened that his *Sinfonietta* was also being engraved at the time, and Prokofiev carried the proofs with him. Seized with a diabolical temptation, I asked him to let me look at the proofs. He agreed, but warned me that I would be wasting my time trying to find errors. This was a supreme challenge to my vanity. There were no wrong notes, but to my delight I found the wrong clef in one of the parts in the score. Prokofiev was visibly annoyed when I showed it to him. He fixed the clef, and the score was published without this embarrassing mistake.

Stravinsky was above all a man of rhythm, and in his orchestral works he extended the rhythm section to an integral part of the score, coequal with strings and winds. He also favoured the dry and hard timbre of the drums. Conducting a rehearsal of *Les Noces*, he asked the drummer to use a harder stick: 'Plus dur, plus dur!' he cried, until the exasperated musician exclaimed: 'Vous voulez que je fasse ça avec ma queue!' and obscenely pointed to his crotch, suggesting that his ithyphallic drumstick would be hardest, whereupon the players erupted in canonic counter-point: 'Tu te flattes, tu te flattes!' Stravinsky remained unruffled.

In all my lengthy association with Koussevitzky I never saw him read a book, and yet in his younger days in Moscow he was surrounded by writers, poets, and multifarious deep-thinkers, among them the philoso-pher Medtner, a brother of the composer. Koussevitzky was also fortu-nate in his friendship with Skriabin, who himself read infrequently. Skriabin's brother-in-law, Boris de Schloezer, tells of Skriabin's lifelong wrestling with the concepts of divinity, eternity, and destiny. The titles of his works, such as *Divine Poem*, *Poem of Ecstasy*, and *Poem of Fire*, had a personal meaning for him. The opening of the *Divine Poem* was to him a declaration of self-being, 'I am', which Skriabin added to the manuscript at Schloezer's suggestion. Skriabin wrote in his diary: 'I want to conquer the world the way a man takes a woman.' At the Moscow Conservatory Skriabin was indeed known as a passionate 'woman-taker'.

Koussevitzky was the first fully to appreciate the genius of Skriabin. He went to see him in Switzerland and offered him a publishing contract with the Éditions Russes on generous financial terms. It came as a lifesaver to Skriabin who, living with Tatiana Schloezer as his common-law wife, was in such financial straits that he sometimes did not have money for a postage stamp. To Skriabin, Koussevitzky was a messenger heaven-sent to serve his messianic destiny. To Koussevitzky, Skriabin was the medium serving to project his own genius as a music-maker. Two messiahs could not exist on the same terrestrial plane, and their relationship gradually deteriorated into an ugly series of mutual recriminations. In the end, Skriabin could not bear to hear Koussevitzky's name even mentioned, and referred to him as 'the unspeakable one'.

Skriabin died in 1915 at the age of 42, of an abscess that could have been cured in twenty-four hours with a few injections of penicillin. Alas, those wonder drugs were not available in his time. Stravinsky remarked acidly in one of his published dialogues that Skriabin's early death was to be lamented, but that one shuddered to think what kind of music Skriabin would have written had he lived longer. Indeed, Skriabin's elfin spirit would not have fitted into the era of Stravinsky and Schoenberg with their set systems. Modern music followed bifurcated roads, retrospective on the fringes of neo-classicism, introspective among the followers of the New Vienna School. The mystical direction of Skriabin, perpendicular to both dimensions, and asymptotic to an astral plane, had lost its audience. I recall an episode at Koussevitzky's Paris villa in 1925; Prokofiev was there for lunch; he picked up the score of Skriabin's *Divine Poem* lying on the piano top, and played over a few pages with a condescending smile on his lips. 'What ought to be done with this music,' he finally declared, 'is to liven it up with a bass drum.' And he demonstrated where he would have used the drum in the score. Skriabin with a bass drum! What blasphemy!

Apart from my duties as a surrogate orchestra for Koussevitzky, I became his *de facto* secretary. His French was lame, ungrammatical, and often unintelligible, and I served as his translator whenever necessary. Once he was interviewed by a French reporter, who wished to know what Koussevitzky thought of French musicians, specifically the violinist

Jacques Thibaud, who was equally renowned for his expertise in the Paris boudoirs. 'Thibaud?' Koussevitzky repeated. 'C'est un grand vertueux!' The reporter was taken aback. 'You mean to say that Thibaud is a virtuous person?' 'Yes,' Koussevitzky insisted, 'and you can put it in your paper that I, Serge Koussevitzky, said that Thibaud is virtuous.' At this juncture I decided to intervene. I explained to Koussevitzky in Russian that he meant to say 'virtuoso', not 'virtuous'. 'But I said "vertueux"!' Koussevitzky exclaimed, still failing to appreciate the difference between the two words. As always in such instances when he thought his dignity or his intelligence were being impugned, he grew red in the face (the redness usually started at the back of his neck) and told me to shut up. I took care to explain to the reporter later what Koussevitzky had intended to say.

With this air of *grand seigneur*, backed by Russian wealth (although Koussevitzky lost most of his wife's inherited fortune after the Revolution) and a reputation as a propagandist of modern music, Koussevitzky was constantly besieged by young (and not so young) French and expatriate Russian composers. Among the youngest, the most talented, and perhaps the most arrogant of these Russians was Vladimir Dukelsky, whose music possessed a certain 'Parisian' charm. He differed from the common run of composers by an affectation of independence. He did not even press Koussevitzky to play his music, an attitude which surprised Koussevitzky and aroused his interest. When Dukelsky went to America, Koussevitzky put his symphonies and ballet suites on his programmes with the Boston Symphony Orchestra, of which he became music director in 1924. At the suggestion of George Gershwin, Dukelsky halved his last name to plain Duke, and changed his first name Vladimir (which means 'master of the world' in Russian) to Vernon. Some of his songs, particularly *April in Paris*, became perennial favourites. But Prokofiev, who liked Dukelsky as a friend and a composer, was disgusted with Dukelsky's plunge into the lucrative field of popular music. 'You have become a prostitute,' he wrote to him. 'When you are paid enough money you spread your legs and invite a client to enter.'

On the opposite pole from Dukelsky among expatriate Russian musicians in Paris was Nicolas Obouhov, a religious fanatic who called himself 'Nicolas l'Illuminé'. His magnum opus was *Le Livre de vie*, scored for voices, orchestra, and two pianos. Koussevitzky played excerpts from it at one of his Paris concerts. The vocal parts included not only straight singing, but moaning, groaning, screaming, shrieking, and hissing. Obouhov and I took over the piano parts, which were accordingly marked in the programme, 'Nicolas Obouhov et Nicolas Slonimsky aux pianos'. During the intermission one of my sarcastic friends suggested that I carry a placard saying 'Je ne suis pas le compositeur', since the programme did not specify which of the two pianists was the composer, and I could be blamed for the music. Not very gallantly, Koussevitzky apologized to the orchestra during a rehearsal for performing the work, but explained that no less a master than Ravel pronounced Obouhov a genius. Obouhov lived in abject poverty in Paris, and I asked Ravel to write a letter appealing for funds on his behalf. Ravel obliged most graciously. I published his letter in America; it brought Obouhov about $250. The original Ravel letter would probably fetch twice as much today as an autograph.

Whether Obouhov was a genius is debatable, but he certainly deserves a footnote in music history as the inventor of 12-tone harmony, which contained all twelve notes of the chromatic scale without duplication. He devised a special notation, replacing sharps by crosses inside a note, symbolic of the crucifix, and he marked tempi and rehearsal numbers with his own blood, symbolic of Christ's martyrdom. The first presentation of Obouhov's 'absolute harmony' was given in Petrograd in February 1916, long before Schoenberg's formulation of dodecaphony. Honegger, among others, thought highly enough of Obouhov's theories to contribute a foreword to Obouhov's book entitled 'Treatise of Tonal, Atonal and Total Harmony'.

Obouhov had a strong, muscular body and made a living in Paris as a bricklayer. He lived with his Russian wife in a tiny apartment, and he kept the manuscript of *Le Livre de vie* in a 'sacred corner' under several icons, with candles burning day and night. Once, in a fit of frenzy, his wife cut up the manuscript, which to her had become a symbol of continued misery. Obouhov reverently bandaged the mutilated parts of the manuscript, and traced the seams of the torn pages with drops of his blood.

A fantastic turn of events changed Obouhov's life. A French countess, Mme Aussenac de Broglie, took an interest in his mystic ideas, rented a house for him, and financed the construction of an electronic instrument in the form of a cross which Obouhov called 'croix sonore' and for which he wrote several works. He dreamed of having his music performed in an open-air amphitheatre, perhaps in the Himalayas, or some other exotic place. This was very much like Skriabin's dream for the production of his *Mystery*, except that Skriabin extended his mystical universe to include dance, religious processions, and colour projections. The Hollywood Bowl would have been an ideal place for such a synthetic spectacle, but, alas, Skriabin died many years before the Hollywood Bowl came into being.

CHAPTER 6

ROCHESTER

In the summer of 1923 I received an offer from America to become opera coach of the newly organised American Opera Company at the Eastman School of Music in Rochester, New York. The enterprise was the creation of the Russian singer Vladimir Rosing, with whom I had toured in 1921 and 1922 as accompanist in France, Belgium, and Spain. Rosing was a remarkable person. He had an expressive but not very strong tenor voice, and he sang Russian songs in a mesmerizing manner, with his eyes closed and his entire body tense with emotion. He left Russia shortly after the outbreak of the First World War and went to London, where his recitals of Russian songs attracted attention in the literary and artistic circles.

Russia was very much in fashion at that time, and Russian artists were welcome in London as messengers of the new and strange art from the North. Rosing contributed to this mystique by his curious notion that a singer must become, in body and in soul, the incarnation of the subject of the song. When he performed Mussorgsky's *Songs of Death,* he became death itself, demonstrating this transformation by drawing in his cheeks, screwing up his bony facial structure, and letting his long nose protrude from his countenance. In the next song he was the village idiot, dropping his jaw to convey an image of imbecility. For Mussorgsky's *Song of the Flea,* Rosing scratched himself all over as if being actually bitten by a flea. At his recitals he introduced each song with a little speech in his rather attractively accented English; this verbal prelude also helped to detract attention from the obvious defects in his vocal technique. Music critics praised him; George Bernard Shaw attended one of his concerts and wrote a penetrating article on Rosing as a representative of the new art of singing. Another admirer was Ezra Pound, who never missed a single concert of Rosing in London, and praised him to the skies in British avant-garde publications.

As a consequence of his London successes, Rosing received a contract for a Canadian tour. On the transatlantic liner he met George Eastman, the American industrialist and inventor of the Kodak film, who had just founded the Eastman School of Music. This contact with an American millionaire gave Rosing an idea. He proposed that Eastman finance an opera company in English at the Eastman School. Accustomed to making decisions on the spur of the moment, Eastman agreed and guaranteed an initial fund of a quarter of a million dollars, an immense sum of money at the time. Rosing was to engage a competent staff, a conductor, an accompanist doubling as a vocal coach, and a stage director; the singers were to be recruited from the student body.

Rosing engaged Rouben Mamoulian, who was then in England, to be stage director of the future American Opera Company. Albert Coates and Eugene Goossens, both distinguished English conductors, were invited to conduct performances of the American Opera Company and also to lead the Rochester Philharmonic. It was at that juncture that I received a cable from Rosing offering me a contract as accompanist and coach. The salary was fabulous: $3,000 a year, something like 40,000 francs in French money, a sum that existed only in fiction for me. I told Koussevitzky about the offer, and he said he was glad for my sake. Rosing sent me money for the boat fare, and soon I was on the ocean.

My great worry was that I spoke no English. I got an English conversation book and memorized some dialogue in it: 'Hello, old boy — you seem to be out of sorts. I came to cheer you up.' How can a boy be old? In my English–French dictionary a boy was a *garçon*. And why cheer up? Was the old boy so sick he could not get up by himself? I translated 'out of sorts' as 'dehors des sorties' — outside of the sorties. Then I tackled irregular plurals. I learned that the plural of sheep was sheep, but that the plural of cow was kine. I also memorized collective nouns for animals: a pride of lions, an exaltation of larks, a skulk of foxes, a volery of birds, a bed of clams, a charm of goldfinches, a knot of toads, and a gaggle of geese. Examples of conversation were most unnatural, replete with circumlocutions. And the pronunciation! Even before learning the most elementary words, I already knew European jokes about English; the worst was that 'ghoti' was pronounced 'fish' ('gh' as in cough, 'o' as in women, 'ti' as in nation). The most intractable sound of all was the diphthong 'th'. This unnatural phoneme had two varieties, the hard one and the soft one. I knew that in order to articulate this sound I had to stick my tongue between my teeth. What civilized nation would accept a language which requires sticking out your tongue every time you use the definite article?

After six days of a wonderfully smooth voyage, the boat docked at New York Harbor, sailing serenely by the Statue of Liberty, familiar to me through numerous reproductions. And the skyscrapers! The Woolworth Building warmed the cockles of my heart, for it had been reproduced on the calendars of my father's Russian insurance policy, printed on glossy American cardboard. I was travelling on a so-called Nansen passport, which was an abomination of desolation, the mark of Cain, the red spot of a pariah. The Nansen passport was named after the Norwegian explorer and philanthropist, Fridtjof Nansen, who became deeply concerned about the fate of 'displaced persons' and did a great deal to alleviate the political disadvantages of such expatriates. I had no trouble getting the US visa as an 'artist', exempt from the national quota. But I envied Americans, who were the first off the boat and who spoke English so fast that I could not understand a single word.

Aunt Isabelle had already settled in New York. She had her own apartment on the West Side, and she had her own telephone. I called her immediately after landing, and she told me to come over at once. I took the elevator to the sixth floor to her apartment and rang the bell. A woman opened the door, and I told her I had come to see my aunt (which I pronounced phonetically a–oo–nt) Isabelle (I never called her Aunt Isabelle, but always by the diminutive Russian name Bellochka, 'little Bella', which in Russian sounded the same as little squirrel). Her familiar presence, massive in body and energetic in manner, gave me at once a sense of psychological stability.

At the end of October 1923, I took the night train to Rochester; the Pullman cars amazed me by their efficiency. A porter fixed an upper berth for me and gave me a ladder to climb in. This was quite an improvement over the night train in which I had travelled between Kharkov and Novorossiysk only three years earlier. I was met at the Rochester railroad station by Vladimir Rosing and several officials of the Eastman School of Music. After an opulent breakfast, we went off in search of an apartment, and found one very fast. It was fantastically modern and comfortable; it had a separate bathroom with a tub and a shower, a luxury that I could not even imagine either in Russia or in Paris. But there was no bed. 'Vheere bet ess?' I asked the janitor. He did not seem to understand, and then exclaimed, 'Oh, the bed?' 'Yes, I sed bet,' I repeated, somewhat ruffled. He opened the closet door and out dropped a fully made bed, a 'Murphy' as I learned later. The rent was $60 a month.

The next day I presented myself at the office of the Eastman School of Music. After I had signed the proper form, the registrar handed me a cheque for $250. Being morbidly honest in financial matters, I explained to him as best I could in my primitive English that I was not entitled to a payment since I had not yet begun my work. No, the cheque was all right, the registrar told me with a smile, showing the word October underneath the signature. I kept repeating, 'Mistek, mistek!' No mistake, the registrar reassured me: my annual payment began in October. Then Rosing came to the rescue. He explained that I was to receive $250 a month, including the summer vacations, and that this sum was reckoned from the total of the annual salary of $3,000.

This episode confirmed my notion of America as a land of unlimited resources populated by smiling men and women of unbounded kindness, a haven for the humble treated as equals even by millionaires, a land of facile friendships, of hearty handshakes, and amiable pats on the shoulder, a society of infinite mutual confidence, a country where I could rent an apartment without paying in advance, and where no one looked at a stranger with suspicion.

George Eastman was a perfect prototype of an American philanthropist, as American millionaires are portrayed in European fiction. He gave generously to causes, even those which he could not quite appreciate. Musicians were among the beneficiaries of his bounties. He admittedly had no knowledge of music, and could well emulate President Ulysses S. Grant in his famous, if possibly aprocryphal pronouncement, 'I know only two tunes: one is Yankee Doodle, and the other isn't.' But Eastman liked to have music played while he had breakfast. I often played for him with a violinist, a cellist, or both in a piano trio. Eastman preferred quiet, classical or romantic music. For these breakfasts, musicians were placed on the balcony of a large hall in Eastman's house in Rochester. He could see us, but we could not see him, which insured his privacy. His breakfast took precisely thirty-five minutes, and he paid $35 per performance to each of us, an amazing largess for the time. To me the name of Eastman was legendary, for as a boy in Russia I owned a 'Brownie' Kodak camera. Could I ever imagine that some day I would shake hands with the inventor of the Kodak camera? America was indeed a fairy-tale land.

The first semester of classes at the Eastman School of Music opened at 9 o'clock in the morning with a class of 'mental training' conducted by Rosing. Rosing recited, in his tense dramatic voice, 'Every day in every way we are getting better and better' (this magic incantation was the invention of a Dr Coué, one of the many European conjurers who invaded the United States in the 1920s). To Rosing the formula possessed a precise meaning, for he was a firm believer in the power of auto-suggestion; he was also a willing convert to any cult that combined pseudo-modern psychology with theosophy thickly enmeshed with fraud.

Special exercises followed mental training. Rosing told the class to flex the muscles of their brains. He knitted his brow. The students did likewise. 'You must make your brain muscles very tense,' Rosing urged. 'Think hard, very hard!' After the class was over, Rouben Mamoulian remarked quietly to Rosing that there are no muscles in the brain. 'Nonsense!' Rosing retorted. 'If there were no muscles in the brain, we couldn't make a mental effort.' He then embarked on an eloquent discourse about mental radio; at that time radio broadcasting was the latest miracle of the age. A hundred years ago, he argued, no one would have believed that a person speaking into empty space could be heard miles away, for it takes hours for the sound to travel such distances, and yet instantaneous voice communication had become a reality. It was going to be the same with mental radio, telepathy, and clairvoyance, which are but natural extensions of wireless communication.

Rosing took me along as his accompanist and guest soloist on a tour of Canada; we played in such fantastic places as Moose Jaw; we also took in towns in northern American states, familiar to me from reading *The Pathfinder* and *The Last of the Mohicans*, novels which were very popular in Russia. No Indians attacked our train, but the territory through which we passed had the essence of a legend. Playing for Rosing was not just a matter of tempo and dynamics. If time had to be kept, it was Rosing's own time, for he treated time signatures as mere academic conventions. One of his favourite numbers was the vocal arrangement of the *Danse macabre* by Saint-Saëns. Instead of coming in immediately after the first beat in the syncopated measure, he would look at me for guidance, or encouragement, and only then make his entrance, one beat too late. He was also apt to get his French words all mixed up; at one of his recitals he kept repeating 'squelette, squelette, squelette', having lost the rest of the text. But when he assumed the appearance of a death mask, with his eyes closed, the audience gasped with appreciation and the critics raved about the mystical Russian art.

In concert recitals Rosing could get away with anything as long as he was confident that his accompanist would follow him through all his vagaries. But a real disaster befell him when he undertook the lead role in an Eastman School production of Gounod's *Faust*. He knew the arias, but the recitatives were beyond his power of retention. He sang in French, and as usual was not sure of the words. For safety's sake he planted scraps of paper with words written on them in the scenery for the garden scene, which had a lot of recitative in it. At the last moment, a misguided stagehand removed the crucial scraps from the trees and bushes. Rosing began his recitative, went to a corresponding bush, fumbled around and found nothing. He had no other recourse but to keep repeating the first line from his aria, 'Salut! Refuge chaste et pure!' It was only thanks to his supreme self-assurance that he pulled through.

Poor Rosing! He failed miserably as administrator of the American Opera Company in Rochester and ran through Eastman's money long before he could stage any opera that would possibly bring in some returns for the investment. George Eastman, a good businessman, refused to pour more funds into Rosing's undertaking, and the American Opera Company, as it was proudly named, expired ingloriously. Rosing, who had married numerous times and somehow managed to attract sympathetic females to take care of his creature comforts, eventually went to California. Unable to make a living, he was reduced to moral and physical misery. In 1960 I received a letter from one of his former students with the news that Rosing was very ill and practically destitute. Would I send him some money? I sent him a cheque for $250 with a letter explaining that this was not a donation, but merely a payment of my debt to him for the initial sum of money I had received from the Eastman School of Music for the month of October 1923, to which I was not entitled, and which was obviously the result of his effort to smooth out the first weeks of my American residency. I was told that Rosing wept when he read my letter.

At the Eastman School I found a kindred soul in Paul Horgan, a talented painter and illustrator who was employed as a stage designer in Rosing's American Opera Company. He also wrote facile verse and clever short stories. I was particularly struck by his novella dealing with a revivalist meeting which he happened to attend. I thought it a perfect satire on American religious frenzy, and I was almost as upset as he was himself by the series of rejections that Horgan received from the various magazines to which he submitted his story. I asked him if he would authorize me to offer the manuscript to a Russian *émigré* paper published in Paris. Horgan, who had a fine sense of incongruity, was delighted at the idea of being published in Russian. Accordingly, I sent Horgan's story to my Paris friend Konstantin Mochulsky, a literary critic and linguist, and asked him if he would translate it and get it published. He did, and so it came to pass that the very first literary work by Paul Horgan (who was to become a multiple Pulitzer Prize winner and a bestselling author) appeared in the Russian language. Horgan himself could not read Russian, but he was bemused by the look of his name and the text of his story in the Cyrillic alphabet. Half a century later, in his memoirs, he recalled this episode, and gave me credit for launching him on his literary career.

My exhibitionism found fertile ground in Rochester. I was aided and abetted in it by Horgan and other whimsical friends. As coach in the opera class, I ostentatiously dispensed with the score and played the music from memory, while giving the necessary cues to the student singers. Impudently, I placed a paperback edition of *Les Dieux ont soif* by Anatole France on the piano rack, pretending to read it while playing *Carmen*, *Faust*, or *Eugene Onegin*. Horgan, who enjoyed the role of my hagiographer, refers in his memoirs to my 'insolent efficiency' in conducting the opera rehearsals.

Horgan and Rouben Mamoulian had a great sense of histrionics. They would put on monocles, click their heels, and spout torrents of ersatz

German in public places. I usually played the role of a deferential companion in such exhibitions. The three of us formed a cult of adoration for Lucile, 'the Venus de Milo with arms', who was the principal harpist of the Rochester Philharmonic, and whose blonde halo and cerulean eyes formed complementary colours to her golden harp, which she fingered ever so innocently. To demonstrate our devotion, we made festive occasions of her periodical departures and arrivals to and from Buffalo, her home town. We accompanied her to the railroad station, laden with costume jewelry purchased at a nickel-and-dime store, hung ruby necklaces around her neck, adorned her fingers with diamond rings, and placed malachite bracelets around her slender wrists. Horgan and Mamoulian put on their usual act, spewing phony German and clicking heels. People at the railroad station looked at us with curiosity; Lucile might well have been a silent film star, and we her German directors.

On occasion we overplayed our parts. In honour of Lucile's birthday, we staged a party in a Rochester coffee shop. We placed a boxful of matches inside the birthday cake; I lit the candles, and as they melted, the matches ignited under the icing and the cake blew up with an impressive bang. We were asked to leave.

Horgan, Mamoulian, and I admired ourselves so pompously that we decided to formalize our mutual admiration in a Society of Unrecognized Geniuses. I was to be President, Mamoulian, Vice-President, and Horgan, Secretary. Regretfully, we voted against including Vladimir Rosing in the Society, for he lacked the quality of boisterous mischief that was the essential characteristic of our collective genius.

Everybody in Rochester tried to teach me English, which was in an embryonic stage of development in 1924. I avoided using the dictionary but proceeded to learn the language as if it were some extinct dialect. Until this day I retain the painful remembrance of trying to figure out just what meaning was conveyed by the recurrent phrase 'of course', which I mentally translated into French as 'de la course', which made no sense at all. It finally dawned on me that the phrase was an intensive locution, corresponding to 'cela va sans dire'. A serious impediment in my progress was the enthusiastic adoption by Horgan and others in my Rochester entourage of my own brand of English, which they thought was 'awfully cute', much as British society adopted the 'small talk' of the heroine in Shaw's *Pygmalion*. I used to say, for instance, that I saw something with my 'proper eyes', which is perfectly all right in Chaucer or Milton, but hardly in Rochester, New York; this gallicism was picked up along with my other aberrations as some sort of baby talk. The worst obstacle in my pilgrim's progress were the English phonetics — I could not tell the difference between 'food' and 'foot', 'hat' and 'head'. The length of each vowel did not register in my ears, and the final 'd' and 't' sounded identical. Other Russians in America had similar trouble. A Russian violinist in the Boston Symphony Orchestra asked the laundryman to wash the bed sheet. Unfortunately he pronounced it 'shit', and the laundryman threatened to punch him in the nose. My poor friend asked me what was wrong. I tried to explain to him the difference between the long and short vowels. 'But I did say *shiit*', he protested.

To exemplify the diversity of English vowels that sounded alike to a non-English ear I devised this sentence: 'Cat, caught on the cot, cut my coat.' I would pronounce cat as ket *à l'anglaise* so as to distinguish it from the other vowels in the sentence, but the rest of the vowels sounded alike to me; when spoken at my request by an American, the sentence came over uniformly like 'Kott, kott on the kott, kott my kott'.

Then there were the idioms. I used to say 'I worked hardly', which sent my friends into spasms of laughter. But if it is right to say 'I walked slowly' rather than 'I walked slow', then, I reasoned, it ought to be similarly correct to say 'I worked hardly'. Logic was on my side, but logic does not rule idiomatic usage.

What gave me a real introduction to the genius of the English language was *HMS Pinafore*, which was the first opera that Rosing put on in rehearsal by the American Opera Company. I savoured the elevated diction of Gilbert's verses; I relished the mock-Bellini music of Sullivan. Some passages in *Pinafore* provided far greater didactic enlightenment to me than all the formal manuals. It was from *Pinafore* that I finally penetrated the meaning of the word 'hardly', gathering it from the marvellous antiphony between the captain and the chorus of his loyal crew: 'And he'd never used the big, big D', with its sceptical rejoinder, 'What, never?' and the concessive, 'Well, hardly ever'. It made it crystal clear to me that the effect of the qualifying adverb here was that of litotes.

It took me a long time to unlearn saying 'When the train goes?' (following the Russian order of the words) or 'When goes the train?' (following the French order), for the auxiliary verb 'do' does not exist in any other language. I practised saying 'Where did he go?' instead of 'Where he went?' or 'Where went he?' The biblical 'where goest thou' was much closer to my linguistic consciousness than its modern equivalent.

I studiously scanned the subtitles in the cinema, and eagerly perused the eloquent advertisements in the *Saturday Evening Post*. The commercial lingo of these advertisements inspired me to compose my first lyrico-dramatic songs to English texts. I fully appreciated the rich verbalization of changing vowels in the resonant appeal 'Make this a day of Pepsodent!' What marvellous sonority is evoked by the promise 'No More Shiny

Nose!' My favourite advertisement was 'Children Cry for Castoria!' Another advertisement extolled the tenderness of Utica sheets and pillowcases. I also appreciated the sombre report 'And Then Her Doctor Told Her', accompanying a scene in which a family doctor, attired in a formal three-piece dark suit, and wearing a gold watch on a chain in his waistcoat pocket, pointed an accusatory finger at a dejected female figure in an armchair. It was pure Aristotle: fear and pity resolved in the catharsis when it was made plain that the patient had nothing more than intestinal irregularity, easily corrected by Pillsbury's natural laxative encapsulated in bran muffins.

I set these poetic effusions to appropriate music. The Pepsodental toothpaste was squeezed out in Mussorgskyan recitative, warning the user that 'film on your teeth ferments and forms acid'. I appreciated the plight of the 'irregular' female, who was 'run down, tired, languid before each day began', and I set this passage to the chime-like progressions borrowed from Rachmaninoff's *Prelude in C-Sharp Minor*. As for the Castoria song, it was to be performed in falsetto. I pulled out all the stops to dramatize the urgent appeal, 'Mother, relieve your constipated child!' When relief came, I made use of such precise expression marks as *peristaltico* and *fecalmente*.

In my own performance, rendered in a voice that could be termed *tenore falsifico*, my advertising songs became a hit at our circle in Rochester. Paul Horgan liked the music of *Utica Sheets* so much that he wrote a new poetic text for it, *'Neath Stars*. Some years later I turned over the entire cycle of my advertising songs to a publisher who thought they would make a wonderful encore group. But when he applied to the companies involved for permission to use the text, they refused. The Pepsodent Company even threatened legal action should the publisher print the song. Eventually I had the songs recorded by a professional singer, with me at the piano. I took the precaution of changing the brand name Pepsodent to Plurodent.

The summit of my Rochester successes was the production of my ballet, with the scenario by (who else?) Paul Horgan, directed by (who else?) Rouben Mamoulian, under the general auspices of (who else?) Vladimir Rosing. The fanciful title was *The Prince Goes a-Hunting*, and the story possessed all the necessary ingredients of a classical ballet, populated by princes and princesses, with a locale in an enchanted forest. The music was unashamedly Rimsky-Korsakovian, but it sounded beautiful to me, Horgan, and all the members of the American Opera Company who took part in the production. My orchestration was rather shaky, and in it I was helped by Vittorio Giannini, an excellent musician who happened to be teaching at the Eastman School at the time. I also profited by advice from Selim Palmgren, the eminent Finnish composer, who was a visiting professor in Rochester. Palmgren told me frankly that my music was 'derivative', but that it was 'nice'. The performances were conducted by Guy Fraser Harrison, a dear friend, who became one of the transient husbands of Lucile, our universally admired, golden-tressed harpist.

In Rochester I received my first lessons in conducting with Albert Coates. I was a singularly inept student. Even Horgan, whose loyalty to me was total, said my conducting was 'jerky'. Among other things, I seemed to be unable to give a decisive first beat, a rather serious handicap for an aspiring conductor. In desperation, I would make a violent downward movement with my right hand, without any preparation, so that the musicians were caught unawares, and came in in a ragged farrago of sounds. Coates was puzzled by my ineptitude. 'How can you be so wonderful at the keyboard', he remarked to me, 'and yet so helpless beating time?' It took me several weeks to comprehend the simple maxim that in order to come down I had first to go up. The upbeat had to set the tempo. But, having once learned that simple truth, I began making my upbeat so decisive that the players mistook it for a misdirected downbeat. Then suddenly I succeeded. I raised my right hand, not too menacingly, and then lowered it, and the student orchestra began to play. It was as simple as that.

Once I had tasted the joy of conducting, I could not be deterred from trying and trying again. Not even my staunchest friends could have foreseen that, seven years after my primitive beginnings, I would dare to lift my baton over the full contingent of the fabled Berlin Philharmonic and receive laudatory reviews from German music critics. Alas, my conducting career proved to be meteoric, sputtering out in dust after a few fleeting moments of deceptively brilliant fireworks.

CHAPTER 7

KOUSSEVITZKIANA

My association with Koussevitzky had not been severed when I went to Rochester. In the spring of 1925 he invited me to Boston, where he had taken root as conductor of the Boston Symphony Orchestra, to spend a few days in his suburban villa in Jamaica Plain. He asked whether I would care to become his bilingual secretary, while retaining my former capacity of rehearsal pianist. Much as I enjoyed the pleasant atmosphere of the Eastman School of Music, a move to Boston was an alluring prospect. Koussevitzky would pay me $50 a week plus meals, a substantial wage in 1925, and I would be able to travel with him to Paris each summer. I was to replace Koussevitzky's former secretary, a Russian journalist and physician named Vladimir Zederbaum. Although Zederbaum's medical degree was not operative in the United States, he prescribed a whole battery of pills and liquids for Koussevitzky's periodical ailments, including one for his recurring fainting spells. Mrs Koussevitzky, the real power behind the throne, remonstrated with Zederbaum for his excessive ministrations. Tensions grew between them, until Mrs Koussevitzky finally told him to pack and leave. For further emphasis, she ordered that Zederbaum's suitcases and other belongings be put out on the porch of their house. Poor Zederbaum, who had a heart condition, had to be hospitalized, and eventually returned to Paris. Still rankling over the manner in which he was dispatched, he bombarded Koussevitzky with letters and telegrams full of abject apologies and assertions of his undying loyalty. He was finally offered, and gladly accepted, a public relations position for Koussevitzky's European affairs.

My departure from Rochester was a riotous affair. At least forty people jammed into my studio apartment. Speeches were delivered, toasts were drunk, tears were shed.

'Partir, c'est mourir un peu', and we all knew we would never reconvene in a similar orgy of *Wahlverwandschaft*, an elective consanguinity of spirits. Paul Horgan recited his epic poem, set in heroic pentameter, 'On the Departure of Colya', using the Russian diminutive of my name. Here is the opening stanza:

And now the Fateful Hour is at hand,
And in the snow a saddened little band
Of friends attempts to stay the Monarch Time.
But he, cruel Emperor, commits the crime,
And Colya takes the New York Central train
Which in itself is something of a bane.

I maintained a lively correspondence with my Rochester friends. Rouben Mamoulian had departed for Hollywood, where he became a prominent film director; rumour had it that he was travelling about with Greta Garbo. Thrilling news came that Paul Horgan had been awarded first prize from Harper's for his novel *The Fault of Angels*. Horgan sent me a copy, inscribed, 'For Colya, to acknowledge again his genius, with the procession of events in the style of our days together.' The book was indeed a chronicle of our Rochester days dealing with a group of artistic people in and about a music school in the town of Dorchester, New York. Among members of the faculty was a Russian named Val, a Russian named Eugene, and a young Irishman, John O'Shaughnessy. There was also a piano player by the name of Nicolai Savinsky, who spoke funny English and liked to invent words. Savinsky wrote a ballet to a scenario by O'Shaughnessy which was produced at the Dorchester School of Music. There was also a beautiful lady of the harp whose golden tresses matched the colour of her celestial instrument.

Publication of Horgan's *The Fault of Angels* coincided with my own little venture into fame as conductor. Our Society of Unrecognized Geniuses was quickly becoming a misnomer. Accordingly, I dispatched an official letter to O'Shaughnessy, Secretary to Paul Horgan:

Dear Mr O'Shaughnessy, I take note of the important prize awarded to your master Paul Horgan for a novel. I also note that one of our former associates in the Society for Unrecognized Geniuses, Rouben Mamoulian, has become a celebrated movie director. My own boss, Nicolas Slonimsky, has achieved some notoriety as an orchestral conductor. In view of these events, I have been instructed by Nicolas Slonimsky, President of the above Society, to inform you in your capacity as Secretary thereof, that the Society of Unrecognized Geniuses is hereby disbanded. Reason: Said geniuses have become recognized. Signed: Nicolai Savinsky, Secretary to Nicolas Slonimsky.

In August 1979 I received a letter from Lucile, adored lady of the harp, acknowledging receipt of some of my recordings:

Dear Nicolai [she wrote]. You really are a genius, even though you ceased being an unrecognized one years ago! Listening to your records gave me the greatest pleasure. Some of the music is just plain beautiful and some of it is extraordinarily witty. How I laughed when I heard the 'ads': after so many years I remembered them perfectly, and they brought you closer to me (and to the wonderful times we had together) than any of the other pieces.

I spent the summer of 1925 in Paris with my mother and sister, the Shestovs, Boris de Schloezer, and a multitude of Russian friends. A near-tragedy darkened our close circle. Schloezer, who like his brother-in-law Skriabin was for ever engrossed in deep philosophical speculations, became possessed with an overwhelming passion for a young Jewish girl. She failed to gauge the metaphysical rhetorics with which he adorned his declarations of immortal love for her, and was confused by his serious approach. Driven to distraction, Schloezer went to Monte Carlo with the firm intention of ending his life. He wrote to Shestov: 'Tomorrow I will cease to exist and will know whether there is another, better world after death.' After a night at the casino, he took the funiculaire to the top of the hill and shot himself through the heart. He was found in the morning, miraculously still breathing, was taken to the hospital, and brought back to life. After his recovery, Schloezer returned to Paris and resumed his work as a writer for the French press and as music critic for the *émigré* Russian daily. He published a remarkable book on Bach, in French, which Ezra Pound, who admired Schloezer's writings, later translated into English. Schloezer died in Paris on 7 October 1969. When, in the last days of his life, a friend asked what preoccupied him most, he said, 'J'étudie ma mort.' Indeed, introspection was a dominant trait of his life; he often spoke of his 'mythic self', which he tried to reduce to realistic terms. Not coincidentally, Schloezer received his 1901 doctorate from the University of Brussels for a dissertation on Egoism.

I continued my work with Koussevitzky. In addition to my duties as rehearsal pianist and secretary, I wrote programme notes for his Paris concerts, for which I was paid by the management. My mother was happy having me close at hand. My sister Julia tried desperately to enter the Paris artistic life. She started a marionette theatre which she called *Les Petits Comédiens de bois*. Milliotti designed the puppets, one of which was modelled after Koussevitzky in a tableau for puppet orchestra. Julia rented a tiny theatre on the *rive gauche*, and manipulated the puppet strings herself. She commissioned several composers to write special scores for her productions. She approached Stravinsky, but he replied coldly, 'Speak to my publisher'. Despite considerable interest in Julia's venture, the attendances were miserably small. The affair ended with an accumulation of unpaid bills, a not uncommon fate of such undertakings in Paris.

Among Koussevitzky's primary tasks in Boston was to inject young blood, mostly French and Russian, into the veins of the ageing personnel of the Boston Symphony Orchestra. Fourteen new orchestra members were recruited, most of them Frenchmen, and a corresponding number of old-timers were not re-engaged, among them the great oboe player, Georges Longy, whose dismissal produced a shock wave among symphony goers. 'New Music Director Shows He's Boss', a Boston paper headlined. The newcomers were given an audition, and, as usual, I served as accompanist. Koussevitzky would ask me in Russian what I thought of each performance; the applicants could easily judge what was said by the tone of my voice, and it gave me a sense of power. I swelled with pride when Koussevitzky asked me to attend to the business details of his commission to Ravel to do an orchestration of Mussorgsky's *Pictures at an Exhibition*, and it was my task to write out a cheque for 10,000 francs for the performance right over five years.

Upon our return to Boston from Paris, I rented a furnished room in Jamaica Plain, not far from Koussevitzky's house. Every morning he would pick me up in his chauffeured limousine and we would drive together to Symphony Hall for a daily rehearsal. Occasionally we would take a walk around Jamaica pond. During one such walk we were suddenly confronted by a ferocious-looking dog. Koussevitzky stopped, his jaw fell, and his neck reddened—symptoms of anger or fear which had become familiar to me over the years. I said something about barking dogs that never bite, but after this episode Koussevitzky discontinued his walks.

Boston became my home town. I enjoyed its intellectual environment; not for nothing was it called the Athens of America. I met several members of the local intelligentsia whose frame of mind harmonized with my own, including Isaac Goldberg, a brilliant literary critic and staunch non-conformist in politics and the arts. When Goldberg visited my rented room in Jamaica Plain, he expressed discomfort at its orderliness. 'I don't like it,' he said, sniffing. 'Everything here is too neat. Something must be very wrong with your psyche.' His observation was astute. There was a great deal wrong with my psyche, but he could not have guessed the origin of this 'wrongness' which lay too far in my Russian past for him, or anyone, to fathom.

Although Goldberg was a Jew, he was very much opposed to the Jewish establishment. He refused an invitation to address a group of Boston rabbis in an offensively outspoken letter in which he characterized rabbis as commercial promoters of an enterprise based on fraud. Goldberg was more lenient towards Catholic and Greek Orthodox priests, he wrote, because they were naturally stupid, whereas the Jews, particularly reformed Jews, were too cunning not to realize that they were engaged in deliberate deception for private gain. Needless to say, this episode did not endear Goldberg to the Boston Jewish community.

Apart from his scholarly pursuits, Goldberg wrote witty verse; one of his pithy epigrams is incorporated in Bartlett's *Familiar Quotations*. He also published a pornographic novel, *Quintet*, in which he vividly described a quintuple sex orgy organized by a group of erotically minded musicians, some of whom were embarrassingly similar to members of the Boston Symphony Orchestra. The book was promptly banned in Boston, but even with this encouragement it did not sell. Goldberg's sex scenes were entirely cerebral, perhaps because his own life was singularly devoid of erotic experience. He married his first cousin; they had no children. He never travelled beyond New York or Maine. He turned down a Guggenheim Foundation grant to South America because he was distrustful of Latin plumbing. When he died at the age of 50, his body showed symptoms of premature senility due to lack of physical exercise. Goldberg may have been an intellectual homunculus, but he also possessed great human compassion and capacity for friendship.

It was in Goldberg's house that I met Dorothy Adlow, a young Radcliffe graduate who subsequently became my constant companion. She told me that she had already seen me from a distance on the boat during her trip to Europe in the summer of 1925, when I was travelling with Koussevitzky. Arthur Fiedler, who had met Dorothy in Boston and who was travelling on the same boat, had pointed me out to her.

I made friends with many Boston Symphony men (there were no women in the orchestra then; even the harpists were men, although one was reputed to be on the borderline of the nominal definition of gender). Koussevitzky was lucky to have Richard Burgin, a Russian Jew and pupil of the famous Professor Auer at the St Petersburg Conservatory, as his leader and assistant conductor. Burgin harboured no conductorial ambitions himself, so Koussevitzky could delegate occasional concerts to him without fear of being upstaged. The personnel of the orchestra numbered few native-born Americans—most were German, French, or Russian. Arthur Fiedler, who was to rise to fame as conductor of the Boston Pops, was a member of the viola section. He was a Jew of German extraction, and both his father and uncle had been Boston Orchestra men. He spoke fluent German, and Koussevitzky could communicate with him in his own ungrammatical Yiddish-inflected brand of the language.

Fiedler's towering ambition was to conduct a pair of concerts in the regular series of the Boston Symphony. Koussevitzky regarded him as a member of an inferior species, however, and never engaged him as guest conductor. He was particularly incensed when Fiedler endorsed a brand of whiskey in an advertisement in the Boston Symphony programme book. (Koussevitzky never drank hard liquor, preferring French red wine and aperitifs.) As time went on Fiedler's popularity with the audiences actually outshone Koussevitzky's. Once a group of young people made their way into Koussevitzky's room in Symphony Hall during intermission, and insolently asked why Fiedler was not conducting. Koussevitzky's outrage can easily be imagined. For his part, Fiedler retaliated by calling Koussevitzky a 'culture vulture' and impugning his musicianship.

Boston was a town of aristocrats. The Brahmins who headed the Board of Trustees of the Boston Symphony Orchestra were inclined to look down upon the lowly Italians and even lowlier Jews. An amusing court case gained newspaper publicity when a Jewish immigrant named Kabotznik decided to shorten his name to Cabot, and opened a grocery store under that distinguished Boston patronymic. A famous jingle about the Brahmins of Boston began to circulate in a revised version: 'And this is good old Boston / The home of the bean and the cod / Where the Lowells talk to the Kabotzniks / And Kabotzniks talk only to God.' The Cabots, greatly annoyed, took Kabotznik to court. They lost, much to the delight of newspaper columnists, who enjoyed this opportunity to punch the Boston snobs on their patrician snouts.

Koussevitzky was no Kabotznik. Actually, his family name is rare in Russia. His father was a Jewish musician who had earned his living by playing the violin at weddings and social occasions. Koussevitzky had three brothers who were also musicians, and together they had organized a working ensemble, with Koussevitzky playing not only the double-bass, the instrument that had brought him fame, but also the trumpet, trombone, and clarinet.

At the age of 14 Koussevitzky had decided to try his fortunes in Moscow, and perhaps enrol in the Moscow Conservatory. He was lost in the big city, and was halted by a police officer who asked for his papers. He produced his passport, which under the rubric of religion said, 'Jewish'. As a Jew, Koussevitzky had no right to be in Moscow. Anticipating the inevitable, he began to cry. 'Don't cry,' the compassionate officer said. 'All you have to do is to have some holy water sprinkled on you in church and you will be as good as any other Christian.' 'But I don't have a godfather,' Koussevitzky whimpered. 'I will be your godfather,' the officer said, and conducted the boy to the nearest church. So it came to pass that Koussevitzky was enabled to enter the class of double-bass players at the Philharmonic Institute in Moscow. And why the double-bass? Because Koussevitzky had no money to pay for tuition, and the only classes that were given free of charge were those of double-bass and trombone.

Koussevitzky was careful to preserve his unique splendour. When his nephew, also a double-bass player, proceeded to give concerts in Russia, advertising his last name in large letters, 'KOUSSEVITZKY', and his first name, 'Fabien', in demure italics, Koussevitzky ordered him to cut off the first syllable of his family name. Fabien Koussevitzky became Fabien Sevitzky. To make matters worse, he drifted into conducting, emigrated to America, and turned up in Boston as conductor of something called People's Symphony, giving concerts in a hall across the street from Koussevitzky's own citadel at Symphony Hall. When the nephew announced a performance of Beethoven's Ninth Symphony during the same week that Koussevitzky was to perform the work with the Boston Symphony Orchestra, Koussevitzky could contain himself no longer. He summoned his nephew into his presence and told him to cancel his performance. Sevitzky dared to talk back at his imperial uncle, and was thrown out of the house. Both Koussevitzky and Sevitzky did the Ninth Symphony without earth-shaking consequences.

Koussevitzky's English was peculiar. He would ask a rhetorical question and supply a rhetorical answer, 'You hev? Mek!' Deciphered, it meant, 'You have it in the music? Then make it!' When a player tried to say something during a rehearsal, Koussevitzky would cut him short with the unequivocal order, 'Me talk, you no speak.' In Russian, a scale is a 'gamma', and Koussevitzky thought that in English it was 'game.' Occasionally he indulged in whimsicalities. Whenever he was dissatisfied with the way the double-basses played he would say: 'Bassi, you play like bassi auf vitch the price is five cents!'

On at least one occasion Koussevitzky was compelled to apologize to one of his players. He stopped a rehearsal when his first cellist had a little solo, and said with a grimace: 'C'est faux!' The cellist, a dignified Frenchman, asked, 'Quelle note?' 'Entre les notes!' Koussevitzky replied. Offended by being told that he played out of tune 'between the notes', the cellist picked up his instrument and left the hall. Koussevitzky was embarrassed. He followed the cellist and apologized, and the rehearsal was resumed.

Occasionally, Koussevitzky was moved to deliver profound philosophical pronouncements. Speaking of Shostakovich, in connection with a performance of his 'Leningrad' Symphony, he made this cryptic statement: 'Nineteen-century génie, Beethoven; twenty-century génie, Shostakovich, Und Haydn? Nu, Kinder?' Translation: 'Each age produces its own genius in music. Beethoven represented the romantic spirit of the nineteenth century in his great symphonies, while Shostakovich reflects the revolutionary world of the twentieth century in his modern creations. But we must not underestimate such masters as Haydn, who composed great works without trying to create new musical universes. Don't you think so?'

One of my prime duties in Boston was to supply symphony programmes to the programme annotator, the venerable Philip Hale, who was also music and drama editor for the *Boston Herald*. Like many conductors before him, Koussevitzky was in the habit of changing his programme at the last moment, after programme notes had already gone to print. Naturally, Hale, and his assistant John N. Burk, were unhappy about this situation. To allay their discomfort, I used to jot down my estimates of the chances that the programme would stay, using such phrases as 'It looks like a picture of health' or 'Guaranteed to last'. Overhearing one of my exchanges with Hale, and noticing my undue animation, Koussevitzky became suspicious. 'Why are they all smiling when they talk to you?' he asked one day, and added, 'You demoralized Hale! He was never like that before.' Koussevitzky decided to hand the programmes over himself. Unfortunately, he could not remember names, and when he did, he pronounced them *à la russe* with disastrous results. The Russian alphabet has no 'H'. Handel is Gendel and Haydn is Gaydn. Koussevitzky certainly knew Gendel from Gaydn, but names like Hale, Hall, Hull, and Hill were all Gaul to him. It was not clear why he could not pronounce the name of Henry F. Gilbert, which could be spelled adequately in the Cyrillic alphabet. He invariably described him to me as 'that friend of yours at Garvard who never washes'. It is true that Gilbert was occasionally negligent in his personal appearance, but he was never at 'Garvard', even though he lived in Cambridge.

Koussevitzky's insistence on handling the programme led to a hilarious mix-up when he was to conduct the world première of *Flivver 10,000,000* by the Boston composer Frederick Converse. The piece was a symphonic dedication to Henry Ford on the occasion of the launching of the ten-millionth Ford automobile. On the day the programme was to be sent to the printer, I received a frenzied telephone call from the symphony librarian. 'What happened?' he asked. 'The boss has cancelled the Converse piece! The publicity is out, and Ford himself is expected to attend!' I was bewildered. 'What do you mean cancelled? We were going over the score last night, and he certainly intends to rehearse it tomorrow.' 'You'd better come over right away,' I was told. I went immediately to Symphony Hall. Koussevitzky was going to play *Adventures in a Perambulator* by John Alden Carpenter, John Burk told me, instead of the Ford piece. 'But he hasn't got the Carpenter score!' I said. 'Where did you get the idea that he will play it?' 'Why, from Mr Koussevitzky himself,' Burk replied. 'You mean to say that Koussevitzky actually uttered the word perambulator?' I asked. 'He does not know what a perambulator is, and would not be able to learn such a word in a hundred years. Besides, the name Carpenter sounds no different to him from Converse.' 'But, he showed it to me,' Burk protested, and demonstrated how Koussevitzky gestured as though pushing a vehicle. 'I asked him whether he meant *Adventures in a Perambulator* by Carpenter,' Burk continued, 'and he said yes.' 'He would have said yes to anything that moves, including *Pacific 231*', I told Burk, referring to Honegger's homage to the American-built locomotive. 'What are we going to do?' he asked. 'Nothing,' I replied. 'Put the *Flivver* back on the programme and don't say a word to Koussevitzky.' *Flivver 10,000,000* had its day of glory, even though Henry Ford never showed up and the critics dismissed the piece with less than faint praise.

Koussevitzky was extremely sensitive to newspaper criticism. He was quite indignant when Boris de Schloezer wrote an unfavourable review of his Paris concert in the Russian *émigré* paper and ordered me to write a rebuttal to the editor. I said it would be unseemly, considering the fact that I was in his employ. On numerous occasions Koussevitzky suggested that I write his biography, which he would dictate to me in Russian. I evaded his requests. Eventually he found a perfect hagiographer in the person of Arthur Lourié, a Russian Jew who for some unfathomable reason described himself as 'of a Catholic family for many generations'. Lourié had published some modernistic piano pieces in the early days of the Revolution, and also served as musical commissar in the Soviet Ministry of Culture. Being a philosopher by inclination, if not by academic training, Lourié filled his book with nebulous speculations about matters metaphysical. He duly noted Koussevitzky's biographical data, omitting his Jewish origin and the fact that Koussevitzky had been married twice. Lourié also made the astonishing statement that Koussevitzky was the first to play Brahms in Boston. There was so much Brahms in Boston long before Koussevitzky that someone once quipped that fire exits in the newly built Symphony Hall should be marked 'Exit in case of Brahms'.

In Russia, and to a certain extent in Paris, Koussevitzky mingled freely with music critics on informal occasions. He was quite surprised to learn that in the United States music critics do not seek social contact with artists. The Boston critics were on the whole laudatory of Koussevitzky, and H. T. Parker of the *Boston Evening Transcript* was apt to wax lyrical in writing his reviews. So it was a shock to Koussevitzky when, trying to penetrate the meaning of a review in the *Boston Herald* which he was reading in the bathroom, he came upon the word 'hysterical'. Not bothering to button up, he emerged from the bathroom with his jaw trembling. 'Did you read what that person wrote about me in the *Gherald?*' he demanded. Of course I had read it, but I replied in the negative, my policy being in such cases to deny any previous knowledge in sensitive matters.

'Then read it!' Koussevitzky screamed, shoving the paper under my nose. I explained to Koussevitzky that the reviewer (not Philip Hale, but one of his assistants) said that, while a listener might have expected a hysterical interpretation of Tchaikovsky's music from a Russian conductor, Dr Koussevitzky (he had in the meantime acquired an honorary doctor's degree from Brown University) gave the audience a sober, measured, and yet eloquent performance. 'You see then', I reasoned, 'that, far from being impertinent, the writer pointed out the great qualities of your interpretation as distinct from the hypothetical hysterical rendition by some other Russian conductor.' 'But the very idea that I might have played Tchaikovsky hysterically!' Koussevitzky screamed. Thereupon he commanded me to take a letter to Philip Hale. I obediently sat down at the typewriter.

Dear Mr Hale' [(pronounced Gaul), he began]. 'I am depriving Europe of my art in order to give your town the best of my artistry. Instead of gratitude, I find myself insulted on the pages of your newspaper. To say that I might have conducted in a hysterical manner is to reveal a total ignorance of my interpretive ideas. I note that the review was signed not by you, but by one of your hirelings. Under the circumstances, I expect you to dismiss the fellow forthwith from his job.'

    He signed the letter with a flourish, and warned me in most imperious tones that he would not countenance any expression of opinion on my part. 'Address it, put a stamp on the envelope, and mail it without delay!' he ordered. Instead of complying, I went to see Mrs Koussevitzky. I told her bluntly that Boston was not Moscow, and that no artist can presume to tell a newspaper editor whom to hire and whom to fire. Indeed, I added, if this letter were to be made public, it could jeopardize Koussevitzky's position with the orchestra. She looked at me with that strange expression that had earned her the nickname 'owl', and said, 'You must have provoked him.' The letter was never posted.

My relationship with Koussevitzky began auspiciously. If anything, he exaggerated my supposed talents and abilities. The qualities he most appreciated were the ones he lacked conspicuously, such as absolute pitch, a fairly retentive memory, an ability to read music at sight, and a flair for languages. I recall my travels with him to Spain and Portugal, where he conducted a Russian opera troupe. In Barcelona we went to a bullfight. A trumpet sounded a signal before the show. Suddenly Koussevitzky asked me in what key they were playing. 'Why, in B-flat major,' I replied, somewhat puzzled by the question. Koussevitzky paused and became strangely pensive. 'You know,' he said, 'if I had your sense of pitch, your memory, and your knowledge of harmony, I would be the greatest conductor in the world.'

Koussevitzky's faith in my linguistic abilities was justified by an amusing episode in Lisbon. During a rehearsal of the last act of *Boris Godunov* with a Russian opera company, when the Czar admonishes the heir to the throne with the words 'Ismenu besposhchadno caray!' ('treason ruthlessly punish'), there was a sudden commotion in the orchestra. 'What is going on?' Koussevitzky asked. The leader explained to me in a mixture of Portuguese, Spanish, and French that 'caray' in Portuguese means penis. I reported this to Koussevitzky, who instructed me, with considerable impatience, to change the word. The challenge stimulated my linguistic imagination. I finally found a Russian synonym for the forbidden word which fitted the melody and had the same stress on the second syllable: 'kazni'. I told the Russian bass singer who had the lead role to change the word, and the rehearsal proceeded without further incident.

Koussevitzky had a most disagreeable habit of diluting his praise with mockery: 'You who know everything, you who hear everything, you who remember everything, will you tell me if there was anything wrong in rehearsal?' I usually replied that it was he, Koussevitzky, who attributed these qualities to me, and that I never made claims to any such omniscience. But I must admit I took advantage of every opportunity to prove him right.

In the summer of 1926 Koussevitzky conducted Mussorgsky's *Khovanshchina* at the Paris Opéra. After a rehearsal he asked if there were any mistakes. I replied with insolent self-assurance: 'Yes, in the seventh bar of the introduction to Martha's aria, the second bassoon played G instead of F.' The familiar red colour filled the back of Koussevitzky's neck. His jaw began to tremble, and I knew a storm was coming up. 'You are going too far,' he said, barely restraining his fury. 'You sit in the hall without a score and you have the gall to tell me that the second bassoon played the wrong note! How could you know what the second bassoon was supposed to play? And how did you know it was in the seventh bar? This time I will call your bluff.' At the next rehearsal, Koussevitzky began with Martha's aria. 'Quelle note avez-vous?' he asked the second bassoon player when he came to the seventh bar in the introduction. 'Sol', the musician replied. Koussevitzky looked at the score and said, 'Non, c'est Fa. Corrigez, s'il vous plaît.' I was greatly relieved that my correction was right.

After lunch at Koussevitzky's Paris house, he asked me with exaggerated politeness: 'How did you know about that error? Did you check out the orchestral parts?' I explained to him that it was an educated guess, or rather an educated bluff on my part, and apologised for being so self-confident. Actually, I did not know for sure that the second bassoon should have played F instead of G, I explained, but, listening to the first rehearsal, I had been struck by the absence of the mandatory passing seventh in the last inversion of the dominant seventh-chord, leading to the first inversion of the tonic triad, a common progression, in which the two bassoons overlap a pair of French horns. It would have been inconceivable if Mussorgsky, or rather Rimsky-Korsakov who orchestrated the score, had missed that all-important passing seventh. Besides, when the passage recurred in another key, the passing seventh was properly there.

Koussevitzky stared at me with glassy eyes. 'I do not understand a word you say. How could you know what Mussorgsky wrote if you did not have the score?' I was about to recapitulate, but decided not to carry on. 'And how did you know the error occurred in the seventh bar?' Koussevitzky insisted. I explained that, since the introduction was eight bars in length, and the segment in question occurred just before the cadence, it had to be in the penultimate bar. Koussevitzky game me a quizzical look, but kept his peace.

In another case of an educated guess, I was able to check my suspicions against the score. Koussevitzky was rehearsing Prokofiev's Fourth Symphony in Paris, and I was struck by the horns that sounded strangely high. Prokofiev was out of town, so I could not check on it with him, but late in the evening, after Koussevitzky had retired, I examined the score. Prokofiev habitually wrote the horn parts in C. Horn players automatically transpose their parts to F, the customary horn pitch, and apparently they had played in F at the rehearsal, a fourth above the intended pitch. But how could it have been that neither Koussevitzky nor the horn players themselves had realized that there was something strange in the transposition? This could be explained by the peculiarity of Prokofiev's harmonies, which are often devoid of chromatic alterations in their diatonic structures. I left a message for Koussevitzky to check on the transposition. At the next rehearsal, he told the horn players to make sure that their parts were written in C. He did not comment on my intervention in this matter, and our relationship remained unruffled.

Despite the dangers, I continued to irritate Koussevitzky, not so much by correcting errors in the music as by my lack of tact in announcing them. The most serious encounter of this nature occurred after Koussevitzky's performance of Rimsky-Korsakov's *Scheherazade*, an occasion honoured by the presence in the audience of no less a celebrity than Charlie Chaplin. Koussevitzky conducted the familiar score with plenty of Russian zest, and was perspiring all over when I joined him in the artist's lounge during the intermission. He began with his customary gambit: 'You who hear everything, you who remember everything, you who . . . '

Once again, like a fool, I made a smart-aleck pronouncement. The second clarinet sounded too weak in holding the bass note in the chord of E minor in the introduction, I said, whereas the bassoon on G sounded too strong. The result was that the harmony registered to the ear as the first inversion of the E minor triad instead of its fundamental position. Koussevitzky was startled by my incontinent stream of words, and stopped wiping his perspiring torso. 'Where? Where? What clarinet?' he demanded. He had the score open and I had no choice but to tell him. 'But the bassoon is below the clarinet part,' Koussevitzky said, 'so how can the clarinet have the bass note?' Yes, I replied, of course the bassoon part is *written* below the clarinet part, but in this bar it *sounds* above the note in the clarinet. Koussevitzky nearly lost his power of speech. 'What are you talking about? The bassoon is in the tenor clef, and the tenor clef transposes a second down!' I continued on my dangerous path. 'The tenor clef does not transpose,' I informed him, 'but if you compare the register of the tenor clef part to that of the treble clef, as I imagine you must be doing, then the sound would be a ninth below, not a second below.' Koussevitzky's jaw began to tremble and his neck grew red. When he had sufficiently recovered, he stammered, 'Are you by any chance . . . Are you trying to . . . trying to teach me elementary harmony?' He retired to his private bathroom, mumbling to himself as if in a catatonic state. I realized I had overplayed my game.

That week I made myself scarce. Fortunately, the orchestra had a New York concert, and Koussevitzky was out of town. When he returned I resumed my secretarial duties, hoping that the *Scheherazade* incident had blown over. Dark clouds continued to gather, however, and the next storm came with thunderous force. Koussevitzky used to praise me so extravagantly in public that rumours spread that I was some sort of mentor to him. I recall meeting a member of the Simon & Schuster Publishing Company in New York. After I had introduced myself, he said: 'I know all about you. You're the person who teaches Koussevitzky how to read scores.' The more I tried to deny such notions, the more rumours grew. It was inevitable that the gossip would eventually reach Koussevitzky, and that he would accuse me of spreading it.

Meanwhile, I was seeking new outlets for my uncertain talents. I played accompaniments, gave piano lessons, and I filled occasional lecture engagements with piano illustrations. I also presented talks on Boston Symphony programmes at the Boston Public Library, strictly *honoris causa*. The audiences consisted mainly of music students and assorted derelicts who came in to enjoy the central heating on cold winter days. My favourite auditor was a middle-aged woman who carried a large burlap sack. She was always first to arrive, and usually occupied a seat in the centre of the front row. She invariably smiled at me as I stepped to the podium, then opened her sack and took out a lot of old newspapers and other rubbish. She carefully folded the newspapers and arranged them in piles on the vacant seats around her. By the end of my talk, she had her rubbish in perfect order, ready to return to her sack.

My English was still imperfect though fluent. At one of my talks, I referred to Pablo Casals as 'The distinguished Spaniel'. Paul Horgan, who attended that particular talk, had no end of fun over my solecism, and made a pastel drawing of a dog playing the cello. I still have it in my collection.

I sought publicity, partly out of vanity but also in the hope of improving my finances, which were in a deplorable state. Leslie Rogers, the friendly librarian of the Boston Symphony, arranged an interview with the *Boston Globe* for me for a feature article dealing with secretaries of famous people. A photographer came to Symphony Hall and took my picture. The reporter asked me all kinds of provocative questions: Was my boss temperamental? Yes, I answered cautiously. Music cannot be pursued without passion. Was it difficult to satisfy him? Yes, but I tried to meet his high standards. Was I doing anything on my own? Yes, I wrote songs which the great singer Roland Hayes had scheduled for performance. I also composed piano pieces.

On the following Sunday, 16 January 1927, I picked up the earliest edition of the *Globe* and turned to the feature page. What I saw made my heart sink. The banner headline proclaimed: 'My Secretary Knows More Than I Do—The Boss.' The quotation was taken out of context from the statement attributed to the President of the United Fruit Company, but the misleading headline was placed right over my picture. My own interview was faithfully reported and contained nothing that could offend Koussevitzky. Just the same, to avoid trouble, I decided not to tell him anything about it. Koussevitzky subscribed to the *Herald*, not the *Globe*, so I believed myself to be safe.

I proceeded nonchalantly to his house for our morning session. We had lunch, and Mrs Koussevitzky obligingly offered me a second helping of delicious Russian blancmange. Then, with ominous formality, Koussevitzky motioned me to repair to the living room, with Mrs Koussevitzky leading the way. He proceeded to speak in measured tones as if addressing a defendant in a court of law: 'I have nothing against your making extra money by playing the piano in clubs and at social functions,' he began. 'But we have a right to demand that you leave my name out of your publicity.' By using the first person plural, Koussevitzky made it plain that he was speaking on behalf of his wife as well. Then Mrs

Koussevitzky broke her silence. 'Like a dirty Odessa Jew,' she remarked icily, 'you are trying to pull your sordid little tricks behind Mr Koussevitzky's back.' Considering that Koussevitzky was himself a Jew, born nearer to Odessa than I, her remark was fantastic in its rudeness. I pointed out to Mrs Koussevitzky that the crucial quotation in the headline referred to the Secretary of the President of the United Fruit Company, not to me. 'If so,' Koussevitzky said, his restraint more chilling than his habitual eruptions of uncontrolled rage, 'then why was your picture placed in the centre of the page under the headline, and the pictures of other secretaries to the right and left of you?' I said it was probably done because my picture was *en face*, and the others in profile. I could not control the placement of the photograph, I explained, which was the business of the man in charge of the layout of the page.

It is of no avail presenting rational arguments to a person whose mind is impervious to reason. I realized that I had reached the end of my rope. I was still coming to the house to file correspondence and to perform other clerical duties, but Koussevitzky no longer asked me to play for his practising. In the spring of 1927, Mrs Koussevitzky gave me my final cheque and said goodbye. We shook hands. Koussevitzky did not appear, and I never met him face to face again.

My embroilment with Koussevitzky did not end with my departure from his employment. Some years later Moses Smith, a Boston journalist, decided to glorify Koussevitzky in a full-fledged biography. Koussevitzky showed interest in the project, and invited Smith to lunch. By that time he could communicate in English, and he retailed to Smith the familiar facts of his life, laying emphasis on his pioneer work in championing new music. Being a journalist, Smith began to ask personal questions. Was it true that he been married to a dancer before he wed the rich Natalie? Was it true that his father was a village fiddler? Was it true that he had hired an orchestra with which to practise in his spacious mansion in Moscow? Koussevitzky signified displeasure at these inquiries. The important thing, he told Smith, was not his early life, but his ideas about music. Not satisfied with these generalities, Smith interviewed some old Russian musicians who had known Koussevitzky in Moscow. They co-operated willingly, adding a few colourful details, some not without malice. Smith was naïve enough to try to check his information with Koussevitzky himself. Koussevitzky bristled and, at the end of an inconclusive discussion, told Smith that he had decided to write his own biography. Thereupon he dismissed Smith from his presence. Smith had a contract for his book, however, and had no intention of abandoning the project. Inevitably his original attitude of awed respect towards Koussevitzky changed to open antagonism.

To my horror, Smith intended to use some rather juicy tales about Koussevitzky that could have come only from me. Yes, the facts were there, but I told Smith he would betray our friendship by reporting them. To this Smith declared in all solemnity: 'Nicolas, you cannot censor history.' I did manage to persuade him to leave out the damaging story about Koussevitzky's letter to Philip Hale. After all, I reasoned, it was never posted and so could not be reported as an accomplished fact.

Koussevitzky's sycophantic friends encouraged him to bring a lawsuit against Smith and his publishers, Allen, Towne & Co., for defamation of character, claiming that the book represented him as 'an incompetent musician and poseur'. The case was thrown out of court. It was common knowledge, the judge ruled, that not all was sweetness and light among musicians, and he found no malice aforethought in Smith's book. Koussevitzky had to pay legal expenses in return for one dollar's worth of moral damages granted to him by the court.

Koussevitzky never doubted his supremacy among conductors. When an excitable Boston matron rushed to congratulate him after a concert and gushed, 'Dr Koussevitzky! I know who you are! You are God!' Koussevitzky replied haughtily, 'I know my *responsabilités*.' Still, he felt uneasy about Toscanini and Stokowski. He told the orchestra that Toscanini was merely 'a good, second-rate conductor of a third-rate opera company in a provincial Italian town', and that Stokowski prostituted his talent by his flamboyant exhibitionism. When a misguided friend sent him a newspaper article extolling 'the great conductor Pierre Monteux', Koussevitzky was not pleased. 'Too many great conductors in this world!' he muttered, pacing the living-room floor. 'Positively too many great conductors in the world!'

He was careful to engage only 'safe' guest conductors for the Boston Symphony Orchestra, including Stravinsky, Ravel, Respighi, Glazunov, Casella, and Goossens. But he made a miscalculation by inviting Dimitri Mitropoulos. Although unknown in America, Mitropoulos conquered both orchestra and audience by the power of his personality. When an English-horn player made a false entrance in the *Alpine Symphony* of Richard Strauss during a rehearsal, Mitropoulos asked, 'My beat not clear?' 'No,' the player quietly replied. 'It was my error.' Mitropoulos inspired great respect among the orchestra men by his fantastic mastery of the scores which he conducted from memory, even in rehearsal. When he appeared to acknowledge applause, the entire orchestra stood up and gave him a 'tusch', the violinists tapping the strings of their instruments with the back of their bows, and the wind players making percussive sounds with their fingers on the frames of their instruments. Koussevitzky did not appreciate this display. He later complained that the orchestra had been 'degraded' by Mitropoulos, who 'rounded up every Greek waiter and shoeshine boy' in town to organize a claque.

After a quarter of a century, the management of the Boston Symphony Orchestra decided to engage a new conductor. Koussevitzky was getting old, suffered frequent infirmities, and repeatedly cancelled concerts. As an ageing monarch about to abdicate the throne, Koussevitzky let it be known that his chosen successor was his immensely talented young student, Leonard Bernstein. Koussevitzky did everything in his power to promote Bernstein. He sent a telegram to Mayor La Guardia of New York City to arrange an invitation for Bernstein to conduct a summer concert at the Lewisohn Stadium (La Guardia himself liked to conduct, and led the orchestra several times in an idiosyncratic rendition of the *Star-spangled Banner*, which he beat in duple rather than triple time). La Guardia was too busy to reply, however. Frustrated by his own ineffectiveness, Koussevitzky told Bernstein to change his Jewish name. A name like Bernstein, he said, is fit for a pushcart peddler, a pants presser, a travelling salesman, or an accountant, but not a conductor. Bernstein bristled. 'If I have to change my name to become a conductor,' he said, 'then the hell with conducting!' As it turned out, Bernstein did rather well with his *echt* Yiddish name!

Koussevitzky never completed his formal academic courses, but he had a great vision of educational institutions for musicians. He established the Berkshire School of Music in Tanglewood, Massachusetts, for composers, instrumentalists, singers, and conductors. It was backed by the regular summer concerts of the mighty Boston Symphony Orchestra, and among its graduates were such talented musicians as Leonard Bernstein, Herbert Blomstedt, Lukas Foss, and Eleasar De Carvalho.

Koussevitzky died in 1951 and was buried in his Tanglewood estate with the full solemnity of the Greek Orthodox ritual. A year before his death he conducted several concerts in Israel, with tremendous emotional acclaim. He no longer denied being Jewish and even concluded his speeches and letters with the word 'Shalom'. I wrote a lengthy article about Koussevitzky for the *Saturday Review of Literature*, in which I paid tribute to his achievements as a musician and proponent of so many worthy causes in Russia, France, and America. The editors of the *Saturday Review* forwarded to me a copy of a letter they had received from the manager of the Boston Symphony Orchestra, in which he voiced his appreciation of my article, adding that it was especially commendable since I had received such shabby treatment from Koussevitzky in return for all the work I had done for him.

CHAPTER 8

BOSTON BEGINNINGS

In the spring of 1927, at the age of 33, I found myself unemployed with dubious prospects for my career. And what career? As a pianist? As a littérateur in uncertain English? As a composer of impressionistic songs with a Russian flavour? As a conductor? As a piano teacher? As a lecturer on modern music? My ambition in every direction was great, my fantasies of recognition in one or all of these pursuits were eager and expansive. In the meantime I had to earn a living, and that was the hardest of my expectations.

I found a manager who believed in my nebulous future. For a starter he got me some jobs as an accompanist, at a fee of $50 for each appearance. The very first time I accompanied a singer in Boston, however, I ran into difficulties — not because I did not play well, but because I played too well! H. T. Parker, reviewing the concert in the *Boston Evening Transcript*, gave the singer due credit, but concluded his review with these words:

However, the attention of the audience was riveted to the accompanist, the able and assured Nicolas Slonimsky wearing his gravest air, faintly suggesting a somber and absorbed young gentleman out of Pushkin's Byronic pages. His piano playing was technically flawless; but it was also poetic and romantic; whenever given an opportunity, he projected a singing tone and dynamic nuances which captivated the listening ear.

My next engagement was with a soprano of considerable abilities, but without a compelling voice. I arranged a modern programme, with songs by Casella and Miaskovsky, a section from *Jonny spielt auf* by Ernst Krenek, an excerpt from the formidable score of *Le Livre de vie* by Obouhov, Prokofiev's long vocal ballad *The Ugly Duckling*, and the concluding song from Stravinsky's *Le Rossignol*. I also included two of my own songs, set to Oscar Wilde's poems, *Silhouettes* and *Impressions*. The singer memorized the entire programme, an uncommon feat for the time, and, not to be upstaged, I memorized my accompaniments as well. When I followed her on to the stage, the piano rack was still in place. With a self-conscious ostentation, I removed the rack and put it on the floor. I cannot be sure whether I was the first to play accompaniments from memory in a song recital, but no one attending that concert mistook the intent of my flamboyant exhibitionism. The Boston critics gave due praise to the singer, but, once again, the greater share of encomiums went to me.

Among my English-speaking Russian friends in Boston was a tenor by the name of Maxim Karolik. He was a person of aristocratic bearing — tall, dark, and curiously nonchalant in his social conduct. He was a Jew from Bessarabia; it was a part of Romania when Karolik received his American citizenship, so that he was required to renounce allegiance to the 'Boy King Michael', then the ruler of the country who reigned in the interim of the two periods in power of his philandering father, King Karol of Romania. Karolik's name had a royal assonance, and many of his friends in the upper echelons of Boston society called him 'Count Karolik'. He never denied explicitly the spuriousness of the title, but carefully explained that in a democracy there should be no titular nobility.

Karolik's brand of English was peculiar, yet he had a gift for language and often found the *mot juste* in conversation. When one of his acquaintances quoted Shakespeare that familiarity breeds contempt, Karolik retorted that, conversely, one cannot breed without familiarity. He gained entry into the upper classes of Boston society, and earned a living by giving private concerts at the homes of such wealthy patrons as the Vanderbilts, DuPonts, and Whitneys. He was a guest at Jacqueline Lee Bouvier's wedding to the future president, and became quite friendly with them. A maiden lady of advanced years, bearing the quintessential Bostonian surname Codman, took a liking to Karolik. She invited him to accompany her to the Riviera, where they were married. He was 34, she was 71. The Codman clan, alarmed by reports of foreign fortune hunters, put detectives on Karolik's trail. He passed inspection without a blemish. The marriage entitled him to half of her not inconsiderable fortune, and when the young bridegroom and his virginal elderly bride installed themselves in her Newport mansion, Karolik proved conclusively the basic decency of his character. While he liked the company of women, he never acquired a mistress, and when kidded by his aristocratic friends about his romantic life, he parried with such forced witticisms as 'I kiss, but I do not tell'.

Mrs Karolik was a frail old lady. She was also somewhat eccentric. Before she married Karolik, she had kept forty cats in her Newport mansion. As Karolik put it, in marrying him she exchanged forty cats for a Russian hound. (Actually, she retained six of the cats even after the marriage.) The Karoliks had a British butler named King, who was formerly employed by the Duke of York, the future King George VI of Great Britain. I was a frequent guest at the Karolik mansion, and always felt slightly nervous when King stood behind me at the table. Once I dropped a fork, and another fork magically materialized to the left of my plate. Karolik acted with total disregard of the royal past of King's servitude. When chicken was served, Karolik asked for a breast cut. 'But don't put a brassiere on it,' he warned. He repeated this several times until Mrs Karolik cried, 'Maxim, if you say that word again, I will leave the table!'

Karolik had the saving ability to laugh at himself. When during a rehearsal I told him that he should not make ritardandos, he replied, 'I didn't make any ritardandos, I just slowed down a little bit.' He also laughed when I said he was the only artist who could fill the Boston Symphony Hall three times in succession during a single season, tripling his ticket sales from the first to the third concert. What I did not make clear was that his manager had sent invitations to schools, colleges, insurance companies, and a nunnery, offering batches of tickets for free. At one concert the entire balcony at Symphony Hall was in black and white—to hear Karolik, the nuns had sent the total membership of their convent. There were also a few innocents who drifted into Symphony Hall by accident and actually bought tickets, so that I was technically correct in saying that the sales tripled during the season—at his first concert the receipts were $17, at the third, $51. As Isaac Goldberg put it, these concerts were Maximum Karolik at minimum prices.

After a few seasons of pointless concertizing, Karolik gave up his singing career. By that time he had become intensely interested in American art. Mrs Karolik owned a number of priceless paintings, among them a couple of Copleys which she had inherited from her father. She also owned some silver pieces which her grandfather had acquired during the French Revolution when he was a member of the American diplomatic corps in Paris.

When Mrs Karolik died at the age of 92, Karolik was disconsolate. She had been the only person in the world who was willing to listen patiently to his self-aggrandizing stories, genuinely believing him to be a great artist. After her death, Karolik donated the major part of her art collection to the Boston Museum of Fine Art. Valuable pieces of Americana, as part of the 'Maxim and Martha Collection', are found in other American museums as well.

Karolik was anxious to issue a definitive statement about the difference between 'singing artists', of which he regarded himself a prominent representative, and mere tenors, 'who had a lot in their throats but not much above'. He liked to quote the Italian degrees of comparison: 'stupido, stupidissimo, tenore.' He died of a massive heart attack in December 1963.

In 1929 I became conductor of the Harvard University student orchestra,

known as Pierian Sodality. It was the oldest symphonic ensemble in the
United States, founded in 1808. Surprisingly, not a single one of the
players knew the meaning of the words Pierian and Sodality. I explained
to them that the Pierian Spring was the fountain where the Muses
congregated, and that Sodality was Latin for Society. *

As conductor of the Harvard orchestra, I did my best to impress the
players by my knowledge of music. Not only did I conduct all rehearsals
from memory, but I also memorized the rehearsal numbers. I would
announce, '4 bars after letter M' or '3 bars before letter D', without
consulting a score. Furthermore, I took pains to memorize the actual
notes played by each orchestral group, or solo instrument, at the beginning of a particular section which I intended to rehearse. Since I selected
the passages for rehearsal, it was not too difficult to stage my amazing
feats of memory with perfect assurance of success.

Not everything I did with the Pierian Sodality was marked by dissimulation or trickery. I really tried to improve the technical standard of
the orchestra. In his book on music at Harvard, Professor Walter Spauld-
ing wrote that I was the first conductor of the Harvard orchestra who
insisted on accurate tuning and precise tempi. Walter Piston, who once
played in the Harvard orchestra himself, told me after one of my concerts
that the orchestra sounded almost like a professional ensemble under my
tutelage.

Forty-five years later I conducted a concert at Yale University. Clar-
ence A. Grimes, former violinist in the Pierian Sodality when I was its
conductor, wrote a letter to the editor of the *New Haven Register* which
gave me real pleasure because of its obvious sincerity.

As a member of the Pierian Sodality [he wrote], I used to marvel at Slonimsky's
expertise. After all, this was his first conducting job in the United States. In the
bull sessions after rehearsals he would amaze us with his ability to read almost
any avant-garde orchestra score at the piano at sight. Even then, this PhD in
mathematics from the University of St Petersburg [did I stoop so low as to brag
about my having studied mathematics in Russia? Anyway, I never got my PhD]
had a phenomenal memory and his encyclopaedic knowledge was no accident.
'How, Nick,' we asked him, 'do you know so many jawbreaker words which most
of us don't use any more?' In his broken English [was my English so badly broken
as to be remembered even through all that polysyllabic accretion?] he replied:
'Every night before I go to bed I memorize twenty of the longest words I can find
in the dictionary.'

Conducting a non-professional orchestra with a changing personnel
was a hazardous undertaking. I recall the dramatic exit during rehearsal of
the *Egmont Overture* of the only viola player I had. 'I am not going to waste
my time playing the same note over and over again!' he announced.

I pleaded with him to be considerate of Beethoven's failure to provide a more important viola part. He finally relented and resumed his seat.

One of the two cello players in the orchestra was incapable of playing in tune, but was very eager to take part in our public concerts. I proposed a compromise: he would play anything he wished in rehearsal, but would move the bow in the air without touching the strings at the concert. He cheerfully agreed.

I recall a horrifying occasion when the cellist (the one who *could* play) did not show up for an engagement in Framingham, a suburb of Boston. Schubert's *Unfinished Symphony* was on the programme, with its famous second theme in the cellos. The situation was critical. I was just about to give up when a miraculous apparition materialized before me in the form of a cellist of the Boston Symphony Orchestra, who, carrying his instrument, was crossing the street towards his car. I ran after him and implored him to help me out. He agreed. The Schubert symphony never sounded so wonderful to me as at that concert.

Even before my stint with the Pierian Sodality (which I conducted for three seasons), I conceived an idea of organizing a chamber orchestra in order to present programmes that would form a missing link between chamber music and symphonic works. My manager was willing to finance the project, for I still retained enough glamour from my Koussevitzky years to attract attention as a conductor in my own right. I issued a polysyllabic manifesto detailing my plans for the new ensemble: it would have only one of each wind instrument, strings in a limited quantity, piano and percussion. Its programmes would emphasize little-known Baroque pieces, or arrangements thereof, and modern compositions. I would also commission works from contemporary composers. Its personnel was recruited from members of the Boston Symphony Orchestra, and the quality of performance was bound to be high. The ensemble would be named the Chamber Orchestra of Boston.

I asked Heinrich Gebhard, a German pianist and resident composer, to write a piano concerto for me and to be soloist in its first performance. He graciously obliged. Another première was a lively foxtrot by the Swiss composer Frank Martin, originally written for my sister's puppet theatre in Paris. And so, on 20 December 1927, I ascended the podium of Jordan Hall, adjacent to the New England Conservatory, to conduct the inaugural concert of my Chamber Orchestra of Boston. H.T. Parker, music and drama critic of the *Boston Evening Transcript* (familiarly known around Symphony Hall by his initials as 'hard to please' and 'hell to pay'), gave me a fine display on the music page with a photograph captioned 'New Hand Upon New Venture'.

I had three rehearsals. Incredibly, my ancient difficulty in giving a clear downbeat without an exaggerated preliminary upbeat came back with a vengeance—I was obviously inhibited by the presence of so many superior musicians under my command. To allay my psychomotoric trouble, I tried mental training of the kind practised by Rosing in Rochester. I uttered a silent soliloquy, reciting in my mind a litany of anticipations. In 72 hours, in 48 hours, in 24 hours, in 12 hours, in 6 hours, in 3 hours, in 1 hour, it would all be over. I mumbled the lines from Virgil's *Aeneid*, 'Forsan et haec olim meminisse iuvabit' ('perhaps even this will be some day remembered with pleasure'). The line refers to the descent into Hades. I also clung tenaciously to my favourite formula of William James, that correlated the strength of remembrance with time elapsed since the event: $M = P/T$. P in this equation can stand either for Pleasure or for Pain, as the case might be. The factor M (for Memory) is directly proportionate to P. The element T (for Time) is in inverse ratio to M; the farther the event recedes in memory, the less painful it becomes.

My Boston friends distributed free tickets for my concert, and the audience turned out in respectable numbers. During the performance I felt so self-conscious that I could barely concentrate on the music. The experienced Boston Symphony players were sympathetic and never betrayed their concern about my lack of expertise. Gebhard played his piece brilliantly, and I faithfully followed his tempi. There were no obvious disasters.

The reviews in the morning papers were lukewarm. But the column, by H. T. P., in the *Boston Evening Transcript*, was devastating. 'Modern Concert / Conductor Clearly at his Beginnings / Mr. Gebhard's Piece Saves the Evening', were the headlines in bold face. But if so, why did Richard Burgin, leader of the Boston Symphony, who attended the concert, say it went all right? And why did the players compliment me on my performance? Were these commendations merely expressions of sympathy for an unfortunate fellow musician?

Some time before my début as conductor, H. T. Parker had asked me to write a feature article for the *Boston Evening Transcript* on Alexandre Tansman, soloist in his piano concerto with Koussevitzky and the Boston Symphony Orchestra. I wrote a discursive piece with a lengthy and largely irrelevant exordium, ending with a flamboyant peroration, very much in the manner of Parker himself. Sesquipedalian polysyllables fairly pullutated in my piece and ottocento vocables grandly adorned the text. This was my first article in the English language, and I was not sure it would be acceptable on purely grammatical grounds. Great was my surprise when, a couple of days later, I received a note in Parker's gnomic hand on an index card, with the logo of the *Boston Evening Transcript* in the top left corner: 'Dear Mr Slonimsky: I received your essay. It has been a long time since anything so admirably devised and so admirably written has come to my desk. I salute you and add that you should write more.' I carried the card with me wherever I went and displayed it proudly to friends.

Word spread that a new little orchestra which promoted ultra-modern music had sprung up in Boston. I began receiving offers of new scores from composers. One of the important contacts I established at this time was with Henry Cowell, a musician of unique originality who had just begun publishing his important series *New Music Quarterly*. Cowell hailed from California, the state of natural wonders not constricted by the fashions (social or artistic) of the effete East. He was a Jack London type—in fact, his father and London were close friends. Cowell never wore a necktie, at that time an indispensable part of male attire, and he ignored the necessity of having his trousers pressed or shoes shined, social embellishments deemed essential for success.

Cowell gave me the score of his *Sinfonietta*, written in dissonant counterpoint and ending with a tone-cluster consisting of dissonantly arranged and closely arrayed notes. Such procedures, common in the wilds of California, I thought, might not be acceptable in the music corridors frequented by proper Bostonians. So much the better, I decided; I liked to shock people.

Cowell asked me to contribute a work to his magazine *New Music Quarterly*, dedicated specifically to ultra-modern compositions. By that time I had abandoned my Russian orientation and began to speculate along modernistic lines. In the 1920s composers were having an orgy of dissonance as a protest against the academic prohibition of unresolved discords. Merely to join this trend would not satisfy my vanity, and in a flash of inspiration I thought, 'Why not write a piece built exclusively on consonances which would sound dissonant because of so-called false relations, forbidden in the conservatory?' The fruit of these elucubrations was a piano suite, *Studies in Black and White*, in which the right hand played on the white keys, and the left hand on the black, 'in mutually exclusive consonant counterpoint'. The black-and-white antinomy represented the physical aspect of my technique; the crucial point of the music was that only consonant intervals (thirds, sixths, and occasional perfect fifths) were used. Fifths occurred only when the left hand played B-flat and the right hand played F, or when the right hand played B-natural and the left hand crossed over to F-sharp. The individual titles of the numbers in my *Suite in Black and White* were typical of the then prevalent modernistic fashion: 'Jazzelette', 'A Penny For Your Thoughts', 'A Happy Farmer', 'Anatomy of Melancholy', 'The Sax

Dreaming Of A Flute', and 'Sin^{2}x + Cos^{2}x = 1', a trigonometrical equation rendered in invertible counterpoint, and ending, by exception, on a unison to illustrate the unity in the second part of the equation. The last piece was called 'Typographical Errors'. Naturally, there were no errors at all, but deliberate simulations of dissonances. A year later I composed a song, 'My Little Pool', based on the same technique of mutually exclusive counterpoint in consonant intervals.

The publication of *Studies in Black and White* was scheduled for the July 1928 issue of *New Music Quarterly*, but was postponed until the following issue to make room for a vocal piece by Aaron Copland, at that time a young 'ultra-modern' composer. I saw Copland often during my Koussevitzky years. Few composers, young or old, were as undemonstrative or unaffected by changes of fortune. In the spring of 1927 Copland was the piano soloist with the Boston Symphony in his so-called 'jazz concerto'. He returned to New York immediately afterwards, and I had the unpleasant task of forwarding to him the perfectly awful reviews of his piece in the Boston papers. Philip Hale said in his review that the concerto displayed a shocking lack of taste and that Copland apparently let his fingers hit the keys at random, in the manner of a child amusing itself by making noise. An editorial in the *Boston Herald* declared that Copland's music belonged to the 'broken crockery school'. But in the *Boston Evening Transcript*, H. T. Parker astutely allowed that 'a serene and distant future, not a clamoring present, will give judgment', suggesting that Copland may be a representative of a new and genuine American music. How right he was!

A less philosophically inclined person than Copland might have been upset by the invective directed against him. Not Copland.

You're a darling to have sent me all those delightful write-ups [he wrote to me]. I went to the mirror to see if I could recognize myself . . . When the Concerto is played again (O horrid thought!) we must see if we can't get the police to raid the concert hall to give a little interest to this 'horrible' experiment.

He wondered whether 'the Maestro will have sufficient courage to perform my music anywhere'. Koussevitzky had plenty of courage, even at the risk of antagonizing his audiences and critics. When he put Copland's *Music for the Theater* on a subsequent programme, there were protests to the management on the ground that the piece employed only a handful of musicians whereas paying subscribers were entitled to hear the full orchestra. Throughout his twenty-five years of tenure as conductor of the Boston Symphony, Koussevitzky remained loyal to Copland, and had the satisfaction of watching his growth from the *enfant terrible* to the status of a great American composer.

Once during an intermission at Koussevitzky's New York concert, I saw George Gershwin standing alone. 'Do you know George?' I asked Aaron, with whom I'd been schmoozing. 'No, I never met him,' he replied. I made the introduction. This was a historic meeting, Copland being a composer who descended to jazz by way of classical music and Gershwin, a jazz composer who ascended to classical music. I had met Gershwin for the first time in Rochester in 1925 when he played his *Rhapsody in Blue*. He had been apprised of my existence by Vladimir Dukelsky, alias Vernon Duke. We had a pleasant conversation. I told him that I had played his song *Swanee* (which he wrote at the age of 19) on my jobs in Constantinople in 1920. He was amused to learn that his tune had travelled so far.

The last time I saw Gershwin was on the day of the first performance of his opera *Porgy and Bess* in Boston on 30 September 1935; the director was my old friend Rouben Mamoulian. Gershwin complained about the annoying reports concerning his lack of technical skill in composition, an imputation based on the fact that his *Rhapsody in Blue* was orchestrated not by him, but by Ferde Grofé, a practical composer and arranger who had acquired fame on the popular circuit. 'Why don't you arrange a news conference,' I suggested to him in my customary frivolous manner, 'write out a complete work in public, and have it projected on the screen?' He met my suggestion halfway. 'Why don't I give a demonstration for you right now,' he said. He took a sheet of manuscript paper from his briefcase and began writing music with extraordinary rapidity. 'This is a funny song I wrote eons ago which was never published,' he said. He filled the page with notes and words of his inimitable satirical ditty about four fiddlers—Jascha, Mischa, Sascha, and Toscha—'whose tone was sour until a man, Professor Auer, came right along and taught 'em all how to pack 'em in Carnegie Hall. They were not lowbrows, they were not highbrows, they were Hebrews.' He handed the page to me.

Two years later Gershwin was dead of brain cancer which started with olfactory hallucinations of burnt rubber, an unmistakable symptom of a cerebral tumour. Not being a collector, I gave away the Gershwin manuscript to a friend. It would have easily fetched a thousand dollars on today's autograph market. But I would never have sold it. My other memorabilia and correspondence eventually went to the Music Division of the Library of Congress.

My own status as an American composer continued to be supported by Henry Cowell in various ways, not least by an article he published in the short-lived *Aesthete Magazine*, under the title, 'Four Little Known Modern Composers: Carlos Chávez, Charles Ives, Nicolas Slonimsky, and

Adolphe Weiss.' An incredible quartet! Charles Ives being little known! Another boost came from Cowell's inclusion of my name in his compilation *American Composers on American Music*. He contributed a chapter on me and I contributed one on him.

I continued my series of concerts with the Chamber Orchestra of Boston. On 11 March 1929 in Jordan Hall, Cowell was soloist in the first performance of his *Suite for Solo String and Percussion Piano with Chamber Orchestra*, a suite comprising three movements: 'The Banshee', 'The Leprechaun', and 'The Fairy Bells'. 'The Banshee', portraying a wailing Irish spirit that predicts death in the family, was to be performed on the bare strings under the lid of the grand piano. There was a gasp in the audience when Cowell got under the lid and began to tickle the naked strings. He also tapped piano strings with rubber-headed drumsticks, plectrum, pencil, and a darning egg. The latter implement inspired the headline writer in the *Boston Post* to say: 'Uses Egg to Show off Piano.' This headline became Cowell's favourite, and he never failed to mention it in his lectures and seminars.

Among Cowell's other tricks was playing a descending scale on the keyboard with his left hand while stopping the piano string with his right hand. He did this so cunningly that a visual downward scale sounded like one ascending. Cowell possessed a weird singing voice ranging from basso profondo to the highest treble in falsetto. He could even sing in quarter-tones.

In 1928 Cowell made a trip to Russia, where he was received as a harbinger of the musical future. Olin Downes, the powerful music critic of *The New York Times*, was also invited to Russia in the same year. Downes combined radical political views with reactionary opposition to new music. Cowell's exercises in altering the natural tones on the piano were particularly repugnant to him, and it was therefore ironic that these two figures were paired in Moscow at artistic events as prominent representatives of American musical culture.

The Soviet attitude towards Cowell changed radically when the Communist Party leadership ruled that modern music was a product of bourgeois decadence. A caricature of Cowell was published in a leading Soviet music journal, representing him as a wild man banging away at the piano with his fists.

CHAPTER 9

THREE PLACES IN NEW ENGLAND

It was through Henry Cowell that I met Charles Ives. In 1928 Ives invited Cowell and me to his brownstone on East 74th Street in New York, and Mrs Ives, providentially named Harmony, graciously served us lunch. They had adopted a girl named Edith. At the time I met him Ives was only 54 years but looked frail, suffering from a variety of ailments, as a result of a massive heart attack in 1918, and he had practically ceased composing. I learned to admire the nobility of his thought, his total lack of selfishness and his faith in the inherent goodness of mankind. There was something endearingly old-fashioned in his way of life; he spoke in trenchant aphorisms, akin to the language of Thoreau and Emerson, and he wrote in a similarly forceful manner. He possessed a natural wisdom combined with an eloquent simplicity of utterance. Amazingly enough, he started his career as a successful insurance man. His achievements in business were postulated, so he explained, on his respect for people at large. Yet Ives was capable of great wrath. He inveighed mightily against self-inflated mediocrity, in politics and art alike. The most disparaging word in his vocabulary was 'nice'. To him it signified smugness, self-satisfaction, lack of imagination. He removed himself from the ephemeral concerns of the world at large. He never read newspapers. He did not own a radio or a phonograph, and he rarely, if ever, attended concerts. The only piece of modern music he ever heard was Stravinsky's *Firebird*; reports differ whether he also heard *La Mer* of Debussy.

Ives was extremely biased in his opinions. Toscanini was a 'nice old lady' and Koussevitzky a 'soft seat'. Some of his aphoristic utterances are fit for an anthology. 'Dissonance is like a man . . .' 'Music is the art of speaking extravagantly . . .' 'A song has a few rights, the same as other ordinary citizens . . .' 'What has sound got to do with music? . . .' 'Beauty in music is too often confused with something that lets the ears lie back in an easy chair . . .' And he urged people to 'stretch their ears'. He was impatient with copyists who questioned rough spots in his manuscript. 'Please don't try to make things nice!' he would admonish. 'All the wrong notes are right!'

Ives was a transcendental rebel in politics. He once circulated a proposal to amend the Constitution of the United States and establish a system of direct vote for President. When Harding was elected President in 1920, Ives gave vent to his indignation in a song damning politicians who betrayed the ideals of the nation. He never participated in active political campaigns; his politics were those of mind and soul. So far removed was he from the reality of the world that he was not aware of the rise of the Nazis. When I told him what evil things Hitler was doing in Germany, Ives rose from his chair to the full height of his stature and exclaimed with rhetorical emphasis: 'Then why does not someone *do* something about this man!'

I told Ives about my chamber orchestra and asked if he could give me one of his works. He suggested *Three Places in New England*. As I looked over the score, I experienced a strange, but unmistakable, feeling that I was looking at a work of genius. I cannot tell precisely why this music produced such an impression on me. The score possessed elements that seemed to be mutually incompatible and even incongruous: a freely flowing melody derived from American folk-songs, set in harmonies that were dense and highly dissonant, but soon resolving into clearances of serene, cerulean beauty in triadic formations that created a spiritual catharsis. In contrast, there were rhythmic patterns of extreme complexity; some asymmetries in the score evoked in my mind by a strange association of ideas the elegant and yet irrational equations connecting the base of natural logarithms and the ratio of the circumference of a circle to its diameter with the so-called imaginary number, a square root of a negative quantity. The polytonalities and polyrhythms in the Ives score seemed incoherent when examined vertically, but simple and logical when viewed horizontally.

The more I absorbed the idiom of *Three Places in New England* the more I became possessed by its power. After conducting the score numerous times in public I felt total identification with the music, so much so that years later, when it became extremely popular, I would turn it off when I heard it on the radio, mumbling, 'It is mine, it is mine.'

The original scoring of *Three Places in New England* exceeded the dimensions of my chamber orchestra, but fortunately most orchestral music of Ives was scored for a 'theatre orchestra', capable of different arrangements. In fact, Ives called *Three Places in New England* an 'orchestral set', implying optional instrumentation. I asked if he could possibly arrange the score to accommodate my chamber orchestra. Yes, he could, and would. In fact, the resulting arrangement became the last orchestral score that Ives wrote out, at least in part, in his own handwriting; later he was unable to handle a pen.

I gave the world première of *Three Places in New England* at the Town

Hall in New York on 10 January 1931. Ives was present; it was one of the few occasions that he came to a concert. By that time my conducting had improved considerably so that I was no longer preoccupied with its technical aspect. And I was also able to control my nerves. I was not disturbed by the whispered refrain of the leader, 'So far, so good,' after each movement. The rest of the programme included Henry Cowell's *Sinfonietta, Men and Mountains* by Carl Ruggles, and a couple of simpler pieces intended to mollify sensitive ears. The final number was Mozart's *Ein musikalischer Spass*, the 'joke' of the title being a polytonal coda. I put it on as if to say, 'Look, listen, Mozart did it too.'

There were a few boos and hisses after the Ruggles piece. I was told that Ives stood up and said to a person who grumbled against Ruggles: 'You sissie, you don't realize that this is a piece of real strong masculine music.' This report found its way into the Ives literature, but I cannot very well believe it. It would have been utterly out of character for him to make such a public display of himself.

The New York concert received mixed reviews, but I was encouraged by the very fact that it went off without incident. Carried on the wings of success, however limited, I was able to get a couple of engagements in Havana, with a similar programme. It was my first trip to a tropical country, and one of my earliest on an aeroplane. I will never forget the amazing sight of a field of green and brown flowers in bloom as the plane was about to land at Havana airport. Incredibly, the flowers turned out to be palm trees, which looked so delicate and minuscule from the air.

I was met at the airport by representatives of the Sociedad de Música Contemporánea which sponsored my appearances in Havana. Cuba was then under the repressive rule of a military dictator, but the arts were left alone. The only restriction as far as music was concerned was the ban on the conga, the large Cuban drum that served as a means of communication between rebellious Afro-Cuban groups in the interior. My Cuban friends had close connections with the revolutionary factions, and they obtained for me a marvellous specimen of the forbidden drum, which I managed to smuggle out of Cuba on my return trip.

I had no trouble whatsoever in rehearsing the dissonant scores of Ives, Ruggles, or Cowell with my Cuban ensemble. The players were not aware that unresolved dissonances or atonal melodies were wrong, and played their parts without objections. To me, the whole Cuban adventure was a voyage into an earthly paradise. I relished the tropical fruits—the mango and papaya—and I was amazed at the sight of tall banana trees. I loved to walk along the beach. On the artistic side I became acquainted with the exotic, freely dissonant music of Amadeo Roldán and Alejandro García

2. My grandfather Haim Selig Slonimski (so spelled in Polish), from a lithograph taken in Warsaw in 1878. He was a man of great learning whose imagination led him to investigate curious and often unsolvable problems. During his very long life (1810–1904) he patented some inventions in telegraphy and proposed a Slonimski Meridian for the proper orientation of wandering Jews. There is a Haim Selig Slonimski Street in Tel Aviv.

1. My great-grandfather Abraham Stern (1761–1840), a portrait painted in 1823, now in the National Museum of Poznań, Poland. He is shown with his invention, a mechanical calculator, which he presented in a personal audience to the Russian Czar Alexander I in 1820.

3. (*top left*) My maternal grandfather Afansyi Wengeroff (Vengerov), who became a respected banker in Minsk.

4. (*top right*) Pauline Wengeroff (Vengerova), my maternal grandmother. In her memoirs she deplored the retreat from Jewish traditions of her grandchildren who 'feared neither God nor the Devil'. The photo was taken in 1913.

5. (*right*) My venerable bearded maternal uncle Semyon Vengerov, whose great work, *Critico-Biographic Dictionary of Writers*, although unpublished, is consulted by generations of Russian scholars. He corresponded with Turgenev, Tolstoy and other great Russian writers. He also edited collected works of Pushkin, Shakespeare and Schiller.

6. (*above*) Zinaïda Vengerova, my maternal aunt, well-known translator of English, French, German and Italian literature into Russian. She published her reports in the intellectual monthly *The Messenger of Europe*, of which my father was an editor. Photo ca. 1900.

7. (*top right*) Isabelle Vengerova, 1930, my maternal aunt and my only piano teacher, who became a celebrated piano pedagogue in America. Among her students were Leonard Bernstein, Samuel Barber, and Lukas Foss.

8. My mother Faina Vengerova as a young woman in the 1870's intent on saving the world by the power of moral suasion.

10. April 1894, St Petersburg. Me, just a few days old in my mother's arms. My mother said she was inspired by an Italian painting of Madonna and Child while pregnant with me and that consequently I looked like the Christ child when I was little.

9. My brother Alexander and my sister Julia, St Petersburg, ca. 1893. The name of the dog is Bobik.

11. The Five Slonimskys, a photograph from the incredible past taken at a summer *dacha* in Pavlovsk, near St Petersburg, in 1902. I am the sole survivor, as of 1987. From left to right: Michael, the future Soviet novelist (1897–1972); me (1894–   ); Vladimir (1895–1916); Julia (1884–1957); Alexander (1881–1964).

12. Mother and father during a summer vacation in Finland, 1910.

13. (*top left*) Me circa 1900. I already knew I was an authentic wunderkind, and the self-admiring expression on my face speaks volumes of my inevitable fall when, a few years later, I realized that the outside world was still not at my feet.

14. (*top right*) Me at a summer *dacha* in Finland in 1910. I was addicted to bilateral symmetry; hence the studied position of hands. On the original photograph I marked my dates 1894–1967, but the anticipated final year proved to be quite off and, in defiance of actuarial tables, I lived on, and on, and on . . .

15. (*left*) My bewildered expression at finding myself in the uniform of the Russian Imperial Army in the First World War is eloquent in its muted absurdity. With warriors like me it is no wonder that the Czar lost both his war and his throne.

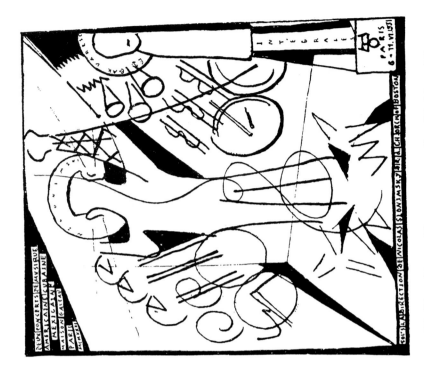

17. "I could see with my own eyes the gilded top of the Eiffel Tower hovering over Slonimsky's head when he spread his arms apart like the wings of an airplane in flight." (A surrealist painting by Alexei Remisoff in his article on Slonimsky's performance of Varèse's music in Paris, June 1931.)

16. Portrait of me made in Paris in 1925 by the Russian painter Vasily Shukhayev, who was fascinated, he said, by the surrealistic asymmetry of my nose bridge.

19. My mother in her Paris apartment, 1932. On the wall, a gallery of family pictures.

18. A silhouette: conducting the Berlin Philharmonic, March 1932.

20. Conducting Varèse's *Ionisation* in Havana, Cuba, in 1933. The Cuban musicians had no difficulties in mastering the acrobatic rhythms in Varèse's score.

21. Publicity picture, 1933, during my stint at the Hollywood Bowl. It did not help, and my Hollywood venture misfired.

22. With Dorothy in Boston shortly after our marriage in 1931. She cleansed me of my Russian neurasthenia and taught me how to live. Professionally she was an art critic, one of the finest.

23. (*below*) A happy nurse and a contented child, Boston, 15 June 1934.

24. Arriving in Peru in the course of a Latin American tour in 1942.

25. (*below*) Trying out Tchaikovsky's piano in 1935 at the Tchaikovsky Museum in Klin, near Moscow, which had been his summer residence.

26. My brother Alexander soliloquizing in his Moscow apartment.
On the wall: various memorabilia of the Pushkin family. Alexander's
wife was a direct descendant of Pushkin's sister. As a devout Pushkinist, Alexander took great pride of this affiliation. The photo was
taken in 1959 by the American photographer Cornell Capa.

27. Leningrad, 31 October 1962. I am sitting between my brother
Michael and his wife Dusia.

28. A demonstration of my ambidextrous conducting. London, Ontario,
March 1979.

29. Orating (in Russian) at the Congress of Soviet Composers in the Grand Hall
of Columns, Moscow, 24 November 1979. The lips form the unpronounceable (to
non-Russians) vowel half-way between the Greek iota and epsilon.

Dear M.S.

You are a Good Boy & a gigantic indifferent job. The book came. Many thanks.

Anybody can write a good symphony — yet it takes a better man to conduct it — But only if you & Sam Johnson can write a Good Encyclopaedia.

Now give your mind & body a good rest — take it easy — just conduct the Boston Symphony for the old ladies for a season — then you will be able to do your life work again — a memorable Day! — Ahoy!

Eva Yours
Chas E Ives

30. Letter from Charles Ives, a characteristically generous response to my
book *Music Since 1900*, which was published in 1937.

IONISATION
(for Percussion Ensemble of 13 Players)

Nicolas Slonimsky

Edgard Varèse

32. Dedication page 'au premier ionizateur—son ami' of Varèse's unique score, of which I gave the first performance, in New York, on 6 March 1933.

31. A page from my guestbook, with comments on my 'Grossmutterakkord'. Ernst Krenek contributed an earnest analysis of inverted dodecaphonic structures, Hindemith extended his wishes for a long life and good progeny to the 'Grossmutterakkord', and Prokofiev, signing his name minus vowels, S Prkfv, wrote, 'To the devil with grandmothers! Let us write music!'

33. With Frank Zappa, 21 December 1981, in the artist room at the
Civic Auditorium, Santa Monica, California

34. With John Cage in Los Angeles, 8 March 1987, enmeshed in the
twisted musical ribbon of my invention, called 'Möbius Strip Tease'.
The orange on Cage's head was used in my defiant performance of
Chopin's 'Black-key Etude à l'orange'. (Photo by Margo Leavin.)

Caturla. Roldán was a mulatto; Caturla was of Spanish extraction, but he was married to a black woman, and his social connections were mainly among Afro-Cubans. He served as a judge in Havana. In 1941 he was assassinated in the court-house by a criminal whom he was about to sentence. In my Cuban programme I included a remarkable Afro-Cuban work by Caturla, *Bembé*, scored for a small ensemble with a lot of Cuban percussion; it was the first original work I ever conducted or heard which was written in an exotic rhythmic manner. I also included *Rítmica* by Roldán. Both Caturla and Roldán were eventually recognized in Cuba as founders of modern Cuban music, and music schools and conservatories were named after them.

I was tendered a reception in Havana by a group of musicians and local officials. The chairman opened the banquet by introducing me in florid Spanish as 'uno de los mas grandes . . .' then stopped and corrected himself, 'no, el mas . . . gran maestro del mundo . . . el maestro . . . el maestro . . .'. There followed a rapid consultation. The chairman whispered something into the ear of another official who shook his head. He turned to another person at the table with similar negative results. The embarrassment was resolved when another official whispered something to the speaker, who was then able to announce my glorious name: 'El maestro . . . Estalinsky!'

My Havana concert went off famously. The Cuban journal *Musicalia* paid tribute to me as a 'músico de gran cultura, profunda musicalidad, magnetismo personal y entusiasmo ilimitado'. Superlatives have a luxuriant sound in the Spanish language.

After the New York concert in January 1931, Cowell and I met with Ives and talked vaguely about more concerts of works by new American composers. To hire an orchestra in New York was too costly, but why not try to export American music to Europe? In 1931 the dollar was still almighty among world currencies, and one could get a lot of French francs or German marks for it. Ives liked the idea and said it would be great to 'rig up' a concert or two of American music in Paris, and volunteered to finance it. (Ives was affluent from the earnings he made as head of the insurance company from which he had recently retired.) His generosity was totally free from any desire to be acknowledged as a musical philanthropist. In fact, the entire transaction was to remain a secret.

On the surface, my concerts in Paris were to be a legitimate extension of my Boston enterprise, and no one was to know any different. And so, in April 1931, I embarked for Cherbourg and Paris. Naturally, I announced my plans to my mother, my sister, and various friends in Paris. Ives gave me a letter of credit to the Paris branch of the Chase Manhattan Bank in the amount of $1,500, an enormous sum of money in French francs at the time.

Edgar Varèse, the formidable musician whose works have literally altered the very substance of musical composition and whose giant figure of a French peasant dominated the minds of other musicians present, was in Paris. He took command of the press, arranged interviews, introduced me to influential people, and encouraged me with grandiloquent pronouncements on the significance of our undertaking. The prestigious Orchestre Straram was engaged for my first Paris concert of American music. Varèse suggested having two concerts, one for a full orchestra and one for chamber orchestra, with four rehearsals for each concert. I had enough money from Ives to take care of the expenses.

Large posters were placed on Paris kiosques and pissoirs announcing my concerts of 'Musique américaine, mexicaine et cubaine' (Mexico was represented by Carlos Chávez, Cuba by Caturla and Roldán). I got in touch with my old friend Boris de Schloezer who promised to cover my concerts in the Russian *émigré* press and in some French publications.

I wrote my own programme notes, and, in my desire to introduce the public to unfamiliar names of composers, I appended a brief description for each of their works. Thus *Three Places in New England* became *Trois Coins de la Nouvelle-Angleterre* with a parenthetical description, 'Géographie transcendentale par un Yankee d'un génie étrange et dense'. For *Men and Mountains* by Carl Ruggles I offered the following: 'Une vision brobdingnague par un inspiré de Blake.' I described Cowell as a Pico de Mirandola of American modern music, but in my extensive programme notes I made an embarrassing blooper by saying that he was a native of Menlo Park, California, 'where Thomas Alva Edison perfected his incandescent electric lamp' (Edison had his laboratory in Menlo Park, New Jersey, not California). For Roldán's Cuban ballet suite, *La Rebambaramba*, the last piece on the programme, I had to import Cuban instruments, which were a novelty for most European musicians at the time. The orchestral musicians had a grand time toying with them at rehearsal.

I had a brilliant audience at my first Paris concert, 6 June 1931. Composers, journalists, painters, Italian futurists—all came at the behest of the indefatigable Varèse. There was applause, but there were also puzzled responses. Paul Le Flem, a long-time friend of Varèse, did his best to draw attention to my concerts; he published a front page review in *Comoedia*. Vuillermoz, doyen of the French music critics and a friend of Debussy, covered the concert in *Excelsior*. A truly philosophical review was published by Boris de Schloezer, in which he discussed the problem of whether Varèse's *Intégrales*, which dispensed with modulations, development, and tonality itself, was, pragmatically considered, a musical work. He arrived at the conclusion that it was undoubtedly music.

My second Paris concert, with a reduced orchestra, took place five days later. The programme included *Energía* by Chávez, which I described as 'une musique énergique et non-jolie'. Most critics readily agreed that the music was indeed 'non-jolie'. Then there was *Bembé* by Caturla, which I described as 'la frénesie afro-cubaine, déchaînée avec un savoir-faire très parisien par un jeune de Cuba'. There followed three canons by Wallingford Riegger ('De la musique pure créée par un esprit inventeur et non-canonique'), and *Intégrales* by Varèse, which I defined by the high-flown phrase: 'Géometrie sonore d'une logique implacable, par un Einstein franco-américain.'

In conducting Riegger's canons I was confronted with a problem. Some instrumental parts were written in 5/8, and others in 2/8. I started beating time in 5/8 whereupon the binary musicians began to gesticulate at me to show their discomfort. They had 2/8 in their parts. What was I to do? Okay, I said, I will conduct 5/8 with my right hand and 2/8 with my left, the least common denominator of an eighth-note being a metrical invariant. I was so proud of my newly found ambidextrous technique that I applied it in other pieces I had to conduct, notably in the second movement of *Three Places in New England.* Someone quipped that my conducting was evangelical, for my right hand knew not what my left hand was doing. As far as I know, no conductor ever tried to emulate my schizophrenic time-beating, a realization that naturally bolstered my ego.

The Paris press gave the concerts a great deal of attention. André Cœuroy published a feature article in *Gringoire,* under the title '*Découverte de l'Amérique*':

We have, *sans blague,* just discovered America, thanks to a Christopher Columbus resident of Boston. This Christopher Columbus is called Slonimsky. Retain this name. It is that of a young musician astonishingly gifted, inventor of a new aesthetic code of piano technique, in which each hand follows its own scale, and a conductor of a promising future. Not only does he possess a specific gift for conducting, authority, puissance, *envol,* but also a finesse of pitch perception that the most consecrated aces of the baton in Europe might well envy. One had to watch him at the rehearsal stopping the orchestra embroiled in an almost inextricable maelstrom of sounds in an atonal score bristling with accidentals and convulsed by multiple rhythms, to point out to the second oboe or the third French horn, 'Monsieur, vous jouez un la bémol, c'est un la naturel!' This does not seem unduly important, but this delicacy of aural perception in the midst of an inhuman uproar, this sovereign assurance in bringing order out of chaos, impresses an orchestra. This is why one can predict without fail an assured career to this young conductor.

There followed a sentence that horrified me: 'Koussevitzky had better look to his laurels.' It was obvious to me that Schloezer, who had his own animus against Koussevitzky, had spread around the story of my break with Koussevitzky, and that Cœuroy thought it would be titillating to bring it up.

Cœuroy's article was translated for Ives, who thenceforth began addressing me in his letters as 'Dear Columbus et Vespuccius', or 'Dear Columerica', or else 'Dear Mr Ambassador'. He wrote to me in pidgin French: 'Dear Monsieur Beaucoup! Mon Dieu! Mon Lisa—Bon Ami (not the mild sapolio)—Bon soir—Cher—Chez,' adding: 'French is too violent a language for me—no good cuss words—I understand it perfectly (when it's translated).' Apparently this verbal eruption exhausted his French vocabulary.

Schloezer's review of my concerts was exuberant. 'Not since the stormy 1920s', he wrote, 'had there been such excitement in the concert hall'. A French critic referred to the 'atmosphere de bataille'. My French manager said about me: 'Il a bouleversé tout Paris.'

Alexei Remisoff, the Russian *émigré* writer whose name is familiar to everyone interested in Russian literature, came to my concert and wrote a surrealist impression of it (he also painted an abstract expressionist portrait of me conducting the Eiffel Tower):

As a perfume expert who has an absolute nose, as a food taster who has an absolute tongue, so Slonimsky possessed an absolute ear. He can tell sounds that differ from one another by 1/16 of a tone. Well, maybe a dog can tell the difference of a 1/64 of a tone, but Slonimsky can tell, listening to the ants in an anthill, which ant hums out of tune.

I am not a specialist, and music for me is not much more than a diversion, and all the sounds I heard in the orchestra were sort of monotonous and boring. But what hit me really in the stomach was the concluding number, *Intégrales* by Edgar Varèse. Did you ever listen to the singing sounds of a sleeping person when he is having nightmares? The source of these sounds seems to come from far away, from distances of thousands of kilometres. Such sounds wake you up, and make your heart beat very fast. Varèse's music takes us to such distant regions, and he twists those sounds in a coil. Human nature has its own stratosphere which cannot be reached in any normal way. And in order to produce such stratospheric sounds, one must use strange new instruments, such as the lion's roar, Chinese blocks, rattles, and even jawbones of a hippopotamus. You have a sense that the whole world is torn apart, and it is then that you perceive your own subconscious deep in your chest cavity. Varèse also imitates the sounds of the city, the clang of metal on concrete platforms. This is his Sounding Geometry. In his *Intégrales* Varèse throws all these sounds into the brass. To protect you from being crushed and deafened, the conductor must grasp them by their throats and pull them down to earthly harmony. I could see with my own eyes the gilded top of the Eiffel

Tower hovering over the conductor's head with its sparkling ornaments, when he spread his arms apart like the wings of an aeroplane in flight.

After the applause toned down, I went backstage. Pushing through the crowded corridor, I particularly remembered Boris de Schloezer, a shiny cranium stuffed with phonograph records. Backstage the mob divided itself into two streams, one around Varèse, and one around Slonimsky. Varèse appeared to me as huge as all of his blaring trumpets, and next to him Slonimsky seemed just like a wunderkind from St Petersburg. But for me Slonimsky was the tamer of the lion's roar in the orchestra. To me this music was a wild phenomenon unlike anything I had ever heard before. On the next day I found a review of the concert in the local Paris paper in the Russian language. The critic wrote: 'Like a ray of sunshine cutting through the fog and bringing joy and hope to one in a prison cell, so the American concert by Nicolas Slonimsky who came specially to Paris from America, brought joy to our Russian colony and dispersed the fog that had hung over it for so many years.'

A sour note came from Florent Schmitt, eminent French composer and critic, who took exception to the parenthetical summaries of American works on my programme. In his lengthy review in *Le Temps* he said that it was 'un manque de modestie, fausse ou réelle' on the part of the composers to tell the critics what they are supposed to think of their music. I immediately dispatched a note to him, pointing out that the parenthetical descriptions were my own and that the composers were in no way responsible for them. He magnanimously printed my demurrer, but added it was an act of arrogance just the same whoever perpetrated it.

Bigelow Ives, nephew of Charles Ives, reminisced of these heroic days of fifty years ago:

I remember how affected Uncle Charlie was by one of the earliest performances in Europe of his music by Nicolas Slonimsky. Nicolas sent him one of the billings that they paste on the walls outside the concert hall, and that went on the door to the music room down in Redding. And how excited Uncle Charlie was over Slonimsky's promotion of his music in Boston! I remember Slonimsky coming to the house at 74th Street, and Uncle Charlie was so delighted to hear him coming. Uncle Charlie's studio was in the attic but he seemed to know when Slonimsky was in the house. He'd shout down to him and Slonimsky would shout back, and there were four floors between them. What a racket was created by those two! They'd get up there in the music room, and Uncle Charlie would go right at it. 'Now what do you think of this?' And then they'd begin experimenting.

Ives was delighted by the Paris reaction to my concert, but he was outraged by the comments in the American press. He was particularly incensed by the Paris dispatch from Henri Prunières published in *The New York Times*. Ives wrote to the pianist Robert E. Schmitz:

Prunières says that I 'know my Schoenberg', interesting information to me as I have never heard nor seen a note of Schoenberg's music. He says that I haven't applied the lessons as well as I might. This statement shows almost human intelligence. It's funny how many men, when they see another man put the breechin' under a horse's tail, wrong or right, think that he must be influenced by someone in Siberia or Neurasthenia. No one man invented the barber's itch. But one thing about the concerts that everyone felt was that Slonimsky was a great conductor.

What really raised Ives's hackles was Philip Hale's editorial entitled 'Mr Slonimsky in Paris', published in *The Boston Herald* on 7 July 1931:

Nicolas Slonimsky of Boston, indefatigable in furthering the cause of the extreme radical composers, has brought out in Paris orchestral compositions by Americans who are looked on by our conservatives as wild-eyed anarchists. He thus proposed to acquaint Parisians with contemporaneous American music. But the composers represented were not those who are regarded by their fellow-countrymen as leaders in the art, nor have they all been so considered by the conductors of our great orchestras. If Mr Slonimsky had chosen a composition by Loeffler, Hill, one of Deems Taylor's suites, Foote's suites, or music by some who, working along traditional lines have nevertheless shown taste, technical skill and a suggestion at least of individuality, his audience in Paris would now have a fairer idea of what Americans are doing in the arts.

Philip Hale further suggested that the American composers on my Paris programmes were followers of European composers of the avant-garde, such as Hindemith and others.

Ives set down some of his thoughts about Philip Hale's editorial in one of his memos:

It is interesting (and perhaps funny) to know that I (as I am included in Philip Hale's sweeping statement) have been influenced by one Hindemith (a nice German boy) who didn't really start to compose until about 1920 and several years after I had completed all of my (good or bad) music which Aunt Hale says is influenced by Hindemith. It happens that the music of mine on this particular program, *Three Places in New England*, was completed almost a decade before Hindemith started to become active as a composer. Again, up to the present writing (August, 1931), I have not seen or heard any of Hindemith's music. During the 20 years ending in 1919, only one conductor had seen any of my music, my first symphony which was completed in college. In 1929 Nicolas Slonimsky saw the score of *Three Places in New England*, and he is the only conductor (at present writing) that has made any adequate and comprehensive study of my music for orchestra. Take these facts, and then take the statement that the old lady makes, and all a man can say is that she, Philip Nathan Hale, is either musically unintelligent or deliberately unfair. To say it quickly, he is either a fool or a crook.

In the meantime my Americanization proceeded apace. In a biographical note inserted in the programme of one of my talks, I said that I was 'thoroughly Americanized in Boston'. The famous Boston novelist John Phillip Marquand, who, to my surprise and delight, happened to attend, said Boston was the last place on Earth in which to become Americanized.

On my thirty-seventh birthday, 27 April 1931, I stood before the judge of the US District Court in Boston and swore allegiance to the United States of America. I gave the correct answer to the question as to the name of the first President of the United States, and I knew that the Declaration of Independence had been signed on 4 July 1776. I replied in the negative to the query, 'Do you advocate the killing of the President of the United States or any government official of the United States?'

I received the precious Certificate of Citizenship No. 3415457, in which I was described as male, white, of dark complexion, brown hair, brown eyes, 5 feet 5¾ inches in height and weighing 122 lbs. My race was stated as Russian, as was my former nationality.

An event took place in Paris that overshadowed all my artistic achievements. On 30 July 1931 I was married by the Mayor of the 16th arrondissement to Dorothy Adlow, who had joined me in Paris to hear my concerts in June. Varèse was our best man. After a brief ceremony, I was handed a marriage booklet, with space provided for twelve children, including an appendix detailing instructions for proper 'allaitement', wet nursing.

Dorothy was seven years younger than I, but an eternity wiser. I was a bundle of nerves when she took me under her protective wing; patiently did she listen to my litanies, and with infinite tact taught me social amenities. Where I was ungovernable, she provided guidance, and where I was suspicious of others, she calmed me by rational argument.

Dorothy's parents were Jewish immigrants from Russia. Her father, who started out as a pushcart peddler, built a flourishing furniture business in Roxbury, a suburb of Boston. His name was Orlow, but to immigration officials the name sounded like Adlow and was thus transcribed. He spoke English with an Irish lilt, since most of his customers were from Ireland, but he never learned to write properly. Dorothy's mother could hardly speak English at all. Uneducated as the parents were, however, they knew the importance of education and sent their three daughters to Radcliffe and their son to Harvard. Dorothy studied art at Radcliffe College. Shortly after graduation, she became an art critic for the *Christian Science Monitor*; later she was appointed head of its art department, the only member of the editorial staff who was not a Christian Scientist.

No sooner had we returned to America than I made plans for another European tour, which was to include Paris, Berlin, and Budapest. Once more, it was Ives who financed my undertaking. My Paris manager had contracted the Orchestre Symphonique de Paris for two concerts in February 1932. I faced this orchestra with trepidation, for I'd heard that its musicians did not take kindly to new conductors. At the first rehearsal I noticed the second oboe player gently rubbing his right cheek with his fingers, a gesture meaning 'rasoir' (razor). I knew enough of French argot to understand that 'rasoir' meant 'no good'. This sort of demonstration was unsettling, but I was determined to counteract such expressions of doubt by my expertise.

My first concert, on 21 February 1932, included the Paris première of a great work, Béla Bartók's First Piano Concerto, with the composer himself at the piano! I had been warned that Bartók was a perfectionist, highly critical of conductors and players who failed to meet his standards. At my first rehearsal, the opening movement passed without much trouble. The second movement, however, which calls for special percussion effects, created difficulties. The score indicated that the suspended cymbal be struck from below rather than from above, and, when the percussionist failed to follow these specific instructions, Bartók walked to his stand to show how the cymbal had to be struck properly. Every minute of rehearsal time cost about two dollars, and I became rather uneasy waiting for Bartók to finish his demonstration. Finally, he returned to the piano, and I could resume the rehearsal. The last movement, in a rapid tempo, went smoothly. Bartók said to me after the concert that, with one more rehearsal, the performance would have been perfect.

On the same programme were three little pieces by Ives, *Appositions* by Henry Cowell, *Vers le Réel* by the astrologer–composer Dane Rudhyar, and *Three Cuban Dances* by Caturla. To mitigate this onslaught of modernity, I placed on the programme a Mozart serenade and *Night on Bald Mountain* of Mussorgsky. The Mussorgsky piece depicts witches riding upon broomsticks, until they are chased away by the sounding of morning chimes. I had been so preoccupied with the Bartók concerto that I had forgotten to order a set of tubular chimes. One can imagine my horror when, on the evening of the performance, I gave a cue to the percussion player to ring the chimes, and realized they were not there. Apparently nobody noticed this absence, and the performance received good reviews.

At my second Paris concert, 25 February 1932, Artur Rubinstein was the soloist in Brahms's Second Piano Concerto. Although I was ambidextrous in modern music, I felt uncomfortable in a straight classical work which seemingly required only setting the right tempo and indicating the proper dynamics. The rehearsal went off smoothly, and I was able to follow Rubinstein's every nuance and every rhythmic figuration. Rubinstein was very popular in Paris, and the applause greeting his appearance on the stage was tumultuous. Immediately after his number he disappeared. Unexpectedly, I got a lot of praise for my part in the concerto. Schloezer was quite enthusiastic; in his review he said that my conducting of the orchestral accompaniment was the finest he'd every heard.

My second Paris concert included the première performance of *The Sun-treader* by Carl Ruggles, rendered into French as *Le Marcheur du Soleil*. It is a tremendously complicated work, bristling with dissonances, and it did not win favour with the orchestra. The first viola player added the pronoun 'il' before the word 'viola' on his part, and 'la musique' after it, which made up the phrase 'Il viola la musique' ('he violated music').

The *pièce de résistance* at this concert was Varèse's formidable *Arcana*. The score calls for a very large orchestra, including a double-bass trombone. There was only one trombone player in Paris who could blow through this breathtaking instrument, and he was already engaged at the Paris Opéra for a production of Richard Strauss's *Elektra* on the very same night. Varèse was beside himself with anxiety. He ran back and forth from the Salle Pleyel, where my concert was to take place, to the Opéra, to see if the double-bass trombonist had time to dart away after the end of the opera in time to play his piece. Fortunately *Elektra* is short, and our precious trombonist managed to make it to the Salle Pleyel in time for *Arcana*.

My Berlin appearances proved even more exciting than those in Paris. My German managers, the prestigious H. Wolff and J. Sachs, engaged for me the great Berlin Philharmonic for a programme which included *Three Places in New England* by Ives, *The Sun-treader* by Ruggles, *Synchrony* by Cowell, *Arcana* by Varèse, and *La Rebambaramba* by Roldán. Never in my unhappily brief career as a conductor did I enjoy such marvellous co-operation. The virtuosity of the individual players was beyond praise. The muted trumpet solo, introducing Cowell's *Synchrony*, was sheer magic; I had never heard anything to equal it in purity of intonation and dynamic fervour. The musicians of the extended percussion section played on the exotic drums like small children enjoying a game. They were particularly fascinated by the *Löwengebrüll* ('lion's roar'), a bucket covered with a drumhead through which a rosined cord is drawn. I had four rehearsals with the Berlin Philharmonic, and never once did the players shown any displeasure with the music or with my conducting. I could not have imagined that, within a year, some of these great players would be forced to wear degrading swastikas and stand up to hail Hitler.

The Beethoven Hall in which my first Berlin concert took place on 5

March 1932 was almost full. For an unknown conductor, my newspaper reviews were incredible. The great Alfred Einstein, not ordinarily given to facile encomiums, wrote in the *Berliner Tageblatt*: 'Das ist ein Talent ersten Ranges, von einer ganz elementaren Fähigkeit, Orchester und Zuhörer zu überzeugen.' I recited the words to myself to absorb their full weight: 'This is a talent of the first rank, of a quite elemental capacity to convince orchestra and audience alike.' Heinrich Strobel wrote: 'No word of praise is too high for the conductor Slonimsky. With astounding knowledge of the scores and astounding energy he set out to promote his fellow Americans.' Paul Schwers, in the *Allgemeine Musikzeitung*, said: 'Astounding was the performance of the conductor Nicolas Slonimsky, who mastered the complex scores still in manuscript with exemplary skill and penetrating musicianship.' Josef Rufer, the Schoenberg authority, wrote: 'The Philharmonic musicians really played to their utmost ability, directed by Nicolas Slonimsky, who is a phenomenon of conducting technique.' Max Marschalk, in the *Vossische Zeitung*: 'In Nicolas Slonimsky we became acquainted with an astounding conductor. Who could emulate him? Who could so courageously and so firmly beat time through the wilderness of this new music?' Hermann Springer, in the *Neue Preussische Kreuz-Zeitung*: 'Nicolas Slonimsky is quite an astounding musician and conductor, who held in hand the Philharmonic players at dangerous moments with precise knowledge of the score and unshakable assurance.' H. H. Stuckenschmidt, in *B. A. am Mittag*: 'Technically Slonimsky is a highly gifted conductor who maintained the beat even in the most intractable rhythms with perfect ease.'

But the Hitlerite critic Paul Zschorlich in *Germania* blasted me and the music in obscene Nazi phraseology:

The leader of this impudent exhibition was naturally a Jew [he wrote]. Slonimsky can call himself a hundred times an American, but one has only to watch his shoulder movements to recognize at once that he is a 100% Polish Jew. He is an experienced time-beater, projecting clear geometric images in space. That is all.

If I ran off with the laurels, the composers on my programme elicited an outpouring of colourful invective from the press. Here is Paul Schwers in the ordinarily dignified *Allgemeine Musikzeitung*: 'Henry Cowell's *Synchrony* begins with a silly little solo of the muted trumpet. The bone-cracking trills of this milk-dripping introduction aroused irrepressible hilarity among the listeners. This screechy and banging piece of so-called music is nothing more than an explosive tonal enema.' Scatological similes marked the same critic's review of the Ruggles piece: '*The Suntreader* by Carl Ruggles should have been titled *Latrine-treader*, which describes more precisely the nature of the music. I for one had a distinct feeling of bowel constriction in an atonal Tristanesque ecstasy.' Schwers ran out of scatological metaphors in writing about Varèse's *Arcana*. 'This tonal monster', he wrote, 'transforms peaceful concert-goers into wild hyenas.' He took occasion, in his peroration, to make a sidesweep at Schoenberg: 'Great Arnold Schoenberg, you are with your famous *Five Orchestral Pieces* fully vindicated! They are utterances of modern classicism beside this barbarous madness.'

Heinrich Strobel wrote in the *Börsen-Courier*:

For two hours Nicolas Slonimsky bore down on the Philharmonic musicians until they finally could no longer conceal their desperation. For an hour and three-quarters the public submitted to the noise. But after the cacophonous tumult of *Arcana* by Varèse, they lost their patience. A pandemonium broke loose. It is understandable. Nobody's ears can stand this kind of noise for any length of time. It has nothing to do with music. It does not shock and it does not amuse. It is simply senseless.

In my programme notes for both the Paris and Berlin concerts, I described Varèse's music as 'sounding geometry'. One of the Berlin reviews came out with the headline, 'With Housekeys Against Sounding Geometry'. Indeed, some disgrunted listeners arranged a little concert of their own after *Arcana*, blowing into their large housekeys. This charivari was duly reported in out-of-town papers, under such headings as 'Scandal in Beethoven Hall!' The story was picked up by the Associated Press. I received a cable from my wife expressing her concern for my safety after the *Boston Herald* published a front page dispatch under the caption, 'Catcalls and Applause for Slonimsky's Berlin Concert'.

As in Paris, so in Berlin, I conducted a second concert for a small ensemble of instruments. For some reason, Wallingford Riegger's *Dichotomy*, a quite innocuous piece of music, evoked the greatest outpouring of invective in the press. Walter Abendroth, a reputable musician in his own right, was moved to describe the work in terms of a striking surrealist landscape: 'It sounded as if a pack of rats were being slowly tortured to death, and, meanwhile, from time to time, a dying cow groaned.'

My concerts in Berlin left lasting memories among those who heard them. For years afterwards I met people who recalled in detail the scenes that took place on those memorable occasions. My Berlin agency, impressed by the praise lavished on me in the press, made plans for me to conduct all over Germany in programmes of 'real' music, with a couple of acceptable moderns. Alas, the agency, largely Jewish in its membership, was swept away by the fateful wave of Hitlerism a few months later. But I had time to conduct in Budapest, again playing Ives, Ruggles, Cowell, and

Varèse. Hungary was still holding off the Nazi tide, and the concerts there went off without disturbance.

In Berlin I was in daily communication with a kindred soul, Roger Sessions, who was there on a Carnegie fellowship. He was a person of inspiring intellect, a philosopher of life, a radical in politics, a linguist (he spoke fluent German, French, and Italian, and even learned Russian). On a less lofty level, he was an amateur sexologist. We used to make regular visits to a Sexualia Shop in Alexanderplatz. Sessions bought stationery with naked women for a logo, and used it in our correspondence for several years.

My European concerts marked the height of my achievements as a symphonic conductor. Gone were the days when I had to worry about technical aspects of conducting. I was just beginning to savour that peculiar pleasure of shaping music with bodily motions, with concentration on the objective thus attained, and free of all egopetal (a possible neologism formed by analogy with centripetal) directive. I experienced this sense of projection with particular force when I conducted *Protée* by Darius Milhaud at my Paris concert on 25 February 1932. Quite spontaneously, I led a section in the score with my right hand alone, then switched to my left to conduct a following contrasting section. The bilateral symmetry of action was not the result of a deliberate plan, but rather a spatial representation of the contrasting motions in music. I dwell on this particular instance because several musicians, and Milhaud himself who was present at the concert, noticed the effectiveness of these gestures. After many years of doubting the value, or indeed the honesty of the art of conducting, I suddenly felt that it constitutes the nearest approximation to music in motion, which in turn governs the physical sound of music.

CHAPTER 10

TIME OUT

The art of conducting is paradoxical, for its skills range from the mechanical to the inspirational. A conductor can be a semaphore endowed with artificial intelligence, or an illuminating spirit of music. The derisive assertion that 'anyone can conduct' is literally true—musicians will play no matter how meaningless or incoherent the gestures of a baton wielder may be. In this respect, conductors stand apart from other performers. A violinist, even a beginner, must be able to play on pitch with a reasonable degree of proficiency. A pianist must have enough technical skill to get through a piece with a minimum of wrong notes. But a conductor is exempt from such obligations. He does not have to play—he orders others to play for him.

Stories about inept conductors are legion. One conductor lost his place while leading an overture. 'Where are we? Where are we?' he whispered frantically to the leader. 'Carnegie Hall, New York,' the other replied. In his attempt to impress an orchestra by his keen ear, a certain conductor put an extra sharp in the third horn part in a *tutti* passage. At the first rehearsal he stopped the orchestra at the designated spot and proclaimed imperiously: 'Third horn, C-natural, not C-sharp!' The musician replied matter-of-factly, 'Yes, some damned fool put C-sharp in my part, but I know the music, and I played C-natural all right!' Another conductor, intent on showing his mastery of the score, kept interrupting rehearsals with pompous observations, until the leader stood up and said, 'Listen, mister! If you go on making such remarks, we will follow your beat at the concert!' This was an ominous threat to the arrogant conductor. Then there is the one about a conductor who was in the habit of running off the podium with the last chord. He miscalculated the number of concluding chords in one particular overture, however, and ran off before the end. The orchestra gave him a loud send-off with two more chords.

Arturo Toscanini was universally admired as The Maestro. He was also known as The Beast of the Baton. He actually had to stand trial in Milan after poking his baton into the leader's eye and nearly blinding him. His defence was temporary insanity, the lawyer arguing that a great artist such as he loses all control when his musical sense is offended. On another occasion, Toscanini, displeased with the singing of a soprano during a rehearsal, grabbed her by the breasts and screamed, 'If only these were brains!'

I attended a rehearsal in which Toscanini prepared for his final concert at Carnegie Hall on 4 April 1954, ten days after his eighty-seventh birthday. He became pathetically confused in the *Siegfried Funeral Music*. He stopped, and hurled imprecations at the orchestra. 'Imbecili!' he stormed. 'La più bella musica del mondo! Tutto è scritto!' He then told the orchestra to repeat the passage 'dopo i corni'.'Which one?' the horn player asked (there were several similar entrances of the horns). Toscanini remained silent, then stepped down from the podium, and slowly made his way to the exit door.

Many conductors were in the habit of addressing the orchestra at rehearsals to explain the meaning of music. Mengelberg once apostrophized his first cello player with a long diatribe expounding the spiritual significance of a certain passage: 'Your soul in distress yearns for salvation,' he recited. 'Your unhappiness mounts with every passing moment. You must pray for surcease of sorrow!' 'Oh, you mean *mezzo forte*,' the cellist interrupted impatiently.

Otto Klemperer indulged in occasional purple prose at rehearsals. Such effusions were decisively brought to a halt when Bruno Labate, clarinet player of the New York Philharmonic, rudely cut him short: 'Hey, Klempy! You talka too much!'

Karl Muck, the very embodiment of Prussian precision, sometimes forgot the order of works on his programmes. On one occasion he gave a decisive downbeat in anticipation of the vigorous opening bars of the *Eroica*, when the number was Schubert's *Unfinished Symphony*, which opens pianissimo. Fortunately, both works were in 3/4 time, and Muck recovered instantly. This brings to mind Mischa Elman's embarrassment when he mistakenly expected to play the Beethoven Violin Concerto which opens with a long orchestral introduction. He was shaken out of his complacency when the orchestra struck the opening E minor chord of the Mendelssohn Concerto, in which the violinist comes in on the upbeat of the very first measure. Elman lost not a beat in picking up his violin and coming in on time.

Mitropoulos caused a sensation in Paris when he played Prokofiev's Third Piano Concerto from memory, conducting from the keyboard at the same time. Prokofiev, who was present, said it was a regular circus show. But, despite his genius, Mitropoulos failed to impress the manager and the board of trustees of the Boston Symphony Orchestra and was never considered as a possible successor to Koussevitzky.

Alfredo Casella, one of the finest musicians I have ever known, lacked popular appeal in his public appearances as conductor. During his engagement with the Boston Pops in the summer of 1928, he presented stimulating programmes, but his podium manners were most unprepossessing. He used to close the score after each number before acknowledging applause, creating an embarrassing hiatus. He was also negligent in indicating when a repeat was to be omitted. I will never forget the mix-up which resulted in the performance of a Strauss waltz, when half the orchestra took the repeat, and the other half went on to then next section. Casella took this imbroglio in his stride. 'It sounded like Stravinsky,' he remarked, 'with the dominant against the subdominant and the tonic against the dominant.' Neither audience nor management, however, found such accidental polytonality amusing. Casella was not re-engaged, and was succeeded by Arthur Fiedler, whose *savoir-faire* in arranging programmes and in dashing off music with great éclat captivated the public and brought fame to the Boston Pops.

Conductors of the old generation were tyrants. Hans von Bülow was often brutal, but his Prussian rudeness was mitigated by a raw sense of humour. It is he who is credited with the line 'Sie sind alle ganz verrückt!' ('You are all completely mad!') to accompany the introductory bars of Liszt's Piano Concerto in E-flat major. Bülow happened to dislike two of the horn players in his orchestra whose names were Schulz and Schmidt. One morning the manager of the orchestra brought him the sad news that Schmidt was dead. 'Und Schulz?' Bülow asked.

For a long time, Stokowski was the only conductor of a major American orchestra whose native language was English. In his perverted sense of values, however, he affected a phoney Polish accent. During his conductorship of the Philadelphia Orchestra, Stokowski liked to lecture his audiences and, dropping his accent for the nonce, would admonish his listeners not to walk out on modern pieces in his programmes. Once he remonstrated with the Philadelphia ladies for bringing their knitting into the concert hall. Naturally, such admonitions made headlines, which pleased Stokowski.

Stokowski's Philadephia successor was Hungarian-born Eugene Ormandy, whose real name was Jenö Blau. His head lacked a radiant halo of Stokowskian chevelure, and he was, in fact, partly bald. He acceded to the throne of the Philadelphia Orchestra unaccompanied by fanfares. He emerged from the plebeian ranks of a film orchestra before joining the violin section of the great Philadelphia Orchestra, and it was from this position that he graduated to the podium. He spoke English with considerable mobility, but for some reason lapsed at rehearsals into a lingua franca—sans syntax, sans grammar, sans sense. A disloyal member of the Philadelphia Orchestra collected a priceless anthology of Ormandian sayings: 'It is not together, but the ensemble is perfect.' 'Suddenly I was in the right tempo, but it wasn't.' 'This is one bar you should take home.' 'There is a number missing. I can see it.' 'Please follow me because I have to follow him and he isn't here.' 'I need one more bass less.' 'I don't want to confuse you more than absolutely necessary.' 'We can't hear to balance it yet because the soloist is still on the aeroplane.' 'Something went wrong. It was correct when I studied it.' 'Who is sitting in that empty chair?' 'He is a wonderful man, and so is his wife.' 'I told him he would have a heart attack a year ago but unfortunately he lived a year longer.' 'It's difficult to remember if the notes are right, but if I listened they would be wrong.' 'The moment you slow down you are behind.' 'The tempo remains pianissimo.' 'The soloist was so sick he almost died for three days.' 'I don't mean to make you nervous, but unfortunately I have to.' 'Even when you are not playing you are holding me back.' 'If you don't have it in your part leave it out because there is enough missing already.' 'Thank you for your co-operation, and vice versa.'

CHAPTER 11

DISASTER IN HOLLYWOOD

My first engagement as guest conductor with a major American orchestra was in December 1932, with the Los Angeles Philharmonic. So as not to antagonize the untutored Californians with splashes of unrelieved dissonance, I seasoned my programme with the mellifluous sounds of Mozart, the dreamy harmonies of Sibelius, and the rousing sonorities of Mussorgsky. It was my hope that these euphonious offerings would offset the impression produced by the rough harmonies of *Three Places in New England* by Charles Ives. I expected no objections to another American piece on the programme—an innocuous and patriotic overture by Roy Harris, *When Johnny Comes Marching Home*, based on a Civil War song.

I established a friendly rapport with members of the Los Angeles Philharmonic, and my concert came off nicely. I had support among younger musicians who infiltrated the press and radio. José Rodriguez published a provocative article in the 7 January 1933 issue of the *Rob Wagner's Script*, entitled 'An Old Lady Gets Three Shots in the Arm'—the old lady being the Los Angeles Philharmonic.

For the first occasion in a long, long time [Rodriguez wrote], the audience had something to dispute about as it left the hall. The three shots were: the local première of Charles Ives's orchestral set, *Three Places in New England*, the local première of Roy Harris's *Overture from the Gayety and Sadness of the American Scene*, and the conducting of Nicolas Slonimsky. Slonimsky is a young, pale-faced man who looks remarkably like the portraits of Napoleon after Marengo, forelock and all. He approaches the rostrum diffidently, holding his baton like a balancing stick. His bow is reticent. But once on the stand, he takes command with astonishing authority and assertiveness. Like a riding-master who mounts a spoiled, fat thoroughbred, he made the Philharmonic go through tricks of phrasing, tonal nuance and virtuosity that most of us did not believe were still in the old horse. We need more conductors like Slonimsky. More men of his imagination, his suppleness, his vivacity, his musicianship, and what is even more important, his courage.

I sent the Rodriguez article to Ives in Taormina, Sicily, where he was having one of his rare European vacations, and he was enchanted.

Buona Bonaparte di Batone [he wrote in his home-made Italian]. You are a good boy, even if you shoot old ladies in the elbow. That article is one of the best we have ever seen. In spite of its ploy of comedy, it is convincing and dignified. Everybody in Boston aged over 38 years 6 months [my age at the time] ought to read it.

Much to my surprise, I received a terrific write-up in the *Citizen News* of Hollywood. Here is the final paragraph: 'Let us not overlook Slonimsky's conducting. Such poetry of motion, such suavity, such fire, such passion—in other words, a spectacle. It would have taken Pierre Monteux six batons and a pair of stilts to get half so far.'

Meanwhile, in New York, I conducted the world première of *Ionisation* by Varèse. It was a fantastic experience. The score included only indefinitely pitched percussion instruments and two sirens. Varèse was still in Paris, and I had to lead the performance without his commanding presence. The process of ionisation, as Varèse had patiently explained to me, is one in which an atom liberates an electron and assumes a positive electric charge. The free electron travels until it is captured by another atom, which then assumes a negative charge. The harmonic tremor of these subatomic events is reflected in the score. The work is unique in the literature of modern music, and I derived considerable pride from the fact that the score was dedicated to me. I also read the proofs of *Ionisation* for publication in Cowell's *New Music Quarterly*.

Dealing with the world of infinitesimal particles, *Ionisation* presented considerable problems to musicians unaccustomed to differential calculus. The metrical divisions were simple, but the rhythmic segments within them were asymmetric, and the players had a difficult time in encapsulating groups of five sixteenth-notes within the metrical unit of a single quarter-note, particularly where Varèse inserted sixteenth-note rests to replace certain notes of the quintol.

Thanks to an extraordinary bit of luck, Columbia Recording Company accepted *Ionisation* for a single disc. Varèse returned to New York in time for the recording session. We engaged the percussion players from the New York Philharmonic, but it soon became clear that they could never master the rhythms. In desperation, we appealed to fellow composers to take over the task; to them the Varèsian asymmetry was child's play. As a result, my ensemble was star-studded. Carlos Salzedo, the great harpist, played the thematically important Chinese blocks. Paul Creston was at the anvils. Wallingford Riegger rubbed the guïro. Henry Cowell pounded tone-clusters on the piano keyboard. William Schuman, then a mere youngster, pulled the cord of the lion's roar. (A third of a century later, Schuman reminisced of the occasion in a public lecture at the University of California, Los Angeles: 'Slonimsky launched me on my musical career', he said, 'when he entrusted to me the part of the lion's roar in *Ionisation*. But apparently I did not do very well, for he never engaged me again.')

Varèse himself was in charge of the sirens for the recording. They had to be of the manually operated type in order to produce the requisite crescendo and diminuendo. Varèse managed to obtain a set from a retired fireman of the New York City Fire Brigade. We planned to have the performance broadcast over the Municipal Radio Network, but hit an unexpected snag: only the fire department was permitted to broadcast a siren call.

The recording of *Ionisation* was just the first step in a grand design for a record album of important American works. We submitted our plan to several phonograph companies, but in vain. Ives, who stood apart from the practical aspect of these negotiations, was disgusted. 'Art and business are hitched together,' he wrote. '$98\frac{3}{8}$ per cent (I like to be precise) of all radio and phonograph records are sebaceous cysts, and soft ones at that, and they sell, though if a 3-year-old is always fed candy for breakfast he will always be a 3-year-old, and the oatmeal market will die.'

We decided to organize a pick-up group under the auspices of the Pan American Association of Composers, an organization of which Varèse, Cowell, and myself were members, and make records to be distributed by Cowell's *New Music Quarterly*. Among the pieces recorded were the 'Barn Dance' from *Washington's Birthday* by Charles Ives and a movement from *Men and Mountains* by Carl Ruggles.

Varèse never doubted the importance of these first steps in projecting his works on the slow march of music history. 'Je sais où je vais. Mon plan est clairement tracé, son développement logique,' he wrote to me on 31 November 1931. 'Tâchez donc de faire le possible et l'impossible,' he added. Varèse believed that the impossible was inevitable, but he had periods of dismay. He spoke of abandoning composition in favour of mathematics and engineering, courses he took as a youth. I recall him showing me an annual royalty statement from his publisher—37 cents in postage stamps (so small an amount did not justify a cheque). Fortunately, Varèse lived to see the footsteps of history catch up with his gigantic strides. A concert of his works given in New York City's Town Hall in the late 1950s attracted a full house.

The most glamorous engagement I received in the wake of my European successes was at the Hollywood Bowl in the summer of 1933. I was endorsed by the leader and all principal players of the Los Angeles Philharmonic who addressed the management with the following words:

Knowing that you were East during the pair of concerts which Mr Nicolas Slonimsky has just conducted, we are sending you this letter especially recommending him to your attention as a good business asset. He has proven conclusively his ability to get fine results in difficult works in a relatively short rehearsal time. The men seem to enjoy playing under him, and the audiences were enthusiastic in their response. We are glad to endorse him in this manner.

This petition clinched the matter. I was tentatively engaged to conduct the entire eight-week season at the fabled Hollywood Bowl!

I wrote to my wife from Hollywood on 21 July 1933:

Last night's concert drew a large crowd, but several players tried to persuade me to cancel some of the more advanced pieces on my programme, particularly Schoenberg's remarkable *Begleitungsmusik zu einer Lichtspielszene*, written for an imaginary film. The first cellist said it was the worst kind of *scheiss* (he used the German word) he ever heard. An even worse complication arose on account of Roy Harris's *Overture* (which I conducted with the Los Angeles Philharmonic last December). After this morning's rehearsal, the chairman of the orchestra said that in my own interests I must take the Harris piece off the program because it was 'ill chosen' for the Hollywood Bowl. The second violinist who represented the program committee said he had just telephoned the manager, and told him the Harris work had been removed. He said I would bear no responsibility for it, since it was a *force majeure*. I went over to the radio station KFI to discuss the matter with Rodriguez. He raised hell with the manager over the phone, and the *Overture* was reinstated. Poor Roy Harris with his ideas of a growing demand for his music!! On what planet does he live?

Alfred Hertz, the bearded German patriarch who had originated the Hollywood Bowl concert series in 1922, came to my rehearsal of *Ionisation* and watched me trying to explain asymmetrical rhythms to bewildered drummers. Getting no satisfaction, I beat the rhythm out on a drum myself. Hertz asked me after the rehearsal whether I was a professional drummer, and seemed surprised when I told him that I had never beaten a drum before in my life.

My Hollywood concerts were broadcast, and I spoke on the radio during the intermission. I got a lot of mail from listeners, some in favour, but most against the modern pieces. Reviews were sour. The editorial pages of *The Los Angeles Times* were filled with letters from disgruntled listeners, with *Ionisation* the main target. Someone, trying to be funny, sent me a postcard signed Iona Lotta Bunk, which read: 'After hearing *Ionisation*, I am anxious that you should examine my composition scored for two stoves and a kitchen sink. I've named it *Concussion Symphony*, descriptive of the disintegration of an Irish potato under the influence of a powerful atomizer.'

The bad reviews and the flight of puzzled and indignant audience members during my performances of works by Ives, Varèse, etc., resulted in an inglorious end to my conducting career. The moneyed dowagers who financed the Hollywood Bowl season declared that they would stop covering the deficit of the Hollywood Bowl unless the management got rid of me. I was paid off and not very delicately told that my further services were not required. The word spread that I was a dangerous musical revolutionary who inflicted hideous noise on concert-goers expecting to hear beautiful music.

How times have changed! In the 1930s, I was a 'martyr for the cause of new music' (as Cowell put in in his book on Ives), but in the 1970s the composers, whose genius I had so stubbornly championed, became favourites with conductors and audiences. Zubin Mehta, conducting the Los Angeles Philharmonic, opened one season with a performance of Varèse's *Arcana* several years after Varèse's death. He asked me to attend a rehearsal to check on the tempi and dynamics. During the intermission, the player in charge of the lion's roar came up to me. 'Mr Varèse,' he started, 'will you tell me what particular effect you intend here?' 'I am not Varèse,' I replied. 'Then why does Mr Mehta keep asking you questions about the music?' he asked.

I remember the philippic of Philip Hale against the programmes of American music I conducted in Paris in June 1931. I should have played pieces by Arthur Foote, Deems Taylor, and Loeffler, he wrote. But who remembers even their names nowadays? In the judgement of history, Ives and Varèse have been proved right. Their names stand high in the pantheon of new music, and, through my association with their genius, I myself have gained a modicum of recognition.

CHAPTER 12

PUELLA

While in California, I received a brief letter from my wife: 'The meteoric showers of Leonids', she wrote, 'left their indelible impression on me, so that I will have a child.' The cryptic reference to the Leonids, a meteoric shower crossing the earth's orbit in November, was an allusion to my patronymic, Leonidovich, son of Leonid. I was a prospective father! All at once the centre of gravity shifted from my inflatable ego to the prospect of an outpost of my own self in another body; I mentally computed the powers of 2 produced by the fantastic mitosis for the moiety of the zygote, which constituted my own gametes: 1024, 2048, 4096, 8192 . . . I had announcements printed, leaving space for the exact date in the putative month of August 1933. My choice of names, in agreement with my wife, was Electra for a girl, and Leonid for a boy.

The name Electra was probably suggested to me by reading about Marconi's yacht, *Elettra*, named after his daughter. There was another possible influence, at least as far as the vowels were concerned. When Dorothy came to Paris, in the summer of 1931, we paid a visit to the famous harpsichordist, Wanda Landowska, who occupied a magnificent estate at Saint-Leu-la-Forêt, a few kilometres from Paris. She kept dozens of girls there, who took care of her creature comforts—plaiting her tresses, fixing her dresses, and preparing her meals. The girls were from everywhere, and French, German, Russian, Polish, and English were spoken. They wore multicoloured dresses, little make-up, and were lively and quick to form new friends. And, of course, they all played the harpsichord. They were like the aristocratic shepherdesses at the Trianon of Marie Antoinette's pastoral scene.

Wanda liked Dorothy. She had an eye for feminine beauty. 'Où l'avez-vous déniché?' she asked. I 'denichéd' Dorothy in Boston, I replied. We had lunch with several of Wanda's girls and a young harpsichord player, Putnam Aldrich, who subsequently abducted one of Wanda's girls to America. (Wanda never forgave him.) They were soon married, and had a daughter, Allegra. If memory serves me, the name Allegra, merged with Elettra, suggested Electra two years later.

I wrote to my mother in Paris of the expected event. She responded with a cornucopia of obstetrical advice:

It's good that Dorothy keeps working. It will enrich the brain of your future heir . . . What shape of abdomen has Dorothy? If it is with a sharp apex, then it's going to be a boy; if it is round, a girl. She must never lift her arms high in the air. She must walk slowly and look only at handsome faces and beautiful pictures. When I carried you, I always looked at the picture of Madonna della Rosa, and, as a result, you looked at birth like the Christ child . . . Give her this very important advice: at the last moment, the most crucial of all, she must not throw back her head, but on the contrary, drop the head on her breast, or else she might have thyroid trouble.

This was a prelude to my mother's cherished plan. 'You will need my knowledge of child care now,' she wrote, 'and it is in your own interest to send me an American visa so that I could come to Boston.'

Electra had a rather difficult birth. Dorothy noted time and duration of the uterine contractions on the cover of the August 1933 issue of the *Atlantic Monthly* at her bedside: '10.00—60 seconds; 10.46—80 seconds; 10.56—70 seconds; 11.12—2 minutes; 11.24—50 seconds; 11.30—50 seconds; 11.40—50 seconds; 11.45—60 seconds.' I kept vigil at the hospital. At last the nurse came in and announced, 'You have a girl.' The hour was 1.06 am Daylight Saving Time, 16 August 1933. At 1.16 I was allowed to see the child. I then went to the Western Union Office and dispatched a telegram to friends: 'Arrived shortly after midnight at the Grand Central Terminal after some delay in making the incline. Stop. Mother was asleep at the time and my poor father waited outside for my arrival. Electra.'

I received letters and telegrams from friends and relatives. H. T. Parker, drama and music critic of the *Boston Evening Transcript*, was disturbed by my choice of name.

Dear Mr Slonimsky [he wrote], I learned that you have chosen to name your daughter Electra, and I am writing to dissuade you from this intention. Why should a young life be saddled with a name that conjures up visions of unquenchable hatred and vindictiveness? Your daughter, when she grows up, will learn of the implications of the name and may become unhappy about it.

H. T. Parker was a literary gnome who rarely voiced personal opinions. I responded immediately:

My dear Mr. Parker, Your letter has just reached me. It will be saved for Electra to read in the year of grace—or, if we are to trust H. G. Wells's prophetic calendar, the year of disgrace—1950. By then morality may be reversed, and Electra will suit the tastes of 1950 modernists. However, for us, her parents, Electra has amber-like associations. Marconi's daughter is named Electra, too.

Soon I shall start conditioning the child according to the best precepts of Pavlov and Watson. Your suggestions are cordially solicited.

I had a highly positive reaction to the selection of Electra's name from Aunt Zinaïda, in a letter she wrote from Paris (in English, of course; she was a prime translator of English literature and lived many years in London as a literary correspondence to my father's magazine, *The Messenger of Europe*):

Dear Dorothy and Nicolas, We congratulate you most heartily on the advent of young Electra and begin—in anticipation of future achievements—to feel proud of our American grandniece. 'Her' cable on arrival was magnetic, and another object of our admiration was the name she has selected for herself. Electra—the poetry of antique age and the symbol of modern science [Electra is amber in Greek] in one—magnificent! I think of starting a family fund for a collection of rare specimens of amber, to present Electra with a necklace of her personal jewels on her sixteenth birthday.

Indeed, once Electra started school, she preferred to be called Lecky or Lucky. It was only when she matured that she came to appreciate the exclusivity of her name.

Dorothy received a charming letter from Henry Cowell: 'Dear Dorothy, So there is Electra! Think of it! How very exciting! Many congratulations on this noble achievement! Hope to view the object in person before too long! Warm greetings to you and the bouncing father (or who is it that bounces?).' When Electra was still an infant, Dorothy made a trip to Russia for the *Christian Science Monitor*, and I was left in charge, with a babysitter. When Electra grew a third tooth, I sent a cable to Dorothy in Leningrad: 'Babikins now tridental.'

I had a good German camera which I had bought in Berlin in 1932, and followed Electra's every step, taking hundreds, if not thousands of pictures—in the crib, on the potty, in the pram. The inevitable outcome of my photographic frenzy was that Electra, as an adolescent, college girl, married women, and mother, developed a deep aversion to having her picture taken under any circumstances.

I concentrated all my capacity for gimmicks on Electra. Dorothy was busy most of the day, lecturing on art and spending hours at the office of the *Christian Science Monitor* whereas I was largely unemployed. In consequence, I was able to spend a lot of time with my little daughter. I began speaking Latin to her, inspired by a Polish couple, both professors of ancient languages in Warsaw who spoke to their offspring exclusively in Latin and Greek. I called Electra 'Puella' and named household objects in Latin for her to learn. I taught her the meaning of such simple imperative sentences as 'Veni huc' and taught her to say 'Da mihi lac' when she wanted milk. I also taught her to count up to seventeen, stopping before the higher two-digit numbers because of their use of a subtrahend, difficult to memorize (as in *duo de viqinti*, or two short of twenty).

Here are some extracts from a 'baby diary' that I methodically kept during Electra's early years, properly documented and dated for authenticity:

June 1936, I sing, 'Dormi, Puella, dormi mi mellita, dormite oculi, dormine auriculi ...'. Electra understood that the verse meant, 'Sleep, girl, sleep my sweet one, sleep eyes ...' She interrupted to ask, 'What is auriculi?' 'Little aures, little ears.'

8 February 1937, 10.05 pm. Electra spotted a feather on the rug: 'Dada, what is it?' 'Pluma.' 'But what is it like Mummy says?' (Meaning: what is it in English?)

21 November 1937. I showed Electra a 1931 picture of myself and Dorothy. 'Where were you when we had this picture taken?' I asked. Her response was, 'Oh, I was nihil.'

Electra's greatest performance as a Latinist occurred during a visit of Professor Hugo Leichtentritt, a famous German–American musicologist. We were having tea when Electra, age $2\frac{1}{2}$, came into the room holding a hand mirror. 'Ecce speculum!' she announced. The syntactic point in this introduction was that, although she knew the word 'speculum' for mirror, and although I had used the indicative pronoun 'ecce' in other contexts, she had put the two words together without any preliminary training in this particular combination. Leichtentritt said that the episode was one of the most memorable of his whole life.

One day Electra announced, with a suspicious look in her eyes, 'Daddy, other kids don't speak Latin at home.' I told her that some kids spoke Italian at home, which was something like Latin, but it didn't impress her. From that day onwards, Electra would give me a blank stare every time I used a Latin word, even one that had become a part of lingua franca in our household.

I also tried to condition Electra to dissonant music. Henry Cowell was especially fond of one anecdote, which he recounted in his lectures and seminars. The story went something like this: When Electra would demand a bottle, I would sit down at the piano and play a Chopin nocturne, completely ignoring her screams. I would allow for a pause, and then play on the piano Schoenberg's Opus 33a, which opens with a dodecaphonic succession of three highly dissonant chords. I would then rush in to give Electra her bottle. Her features would relax, her crying would cease, and she would suck contentedly. This was to establish a conditioned reflex in favour of dissonant music.

I also introduced music into Electra's curriculum in my own perverse way. I taught her notes in neumatic notation with Latin terms in medieval terminology: *clivis, torculus, climacus, scandicus*. I taught her the formation of basic chords, as well as the art of embellishing a melody by sticking a *clivis* or a *torculus* upon it to form rudimentary variations. She was seven years old when she wrote, under my guidance, a sophisticated little piano piece in variation form. I showed the manuscript to Lukas Foss, and told him that it was written by a seven-year-old girl. 'Either the child or the teacher is a genius,' he said. I bowed modestly.

I taught Electra the names of medieval modes, and she was soon able to write out and harmonize a tune in a Dorian mode as easily as one in C major. One day she came home from grade school rather upset. 'Daddy, isn't the mode from G to G on white keys a Mixolydian mode?' she asked. 'Of course it is,' I replied. 'Why?' Electra explained that the teacher had written out a scale from G to G on the blackboard, and asked the class to identify it. 'So I raised my grimy hand,' Electra continued, 'and said it was the Mixolydian mode, but the teacher looked kind of funny at me and said, "Okay, we will talk about it later." ' The teacher probably intended this to be a G major scale, but failed to enter the obligatory F-sharp. It was obvious that she had no idea what the Mixolydian mode was.

When Electra started school, we decided to register her under Adlow, Dorothy's maiden name and also the name she retained professionally after our marriage—it was too laborious to use an un-American name like Slonimsky. Our postbox at home listed two names, Adlow and Slonimsky. Word went around among Electra's friends that her father and mother were not married. This caused Electra much embarrassment, but she eventually adapted.

During Electra's infancy, Dorothy arranged for me to contribute occasional articles to the *Christian Science Monitor*. This required some adjusting to the peculiar taboos inherent in the doctrine of Christian Science. References to alcohol, cigarettes, tea, or coffee were out. An illness was an error in one's mind. There was no death.

In 1936 I started a series of articles on the children's page of the paper, in which I attempted to present rules of music theory in a graphic manner, using simple diagrams and vivid illustrations. Some of them were rather corny. How could I have stooped so low as to make a drawing of two nuts on two opposite sides of a stalk and next to it a drawing of two notes on a stem at an interval of a second, and caption the result, 'Nuts and notes'? Another illustration represented a 'rest-ful house'. It was indeed a house, but its walls, windows, roof and chimney were all made of wiggly rests. I indulged in outrageous puns. To demonstrate the technique of figured bass, I said that, 'The bass is the boss'. My jingles were inexcusable. Here is one:

> Consecutive octaves or fifths in good harmony
> Ought not to be used lest ears they might harm any.

In an article on the fugue, I offered a limerick, purloined from somewhere and rearranged to suit my perverse tastes:

> There was a young woman named Hatch
> Who was fond of the music of Batch.
> It isn't so fussy
> As that of Debussy
> Sit down, I'll play you a snatch.

I allowed myself to wax poetic in a wretched poem, *The Mad Celesta Player*:

> Would you care to play the flute?
> He replied in French: *Ah zût!*
> How about the clarinet?
> He shot back in Russian: *Nyet!*
> Would you then take up the cello?
> But he membled: *Non è bello.*
> Then he spotted the celesta
> And exclaimed in Spanish: *Esta!*

In one article on orchestration I reproduced the entire score of one of the marvellously concise orchestral pieces by Anton von Webern, adorning each individual part with a drawing of the instrument involved, a trombone, a mandolin, a celesta, a harp, a trumpet, and a drum. I sent the page to Webern in Vienna, and received a most gracious reply:

Your friendly letter with enclosures brought me very special joy [he wrote]. To think that you have taken the trouble of making my music accessible to children, and that you have actually succeeded in doing so gives me uncommon satisfaction and real consolation. It makes me happy that the notes that I have written appear on a page dedicated specially to children. If only the so-called adults had as little prejudice against anything new as children, then our lives would be quite different.

These articles were eventually published in book form under the title *The Road to Music*. The book bore the dedication: 'To Electra, Against Her Will.'

CHAPTER 13

LOFTY BATON TO LOWLY PEN

Like gaseous remnants of a shattered comet lost in an erratic orbit, occasional conducting engagements came my way. On 15 April 1934, I conducted in New York my last engagement under the auspices of the Pan American Association of Composers, with works by Ives and Varèse. Anxious to give me some financial support, Ives asked me to orchestrate accompaniments for several of his songs for his concert; he offered me a fee far in excess of the fair amount for such a task. We worked on the orchestration together in his country house in West Redding, Connecticut. The Varèse piece, *Ecuatorial*, to Spanish words, was a ballad for solo baritone accompanied by an instrumental ensemble. The singer was plainly incapable of mastering Varèse's intricate melodic patterns, and the rehearsals were dismal. At the final rehearsal, Varèse lost his patience. 'Je ne permettrai pas de massacrer l'œuvre!' he cried out. The concert went without catastrophe only because the music was unfamiliar to the small audience which had assembled for the occasion.

Another orbit of my shattered comet took me to Denver, Colorado, where I conducted a programme of American music with a local chamber orchestra. I arranged a 'balanced' programme, with pieces by Copland, William Grant Still, Burrill Phillips, Roy Harris, Ernest Bloch, and *Three Places in New England* by Ives. I also included a piece by Cowell, but it was vetoed by the Technical Board of Pro Musica, which sponsored the concert. Cowell wrote to me ruefully:

I am so delighted at your Denver program, and hope you will open up a field there. It looks very diversified, if not too powerful. I knew I was *persona non grata* there, but I find it very amusing that my piano recital in a private house fifteen years ago should, in the minds of the committee, make me ineligible to have an orchestral work performed now! The impact must have been great if it required such an anticlimax now!

My last service for Charles Ives was to arrange for the publication of *Three Places in New England*. I knew that no commercial publisher would consider printing it. Aaron Copland, who never met Ives but who none the less understood his greatness, tried to persuade Koussevitzky to perform one of his pieces. Koussevitzky told Copland that he simply could not make head or tail of the score. Under these circumstances, the only way of getting an Ives score published was to approach a liberal publisher willing to take a chance. I knew such a publisher, C. C. Birchard of Boston, a cultured and friendly person with whom I could converse on intellectual terms. I brought the manuscript of *Three Places in New England* to him, along with European programmes and reviews, and told him that Ives would pay the costs involved in engraving and printing. He agreed to undertake the project. Characteristically, Ives waived all performance rights.

It apparently often means a lawsuit, and prevents performance [he wrote to me from West Redding on 4 November 1933]. Henry Cowell says that Stokowski returned his score to him saying that the Philadelphia Orchestra would not pay fees. I would be willing to make any business arrangement that Mr Birchard would suggest so that performance fees could be cut out. If this can be done, I think I might as well go ahead and have the score made. I greatly appreciate your willingness to help me correct the proofs. I can't see that green–white proof paper. Can't find a score here but have one in New York. Have extra pencil—I revert to it—can steer it with less vibrato than pen.

I suggested to Ives that the polymetric section of the second movement be engraved in two parallel staves, with four bars of the faster march corresponding to three measures of the slower march. Ives, however, who usually minimized the importance of notational details, was unwilling to make the change. 'Generally speaking, I don't like to change anything . . . once finished,' he wrote to me on 5 December 1933. 'But you may be right. We can tell better when we see the proofs.' He wrote again a week later: 'Dear Padre [a salutation in reference to my recent parenthood], you are a good boy to take so much trouble over the score. Most of the ways you suggest are advisable, I think. The work looks well done. I will start today to go over the proofs and will get them back in a week or so.'

Still hoping that Ives would agree to the alternative notation in the march movement, I sent him a 'conductor's note' which explained how to beat time ambidextrously. Ives was reluctant to accept it.

Your conductor's note is well put [he wrote]. For some conductors it will be a help and for others it will (according to what I hear of some conductors) mix them up, so they will sidestep the job—it will make them sour. If used, I think it better be sent out when parts are asked for. I wouldn't like to have them think (as it came ostensibly from me) that I underrate their intelligence, for instance Goossens. There are very few, if any, conductors with your gifts. I think most of them could not learn to beat two ups, and if they tried to would make things worse.

Ives returned to my controversial 'conductor's note' in his letter of 26 December 1933:

I think your note about beating two rhythms is excellent and well put, even as it stands, if it got before men of your genius, brains and courage—but where are they? Most conductors, if they should be told to beat two together, would fall over in a nice-looking swoon and give up the whole job, and it would give them another excuse for not playing anything.

A compromise was finally reached. The polymetric section would be engraved with an 'ossia' part in smaller notes designed especially for ambidextrous conductors. The score thus arranged became standard in all performances and recordings of the works. It was not until the Ives Centennial in 1974 that the original score for large orchestra was published and performed.

Just as the Russian language was still the natural medium for my thinking and my correspondence while my family was still alive, so the musical language of Tchaikovsky, Rachmaninoff, and Glazunov was for me the natural mode of melodic and harmonic expression. So deeply was this musical grammar and syntax ingrained in my psycho-musical make-up, that any other style of composition was to me as alien as an imperfectly absorbed foreign language. But gradually I realized that there were other possible musical languages, some natural though alien, and some artificial though plausible.

Cowell, Ives, and Varèse were the principal mentors in the revolution of my musical aesthetics, and they were soon joined by Leon Theremin, whose acquaintance I made in New York, and Joseph Schillinger, the iconoclastic theoretician. With them I could discuss the creation of mathematically organized melodies, harmonies, and rhythms. Theremin was an electrical engineer who invented the first electronic musical instrument, activated by a movement of the hand which caused a hetero-dynamic effect, resulting in the alteration of frequency and a change of pitch. Theremin demonstrated his instrument to Lenin in 1920, and Lenin, whose slogan was 'Communism is Soviet power plus electrification', said a few kind words about the invention. (Incidentally, Theremin is the French version of his Russian name Termen; in French the name should bear two *accents aigus*, Thérémin.)

In the 1920s Theremin gave demonstrations of his electronic instrument in Europe and America. Stokowski asked him to construct an instrument that would lend support to the low bass notes in the orchestra, and Theremin manufactured one that produced frequencies at the threshold of audibility. The infrasonic vibrations were so powerful, in fact, that they hit the stomach physically, causing near-nausea in the double-bass section of the orchestra. Stokowski abandoned the project.

Theremin's instrument was patented in America under the name

Thereminovox. Its great advantage was that it could produce any frequency by changing the resistance of the rheostatic environment. It
possessed an inherent defect, however—its tones were not precise as to
pitch. Worse still, the transition from one tone to another carried with it
an unwelcome glissando. Theremin, who was also a professional cellist,
developed a fairly good technique on the Thereminovox, as did several
other musicians in New York. Joseph Achron, a fine violinist and composer, fared rather poorly because, so he joked, his long Jewish nose
produced an interference that threw the Thereminovox off pitch. I tried
my luck as well, and composed a piece for Therminovox which was duly
performed at Carnegie Hall.

Cowell found a kindred spirit in Theremin. He asked him to manufacture an electric instrument that would produce a series of natural overtones up to the sixteenth partial, with the specification that each of the
partial tones would carry beats numerically proportional to its place in the
overtone series. Thus the fundamental tone occupied a complete rhythmic unit, the octave above had two beats per time unit, the next partial
tone (a fifth above the octave) had three beats to a time unit, and so on.
When all the overtones were sounded together, the effect was that of
accelerating ascending scales alternating with decelerating descending
scales in the upper register of the series, sounding to untutored ears like
an Indonesian gamelan. Its power was generated by cranking the rheostat;
when cranked a little faster, the pitch of the entire column of overtones
went up with fantastic effect.

Cowell called this instrument Rhythmicon, and composed a special
Rhythmicon concerto. He wrote it in the hope that I would present it at
one of my European concerts. The Rhythmicon was capricious and
subject to fits of musical distemper, however, and I was not sure that the
voltage could be adjusted to the European current. There was also the
problem of money for its manufacture. Cowell approached Ives, who in
turn apprised me of his thoughts on the subject in a letter from New York
in January 1932:

I had a long talk with Henry about the Rhythmicon situation. It relieves my mind
to know especially that the new instrument would really be nearer to an instrument than a machine. There will be a lever that can readily change the tempo,
with pedals and tones, etc. It was not so much the question of having one made,
but whether it is yet time to present it in Paris. I sent the remitted check to Mr
Theremin yesterday, and he has started the building. It will be yours and
Henry's. I just want to help, and sit under the shadow on a nice day.

Like many a futuristic contraption, the Rhythmicon was wonderful in
every respect, except that it did not work. It was not until forty years later
that an electronic instrument with similar specifications was constructed

at Stanford University. It could do everything that Cowell and Theremin had wanted it to do and more, but it lacked the emotional quality essential to music. It sounded sterile, antiseptic, lifeless—like a robot with a synthetic voice. The emotional appeal of instrumental music depends on the human imprecision of performance. If an orchestra were to play in perfect intonation, the resulting pure overtones and differential 'wolf' tones would create a bewildering cacophony of conflicting harmonies. The paradox of good performance is that it must be slightly out of tune.

Theremin and I indulged in fantasies about automated composition. I discussed with him the possibility of manufacturing a fugue machine, wherein the composer would put a subject into a slot and the machine would automatically generate a fugal answer, countersubject, stretto, and coda. Of course, this was long before the advent of computer technology, but the unfeasibility of the thing only enhanced its attraction.

I wrote to my wife in Boston from New York on 29 September 1933:

Theremin seems to be more prosperous than previously. He builds advertising machines worked by radio: you come near the mirror and it lights up and talks back to you extolling the qualities of the advertised product. I asked Theremin about automatic feeding for my baby-sitting with Electra. When she cries for food, the cry is picked up by a sensitive microphone, is magnified and relayed to the refrigerator, or, better still, to the thermos bottle, and starts a current, which is automatically switched off the moment the milk reaches the desired temperature. We discussed mechanization . . . I spent the morning rushing around with Varèse who is full of his Quatrième Internationale des Arts, with Spain as headquarters. He appointed Stokowski and me as his conductors, but he will warn Stokowski that unless he applies himself seriously to performances of Varèse's music, he won't have him. He received Electra's birth notice in Madrid, and he thought Electra a marvelous name.

Theremin was a blithe spirit—a scientist whose imagination spilled over into science fiction. When a young woman employed in his laboratory in Petrograd in 1919 died, and her colleagues arranged a memorial service, Theremin protested against any funeral orations. 'As scientists,' he declared, 'we must not take her death as a finality, but start work immediately and unremittingly on the problem of the restoration of the biological mechanism of her body so as to return her to useful life.'

In his personal affairs, Theremin was incautious. Rumour had it that he was simultaneously married to a society woman in New York and a black woman in North Carolina. One day he simply disappeared. A report circulated in New York that he had returned to Russia and was shot for his dealings with the German embassy in Washington. What was really ominous was that Theremin's name disappeared from the Soviet press—he was not even mentioned in special Soviet articles dealing with electronic musical instruments, and this in spite of his approbation by Lenin. When I asked Shostakovich in 1959 whether he could shed light on Theremin's whereabouts, he merely blinked and said, 'About Theremin I can say nothing'. Theremin eventually surfaced, very much alive and teaching at the Moscow Technological Institute.

Another blithe spirit with whom I spent much time in New York was Joseph Schillinger, who arrived in America at nearly the same time as Theremin. They had much in common; both believed that music ought to be based on scientific principles and that performances must be electronically controlled. Like Theremin, Schillinger was constantly in debt. Schillinger expounded to me his table of priorities in life: a place to live, a woman, and food. All else was insignificant. He found women to live with in vacated apartments, and was invited to take his meals with affluent friends.

Schillinger's attitude towards his own theories was a mixture of cynicism and megalomania. He earnestly believed that he held the key to the evolution of music according to mathematical principles. He used to say, quite seriously, that Bach missed a chance to write really great music because of his lack of knowledge of the theory of combinations and permutations. He dismissed Chopin, Schumann, and Verdi as mere amateurs. With such notions he was unable to secure a teaching job. Then, in a peripiteia worthy of classical comedy, Schillinger drew into his orbit a number of popular musicians who sought knowledge free from academic tedium. He taught harmony and counterpoint using graph paper, in which each unit corresponded to a given interval. Jazz players loved it, and Schillinger became a sort of musical guru. George Gershwin, among others, came to him for contrapuntal 'therapy'. Schillinger instructed him to fill graph paper with dots, lines and squares, which purportedly gave Gershwin a new creative energy. Actually, Schillinger's 'science' did not go beyond elementary algebra with a somewhat incongruous emphasis on the binomial theorem. His high-falutin terms, however, sounded grand to untutored popular musicians, who savoured the big words as magic symbols. Gershwin treated his involvement with Schillinger as a diversion. He had gone into psychoanalysis, so why not try its musical counterpart? But the only device Gershwin borrowed from Schillinger was some scientific-sounding propaedeutics about harmonic 'layers'.

However that might be, Schillinger rose from abject poverty to luxuriant affluence and became a cult figure in the lower echelons of composers. He boldly assured his disciples that no talent was required to be commercially successful (an assertion that may conceal ironical truth).

Some aspirants travelled great distances for an afternoon session with him. Then, at the height of his success, Schillinger died of an intestinal constriction. His monumental work, *The Schillinger System of Composition*, was submitted posthumously to several publishers, but was rejected as impractical. Hindemith thought it was preposterous. But a group of Schillinger's disciples decided to publish the book on a purely subscription basis, and the list of people (many of them famous) who were willing to pay $35 in advance for the projected two-volume edition sufficiently impressed Carl Fischer of New York to accept it for publication. It went into several printings and continued to sell at a brisk rate even when composers turned away from creating music by mathematics.

Pondering the savage reception of new music by critics and audiences, I became interested in the problem of the methodology of music criticism. I found a treasure trove for my research in the Music Division of the Boston Public Library, which contained a unique collection of contemporary newspaper reviews pasted in individual scores. Many were astonishing in their faulty judgement, but fascinating in their skill in invective.

Gradually an idea for a new book took shape in my imagination. It was to be called *Music Since 1900*. Its premise was to be a musical chronology listing significant events of twentieth-century music, year by year, month by month, day by day, including first performances of major works, the dates of birth and death of composers, and other relevant matters. To this I planned to add an appendix with texts of declarations of modern music groups, and letters on musical subjects which I solicited from famous persons, including George Bernard Shaw. I also obtained a statement on the origin of the 12-tone method of composition from Schoenberg. I could not refrain from quoting a letter from a Japanese composer, intact in its pristine beauty: 'We feel so many happies that we are musician, such a international artist.' The Japanese letter concluded with this priceless envoi: 'My honorable Conductor! Please teach us hereafter!' It was signed, 'Good-bye!'

Henry Cowell wrote to me:

The work on your book sounds perfectly stupendous. The title which you propose, *Music Since 1900*, describes it perfectly. But I find it dry, and it will appeal only to highbrow librarians. You should have a title such as *20th Century Dated Up* or some such thing in order to make it a best-seller. Or make two editions, one with each title, the one for libraries and colleges, and the one with the flashy title for the more gullible ones. . . . Your next work should be *Music From 1999 to 1937*, listing all the events that are going to happen, beginning at the end of this century and working backwards. Everyone would have a real good time if you would do this!

I submitted the book to W. W. Norton, a cultured and forward-looking publisher who was interested in new trends in music, literature, and art. It was accepted for publication, and released in September 1937. I sent a copy to Ives. He responded in his own seismic handwriting: 'You are a good boy! A gigantic and difficult job! Anybody can write a good symphony—yet it takes a better man to conduct it. But only you and Sam Johnson can write a good encyclopedia. A memorable day! Ahoy!'

There was also a British edition. M. D. Calvocoressi opened his review in *The Musical Times* with the words, 'Like everybody, I have been reading Nicolas Slonimsky's astounding *Music Since 1900*.' American reviews were equally encouraging.

I gave a copy of *Music Since 1900* to Prokofiev during his last visit to America in 1938. Electra tried to snatch the book from him, and Prokofiev reprimanded her sternly. He then picked her up and held her in his arms. I had taken so many pictures of Electra in various situations—what a pity I missed that particular pose! Prokofiev told his Russian friends in Moscow that he read *Music Since 1900* from cover to cover on his return boat trip to Europe, and found it absorbing. Much of the information on his own music I got from Prokofiev himself, so that the data were accurate. In fact, when queried about the dates of composition of his works, he would refer to me: 'Write to Slonimsky in Boston—he has more information about me than I have myself.' Prokofiev's friend, Nicolai Miaskovsky, used the same quip whenever he was importuned for his dates, and a reference to my reliability in the matter of chronology is contained in one of Miaskovsky's biographies published in Russia. Miaskovsky was a most punctilious correspondent in this respect. On the very day he put the final touch on one of his twenty-seven symphonies, he would write to me to say: 'This morning I finished my symphony No. X.' Thanks to his exemplary accounting, I have been able to give exact dates of inception and completion of each of his many symphonies and the exact dates of their first performances in consecutive editions of *Music Since 1900*. The single exception was his Symphony No. 13, for which he did not have the date of performance because it was first given in Wintenthur, Switzerland. I obtained it from the Musikkollegium there.

In 1971 I brought out a new edition of *Music Since 1900*, updating the chronology to 20 July 1969, the date of the landing on the moon. What did the moon have to do with modern music? The way I rationalized it was as follows: '20 July 1969: The Harmony of the Spheres of the Pythagorean doctrine that interprets the position and movement of celestial bodies in terms of musical concordance is mystically manifested as first men step on the silent surface of the moon.' But is silence music?

Shall I confess a really outrageous hoax? In the 1971 edition of *Music*

Since 1900 I inserted, with malice aforethought, the following entry under 27 April 1905:

On his eleventh birthday Sol Mysnik stages in St Petersburg the world première of his opera *The X-ray Vindicator*, dealing with a young scientist jailed for advocating the extermination of the Czar, who escapes by directing a stream of Roentgen rays at himself, inducing horror on the guard by appearing as a skeleton, and then calmly walking through the open gate to resume his terroristic propaganda, and singing 'The Sun Goes Up, The Sun Goes Down, I Wish the Czar Would Lose His Crown.'

Sol Mysnik is, of course, an anagram of my last name. I was 11 years old on the given date. Nobody became especially interested in this alleged opera except Boris Steinpress of Moscow, editor of music encyclopaedias, who was working on a grandiose dictionary of operas. He wrote to me saying he could find no reference to the *The X-Ray Vindicator* in any St Petersburg newspaper for April 1905. Would I enlighten him on the source of my information about that opera? I had no choice but to confess.

A spin-off of *Music Since 1900* was my *Lexicon of Musical Invective*. To compile it I went through the newspaper and magazine clippings in the Boston Public Library and the New York Public Library, covering not only twentieth-century composers, but those of the classical period as well, beginning with Beethoven.

Among my favourite finds was a review of Chopin's 1841 London recital describing Chopin's music as 'a motley surface of ranting hyperbole and excruciating cacophony', and expressing wonderment as to how 'that archenchantress, George Sand, could be content to wanton away her dreamlike existence with an artistical nonentity like Chopin'. The Boston critic W. F. Apthorp contributed the following analysis on Tchaikovsky's *Pathétique*:

The work threads all the foul ditches and sewers of human despair; it is as unclean as music well can be. The unspeakable second theme may tell of the impotent senile remembrance of calf love. In the finale, bleary-eyed paresis meets us face to face, and that solemn closing epitaph of the trombones might begin here: Here continues to rot . . .

In his 1907 review of *Salomé* in the *New York Tribune*, H. E. Krehbiel shrank away in horror from 'the moral stench with which Richard Strauss fills the nostrils of humanity and makes us retch'. The *London Spectator* warned in 1856 against attending performances of *La Traviata* as 'an outrage on the ladies of the aristocracy who support the theatre' and expressed horror at watching 'a very young and innocent-looking lady impersonate the heroine of an infamous French novel who varies her prostitution by a frantic passion'.

The Boston critic and historian Louis Elson suggested that Debussy's *La Mer* ought to be renamed *Le Mal de mer*, and he volunteered subtitles for its three movements: the first bringing on a headache, the second expressing an anxious doubt, and the third, throwing up.

The obloquy to which Schoenberg was subjected by critics, both in Europe and America, was extraordinary. I made a selection of the more outrageous reviews of his works for a dedicatory volume published for his seventieth birthday in 1944, and Schoenberg graciously acknowledged my contribution in a friendly letter.

A French critic wrote that Stravinsky's *Le Sacre du printemps* should be renamed *Le Massacre du printemps*. An outraged Bostonian broke into verse in the *Boston Herald* after its first performance by the Boston Symphony:

> Who wrote this fiendish *Rite of Spring*?
> What right had he to write the thing?
> Against our helpless ears to fling
> Its crash, clash, cling, clang, bing, bang, bing?

Interestingly enough, another newspaper poet had delivered himself of a similar outcry against Wagner some forty years earlier, in which he complained that Wagner 'let key be blent with key in hideous hash'. The anti-Wagner poem ended with a line almost identical with the anti-Stravinsky one, 'And clang, clash, clatter, clatter, clang and clash.' Henry Cowell set both poems to music with an acute sense of parody.

To supplement my meagre earnings from teaching piano, I published piano pieces with such catchy titles as *Dreams and Drums* and *Kiddies on the Keys*. I also wrote vapid songs about flowers. The only piece in my 'popular' genre that I can recall without cringing was something called *The Opening of the Piano*, with a motto from a poem by Oliver Wendell Holmes: 'Ah me! How I remember the evening when it came! / When the wondrous box was opened that had come from overseas / With its smell of mastic varnish and its flash of ivory keys!' I found a publisher in Providence, Rhode Island, who not only published my stuff but also paid me $50 down for each. Soon he went out of business.

Still hoping to make a hit as a composer of semi-classical piano pieces, I approached Gustave Schirmer. He was a hulk of a man, weighing about 300 lbs. When he rose from a chair, coins dropped from the holes in his pockets, making a fine tinkling sound on the tiled floor. Schirmer was in a talkative mood the day I visited, and he boasted to me about his infallible sense of musical values. His happiest discovery was made at a music teachers' convention in Kansas City, where he corralled an educationist who made arrangements of familiar classical tunes, reducing them to the uniform length of sixteen bars each. Schirmer commissioned him to compile several albums of such arrangements, and published them under the title *Magic Fingers*. Schirmer's sense of musical values did not deceive him, for the albums sold into millions. He gave me a copy of one of these collections, and I was amazed at the poverty of the arranger's technique. 'Give me one afternoon,' I said to Schirmer, 'and I will manufacture such pieces by the dozen.' 'Oh no,' he retorted, 'for this you must have talent!'

It had long been clear to me, and it was painfully obvious to my wife, that I could not make a decent living with my variegated talents. When I returned from a 1931 conducting engagement in Havana, laden with bongos, congas, maracas, and other exotic noise-makers, my father-in-law asked me, 'Is this a good investment?' There was no sarcasm implied in this remark; he sold furniture, and to him all material things, including my Cuban instruments, held a promise of profitable returns. Still, he realized that a little help would be welcome, and began sending weekly cheques of $50 to my wife. An unpleasant rumour grew in the Boston Jewish community that Dorothy had married a no-goodnik. Her older sister's husband was a successful physician. Her younger sister was married to a mining engineer who made a fortune in Labrador. I was the only Adlow acquisition who had failed to achieve financial success. Worse still, the ugly rumour spread that I was a *goy*. Dorothy had married an uncircumcized dog! I never went to the synagogue. I never lit candles on Yom Kippur. I observed Christmas and Easter in the company of non-Jewish Russians in New York. My wife loyally declined to discuss my personal affairs with any of her intrusive friends, and ceased social contact with some of the more importune questioners.

My Job's comforters knew that I had to support my mother in Paris. In the meantime, she stepped up her demands to be brought to America, describing in melodramatic detail the hazards of her remaining in Paris alone. Could it be that the Christ-like child she bore in such travail would be so ungrateful as to refuse her shelter with his new family?

I had to have a hundred stitches put on my wretched guts torn by years of continuous childbearing [she wrote]. Here I am, a 77-year-old hag discarded like an empty can and thrown into the garbage to await disposal. But what's the use of pleading with my children who no longer need me and to whom my desperate cries for help fall on deaf ears? If you will not take me to Boston, I might consider moving to New York to stay with Isabelle, even if I have to sleep in the corridor of her apartment. At least I will not go hungry. This is not a trick to force you to take me to Boston. I have no intention of intruding into your domestic life, even though you are my own son, and even though my daughter-in-law seems to be well disposed towards me.

I kept Dorothy informed of my mother's situation. One day, in the spring of 1938, Dorothy suddenly said, 'I have decided to ask your mother to come live with us.' This was a noble decision. There were objective considerations in favour of my mother's leaving Paris, for the possibility of war was very real. Had my mother remained in Paris during the Nazi occupation, she would surely have perished, and her dire prophecies would have come true.

Isabelle went to Europe every summer, and she volunteered to bring my mother to America. There was no problem about a visa, since I was an American citizen and therefore entitled to bring my mother in. She embarked for New York, accompanied by Aunt Isabelle.

We found an apartment for my mother on the same floor as ours of Hemenway Street in Boston. She hung family photographs all over the walls, and settled down to a happy existence, enjoying an ideal relationship with Dorothy, whom she had favoured as my spouse from their very first meeting in Paris. She spoke German to Dorothy, who spoke Yiddish to her. Electra was five years old and listened to this conversation in bewilderment. They played Lotto together, calling out numbers in Latin. I was very much amused hearing Electra say 'quinque, octo, viginti', etc. German-speaking friends occasionally dropped in; my mother's German, acquired during her stay in Dresden in the 1870s, was excellent. Sometimes I played chamber music with Boston Symphony men, with my mother listening with great pleasure to this artistic entertainment.

Idylls seldom last. It was not long before my mother began to complain about everything. Her guts were falling out, she said, from repeated childbirths during the nineteenth century. Dorothy bought her a girdle, but it proved unsatisfactory. If that particular complaint was contrived, my mother's eye trouble was all too real. She had a cataract. We engaged an eye specialist who removed the lenses under local anaesthesia. My mother displayed remarkable fortitude during the operation; she seemed to enjoy being the centre of attention. She was fitted with a pair of bifocal glasses, and was genuinely amazed at the clarity of her regained vision. 'But you are Sasha!' she exclaimed when she saw me clearly for the first time. Indeed, the physical resemblance between me and my older brother Alexander was very great—we were both genetic replicas of my mother, a pair of Mendel's pea pods demonstrating the combinatorial principles of heredity.

For her age, my mother was remarkably spry, and she began to complain of her forced inactivity in Boston. Suddenly she declared that she would have better chances to do her work in New York. She never made clear what kind of work she proposed to do without knowledge of language and without any specific manual skill, but I had no objections to her going to New York, particularly since I was about to embark on a South American tour. I accompanied her to New York by train, where she joined Aunt Isabelle and Aunt Zinaïda. I took a picture of the three sisters together in Aunt Isabelle's apartment, in full realization that it was to be the last of all three of them together.

CHAPTER 14

JAILED FRIEND

Through the years, Henry Cowell was my Rock of Gibraltar. In his words, we were 'thick as thieves'. His integrity was total, making it all the more tragic when he became a victim of social bigotry.

Cowell owned a shack in Menlo Park, California. Each time he went away, he let young boys in the neighbourhood use the place, ride his ramshackled jalopy (which could not go uphill unless put in reverse and driven backwards), and swim in his small pond. In the spring of 1936, while Cowell was in New York, the police received complaints about kids running wild around his grounds. When questioned, the older ones claimed they had permission from the owner to use the facilities. The police investigated the Cowell case *in absentia*, and found that he had been to Russia, and that he was a musician with bizarre characteristics. Furthermore, he was the object of a complaint by a wealthy Californian landowner whose name happened also to be Henry Cowell, and who suspected that his lowly namesake was using his name for iniquitous purposes. Ironically, it was the rich Henry Cowell who was not genuine; his real name was something like Kowelski, whereas 'our' Cowell was a true American. The authorities also found out that Cowell contributed to radical magazines, such as the *New Masses*, which figured on the district attorney's list of subversive publications. Indeed, Cowell published an article in the magazine, pointedly entitled 'The Kept Composer', in which he deplored the precarious situation of American composers who had to kowtow to wealthy people in order to survive. This was long before the days of the beneficent ASCAP and BMI, with the Guggenheim Foundation the only philanthropic organization providing help to impecunious composers.

With Cowell still in New York, the police concentrated on a 17-year-old boy who claimed to have a special relationship with Cowell. He was a ward of his aunt, and the police put pressure on her, threatening to send the boy to reform school if he refused to talk. When, unaware of all this, Cowell returned to Menlo Park on Friday, 22 May 1936, he was taken into custody and charged with impairment of the morals of a minor,

sodomy, and an assortment of cognate offences. After preliminary inter-
rogation, Cowell was advised to plead guilty to a limited charge, with a
promise that he would then be placed in a psychiatric institution for a few
weeks and released without prejudice. In the meantime, he was remanded
to the sheriff of Redwood City, California. I received a heart-rending
postcard from him, asking me if I still wanted to be his friend under the
circumstances. I replied passionately that I would, for ever, and our
correspondence continued.

In a card dated 29 June 1936, Cowell wrote:

Dear Nicolas: It is most comforting to hear from you so frequently, and to have
further reassurances of your friendship! In a week, if all goes according to
schedule, I will be sentenced. There will be no trial; a trial would be very harmful
to a number of perfectly innocent people. My sole hope lies in the nature of the
sentence. According to California law, I can be given, I believe, from 1 to 15 years
in the pen. I hope, however, for some sort of probation which would alleviate the
harshness of the term. In case I win probation then whenever I am released I will,
if permitted, go East, where I will need all the offices of my good friends. I am
trying to sell all property and will without doubt be legally restricted against
entering the Menlo Park district.

More communications followed in quick succession: 'Dear Nicolas:
Many thanks for your fine note. I will wire if I need your aid in character
recommendation, etc. In the meantime, please discuss as little as possible.
No publicity is good publicity, and don't believe the newspaper reports!'

The newspaper reports were vile. The Hearst papers published a photo
of Cowell behind bars with a banner headline: 'California Oscar Wilde
Jailed!' There was also a photograph showing Cowell in a pickup truck
crowded with kids in the back. The caption explained that Cowell was
taking them to boys' camp in Arizona where he served as music instructor,
but the implication was clear: Cowell was taking a truckful of kids across
the state line for immoral purposes.

A letter dated 6 July 1936 read: 'Dear Nicolas: Today received sentence of 1 to 15 years in San Quentin prison—my new address . . . All
need for keeping quiet is now removed. Warmest affection, Henry.'
Cowell wrote to me to keep in touch with his father Harry Cowell, and
with Harry's second wife, Olive, Henry's stepmother. Olive kept me
informed of the situation. She wrote on 13 July 1936:

Don't worry about Henry. He's making his adjustment; we have already had two
letters from him, and will visit him tomorrow. He is allowed a typewriter, books,
periodicals, and newspapers from outside the state, if sent direct from publishers.
He is taking the whole thing philosophically, and his physician says he will come
out all right, and live down the thing completely. He pleaded guilty to a morals

charge involving a 17-year-old boy, and fully expected either probation or hospitalization. At the last moment some kind of opposition developed, and the judge sent him to San Quentin. It was a great shock to us all, as it was not expected. But we have to keep it very still, in order not to fan the opposition. No publicity at this time. Later all his friends will be called upon to help. Everyone has been so loyal, and there are very influential people back of him. We engaged two physicians, both of whom went over his whole life, and found the cause of the irregularity in certain shocks and strains which have befallen him; but both of them found him normal now. He's in fine shape emotionally and spiritually. His life is the life of the artist, one disappointment after another. Write him often; there seems to be no limit to mail he receives, but he cannot write much. Do not discuss his case at all as the letters are censored, but tell him what is going on in the musical world, and so on, with all your characteristic humor. While he was in Redwood City jail he wrote two compositions with long articles expounding the esthetic theory upon which they are built. He says it is an entirely new departure for him.

While in San Quentin, Cowell wrote a string quartet, which he described in a letter dated 16 July 1936:

In this quartet, I tried to make a first step toward a style which is not an imitation of that of any nationality, but which is based on the least common denominator of musical elements, which are drawn from the peoples of the whole world, which are simple enough to be understood universally. If the music is a success in this attempt it may sound a bit odd, but it should be equally understood by Americans, Europeans, Chinese, Indians, or primitives. If you know any organizations who might wish to perform the quartet or other works of mine, it would be fine. I am hoping that my music will not be boycotted. I have a certain amount of time in my cell when I may study, and I can write music then if I feel like it, but I am not sure I could get permission to send it out. I am rather tired by the time I have my cell time as I work in the jute mill from before 7.00 am to about 3.45 pm, except for lunch. The work, thank goodness, is not injurious to my hands. It is spooling, transferring jute from small to large spools. Each individual must operate 20 spools, which whirr to a deafening machine sound. I am a novice and marvel at the skill required to handle the whole machine. There are nearly 6,000 men in this prison, and I am sure over half must be in this mill. It is an amazing place. As to the rest of the conditions here they are not unlike the army life I remember. It is a relief here, after the Redwood jail. The food is better, and there is at least activity. I don't mind being a mill-hand! It's a genuine experience!

From a letter dated 14 August 1936:

It will interest you to know that there is contact here with the State Library of Sacramento and prisoners may order books from it. I discovered that my book, *American Composers on American Music*, has been here twelve times, ordered by different men. The bandleader here, a prisoner, has fully digested all the details of your article on me. You ask whether the prisoners are of the type portrayed in the movies. I must frankly say that I haven't seen one! On the surface they impress one as being a rather rough-and-ready, good-natured group, something like army men. It is only when one becomes better acquainted with them, that their lack of feeling for ethical behavior becomes evident. In a group of about fifteen men, one will find some who really have a strong moral sense; ten or twelve who seem to be rather childish, good-natured morons; and one or two really tough eggs, bad men of whom one has to be careful. I cannot convey to you how extraordinary is the experience of being thrown in with such a motley crew. The whole thing is really an experience which, if not too protracted, one would not wish to have missed . . . I have heard not a word from Ives. Do you have any news of him? I am worried. I wrote to Mrs Ives when I was sent here. She has not answered. It does not seem in the least like them to turn against me in such fashion as to remain silent on account of the present condition, and so I worry for fear he is very ill.

From a letter of Olive Cowell dated San Francisco, 28 October 1936:

Henry is in very good spirits and is working. He is proving what a great human being he is, never complaining, and making the best of everything. He has lots of visitors and enjoys letters, but can write only one letter a day. His physician says he has been suffering from a sexual neurosis which had its origin in a misguided and delayed emotional development, and which was provoked by definitely known shocks in his personal life. The cure of this condition is effected by re-education and treatment through psychotherapy. His understanding of his case, his unusual intelligence and strength of character, as well as his eagerness to co-operate, provide the basis for a favorable outcome. We can therefore assume that he will be able to make a satisfactory adjustment leading to emotional maturity and normal sex life. No recurrence of the offense need be feared, if he were released today.

Several prominent musicians sent testimonials in Cowell's behalf to prison authorities. During his lecture tour in California, Varèse went to see Cowell and to speak with his warden about prospects for parole. The warden told him not to worry, and made a gross and gratuitous remark to the effect that, for Cowell, doing time in the company of cons is like going to the Ziegfeld Follies.

From Cowell, dated San Quentin, 15 December 1936:

Dear Nicolas: I was glad to hear that you received my music autograph okay. I do hope that you will ask the *Christian Science Monitor* to send me a copy of the magazine section when your article on modern American composers is printed. Remember, a publisher can always send me his publication. The *Monitor* is widely read among the inmates. Let me know the dates of your articles on the children's page, and I will probably be able to find them. The *Monitor* is an ideal paper for penal institutions, and it is the most favored here by the authorities . . .

Do you hear from Ives? I have not had a word from him. I naturally feel very badly. I wrote the whole thing to Mrs Ives, with a letter to give Mr Ives if she felt it would not be too much of a shock for his health. I wonder very much whether she gave it to him, or what he himself knows of my case. I asked them to please not form judgment until I have had a chance to tell them of the matter myself. It is very unlike Ives to suddenly cut me off from all communication. I can't conceive of it at all. I know that his eyes are very bad and that he probably cannot write or read the letters himself. Mrs Ives wrote to Gerald Strang a formal note saying that Ives was interested to continue doing something for *New Music Quarterly*. I was not mentioned. Since the matter is very delicate and I have no way of finding out anything about him, perhaps you would know something of what happened? If you do, good or bad, I wish you would let me know. Not hearing anything at all is really torturing, because as you know, I regard Ives the same as a father; no one who had ever known him could fail to be attached.

Anguished inquiries from Cowell about Ives continued. I suggested to him that perhaps Ives was biding his time to recover from the shock at the news of Cowell's incarceration. Cowell accepted my theory as plausible:

Your idea that Ives is waiting to have enough strength to write himself is, I hope, the correct solution. I wrote Ives again last night, however, telling of my life in prison, hoping to have news because Ives is very close to me and I worry about his health . . . He is surely unique among men for his altruism and such generosity that its recipients, not he, must put on the brakes!

And again:'I wrote Ives a letter after a year and half or so of not writing, saying how pleased I have been with the progress of his performances, but I did not have a reply.'

I never asked Ives for his reaction to Henry Cowell, but, as a puritan at heart, he was profoundly shocked and could find no forgiveness in his soul. Harmony Ives wrote to a mutual friend on 12 July 1936: 'Charles will never willingly see Henry again—he can't. He doesn't want to hear of the thing. The shock used him up and he hasn't had a long breath since.' If reports could be trusted, Ives said that Cowell ought to get a gun and shoot himself.

The most extraordinary testimony of Cowell's fortitude was his vivid interest in intellectual and artistic matters in time of personal humiliation and misfortune. Here are some of his letters from San Quentin:

I am delighted that you are interested in the ideas behind my new *United Quartet*. I think that the idea of choosing materials that are more world-wide is a good practical way in which to use my knowledge of comparative musicology, and I am also interested in the ideas of cohesive form and tonal relationships. Concerning the symphony in different styles by Spohr, I did not know about it, but it is interesting to me, for when I was 15 years old I composed a 'résumé' for piano in sixteen movements, embracing a complete sonata to represent the classical style, different folk-type movements, etc. It takes a whole evening to perform, and I gave concerts twice during my early career in which it was the only work on the program. I certainly did not know that anyone had done this sort of thing before! But your new idea is most attractive, and I am quite fascinated by it. . . .

Your children's articles in the *Christian Science Monitor* are read very eagerly, and my music students constantly bring them to me, not knowing that I am a friend of yours. But the way, with your eye for statistics, you will be interested to know that during the two years I have been teaching in the education department in San Quentin, I have had 1,549 registrations in my music classes, 343 registrations in my elementary work, and 59 registrations in my harmony course. In the classes, 138 were for music history and appreciation, and the rest were all actual study courses in reading, writing, and playing. I teach 22 hours a week, rehearse the band for 5 hours, rehearse about $7\frac{1}{2}$ hours with the band myself playing flute, take 4 hours a week in studying Japanese, etc. My composing is all done in my cell, of course. . . .

I have just completed the cycle of three songs to the texts of the *Anti-Modernist Poems* from your book. The style of each song smacks faintly of that of the composer who is being derided, but not to the extent of taking actual themes. By the way, I saw that you have invaded the *Étude* magazine lately. How do you do it? Do let me know the secret! A violin has been sent in to me, and I am trying to learn it. I am also practising on the flute. I have never tried to blow into one before, and so find it of interest. Having only one hour per day in which I am permitted to practise at all, I have a great time, dividing it between the violin and the flute . . . My cell partner is to leave next week, and I wait with great anxiety to see who will be put in with me afterward, as the whole question of whether I am able to compose or not hinges on what sort of person he may be . . .

Recently your publisher sent me a copy of your violin piece. It is very clever, witty and interesting throughout, and extremely effective. It is truly amazing how you have been able to coax your theoretical constructions into anything so well adapted to the instrument, and so painless to take! I think I told you that I work here with a very good violinist who was a pupil of Joachim. He is greatly attracted to the piece, and although he mutters about key changes, he is very enthusiastic over it, much more so than I would ever have expected from an old-school man. We are to perform it at our next concert together, and I hope to be able to send you a program.

In March 1937 I sent Cowell a copy of the book *Life Begins at Forty* (Cowell was born on 11 March 1897). Our correspondence continued vigorously. He wrote to me regularly every fifteen days, which was his quota to any one individual. The prison failed to undermine Cowell's imaginative plans. He completed a melody book there, and also a 'reel' for Percy Grainger:

He is to play it over a NBC hook-up this Sunday. He says it sounds splendidly.

Wish I could hear it, but we are not permitted to have radios. Martha Graham gave a première of a new dance for which I wrote music here, and Riegger wrote it was a success. It is written in the 'flexible' form, so that any section can be pulled out or pushed in to any length. It seems to work. Martha Graham used the music and said it fitted with the dance she did before receiving the score, and I did not even know the length of the dance!

The California authorities refused to give Cowell credit for the fine work he was doing in prison, and sentenced him to the maximum term. In September 1937 I received a letter from Henry's stepmother:

Well, the worst has happened. They paid no attention to anything that we presented regarding Henry's case. They treated him as if he were a confirmed homosexual, a degenerate who seduces the young with violence, none of which is true. They gave him fifteen years, with parole denied until half his term is served. If he gets time off for good behaviour, it will be reduced to nine and a half years, with an application for parole due in three and a half years from now. Of course they can change their mind and grant him parole at any time, but that is how it stands at present. I saw Henry after he had received word of the outcome and he was in excellent condition. He was ready for it, so it did not overwhelm him. He has amazing courage and fortitude. And he has a great calmness, remarkable spiritual poise.

In 1940 Cowell was granted parole. In 1941 he married Sidney Robertson, a folklore specialist. The marriage reconciled Ives to him. He even consented to have a picture taken with him, an extraordinary favour considering the almost pathological aversion Ives had to photography.

Dorothy wrote to me in Managua, Nicaragua, on 5 January 1942:

Henry Cowell came with his wife last night unexpectedly. We had some supper and he played his new concerto with his elbows, and within the piano. Electra was fascinated as she looked into the piano's viscera which he operated with a manicure file, gaspingly. His wife is a fine person, very cultured and good natured. Henry looks grand and very happy. The Cowells will stay at our place.

At his death in December 1965, Cowell had written nineteen symphonies and hundreds of works of smaller dimensions. His greatest victory was the wide recognition of his importance as a composer, a theorist, and as an inventive philosopher of modern music.

CHAPTER 15

EXOTIC JOURNEYS

My musical excursions to Cuba had whetted my appetite for a wider exploration of Latin America. I received a grant from a retired Phila-delphia businessman named Edwin A. Fleisher to travel to the countries of Latin America in order to collect symphonic scores for the Free Library of Philadelphia. I embarked on the *SS Uruguay* in July 1941 for Rio de Janeiro. Dorothy sent me a characteristic missive in care of the boat purser: 'I hope you will get a good rest on the boat, and dismiss your various symptoms of nervousness and oppressiveness. Try to grow up completely as you approach your sixth decade.' I was 47 years old at the time.

Rio de Janeiro was the city of Villa-Lobos, who possessed a truly tropical imagination. He liked to recount his adventure among the can-nibals of the Amazon River where he went in search of folklore. An excellent cellist, he took his instrument with him. He was captured by cannibals, and they heated a huge cauldron in anticipation of a fine meal (Villa-Lobos was meaty in his physique). As a sort of swan-song, Villa-Lobos took his cello and began playing an Indian tune. Suddenly, the chief cannibal and several of his wives fell down on the ground and prostrated themselves before him. The sounds of the cello convinced them that Villa-Lobos was divine. He spent many happy days with the cannibals before bidding them farewell.

His musical stories were equally incredible. He told me, for instance, that the inverted organ point on the high B-flat in one of his enchanting Brazilian pieces represented the cry of the jungle bird Araponga. To check up on that, I went to a bird shop and asked the owner in my rudimentary Portuguese whether he had any Arapongas for sale. He certainly had, and he brought out a stuffed parrot. No, I said, I wanted a living bird. For that, he told me, I would have to travel deep into the forest. But I had heard too many horrifying tales about the perils of the jungle, about ticks that lay eggs in the pores of the skin causing indescribable torment, and about malaria-bearing insects. I decided not to venture forth.

I returned to the Government Office of Music Education in Rio de

Janeiro where Villa-Lobos served as Director and I reported to him my failure to find an Araponga. He called in one of his assistants and asked him, 'What is the high note that the Araponga sings?' 'Si bemol!' the other answered with assurance. 'Vous voyez?' Villa-Lobos said to me. Observing that I was still unconvinced, he called in another person of his staff and repeated the same question. 'Si bemol!' came the immediate reply. He turned to me and said again, 'Vous voyez?' The more evidence he produced, the less I believed it; I even harboured the sneaking suspicion that the whole scene had been carefully rehearsed for my benefit.

Apart from his preoccupation with Brazilian birds and cannibals, Villa-Lobos also fancied himself a musical scientist. He wrote a piano cycle entitled *Bachianas brasileiras* because he felt that Brazil had a mysterious kinship with Bach's counterpoint, symbolized by the fact that the words Brazil and Bach begin with the same letter of the alphabet. He invented a 'graphical millimetrization' by which he could turn diagrams, landscapes, and photographs into melodies. He readily agreed to 'millimetrize' a picture of my family at breakfast. Busy as he was, he sat down and patiently drew on graph paper a curve corresponding to the outlines of myself, Dorothy, and Electra, and made them into a tune. He dated it 'Rio. 3/10/41, 18.15 hours'. The resulting melody was rather angular and difficult to sing—my family was apparently not photogenic. Villa-Lobos was selective in his 'millimetrization'. When a woman asked him to turn an X-ray picture of her heart into a melody, he declined. Her heart, he said, was millimetrically unmelodic.

In my travels I followed the geography of South America country by country—Argentina, Chile, Peru, Ecuador. Every new place was a discovery. In Buenos Aires I met the oldest and the youngest composers of Argentina, Alberto Williams, a grandson of a British immigrant, and Alberto Ginastera. Williams studied in Paris and wrote symphonies in an impressionistic vein. Ginastera wrote authentic tunes in an indigenous manner, but later in his career adopted a serial manner of composition. In Chile I collected a number of interesting works, both in the folkloric and cosmopolitan styles. Peruvian music was pentatonic and austere. Even more severe was the native music of Ecuador. Comparing the musical productions of the Atlantic and Pacific coasts of South America, I came to an interesting conclusion: the music of Brazil and Argentina was luxuriantly tropical, much influenced by the injection of Italian and Portuguese folklore, melodious in lyric productions and fast and lively in dance forms, while the songs and dances of the West Coast were impressed with aboriginal Indian folklore. I also found that the music of the high Andes was slow and deliberate, confined to a few modes of the pentatonic scale, as though breathing at that altitude required deeper inhalation. I almost fell victim myself to the thin air of Quito, the capital city of Ecuador, as I banged away the piano version of Gershwin's *I Got Rhythm* during a recital in a local club. At the end of the piece I nearly passed out because of the lack of oxygen.

Panama, my next step, was at sea level and at least I could breathe, but the heat was inhuman, only occasionally relieved by a cloudburst lasting a minute or two. Once I was drenched while crossing the street, but the rain had stopped by the time I reached the other side, and the hot sun dried my shirt in a matter of seconds. I was given a guided tour of the red light district of Panama by a local musician. It was unlike anything I had ever seen. The street was lined by what seemed to be a row of furniture stores with huge beds on display. They were not furniture stores, however. In the doorways an assortment of incredibly large women solicited trade in several languages at a uniform price of $5 a head. The beds were apparently never used; they were just window displays. Action took place behind the stores. I was also taken to a leper colony. I knew that leprosy is not contagious, but cringed none the less when shaking hands with people whose fingers seemed to be falling off like dry twigs.

Moving up the isthmus, I reached Costa Rica, where I was given a chance to conduct an orchestra. The country has the most wonderful weather in all Latin America, and also produces the most wonderful coffee in the world. When I got to Managua, Nicaragua, the local paper greeted me with front-page headlines and salutations:

You come to Managua, oh Nicolas Slonimsky, at the time when the soul of Russia flies on the heroic wings of liberty in defence of the alert spirit of democracy. You bring us a message of immortal Russia, the Russia of the arts, and a reflection of the epical accomplishment of a nation that knows how to protect the integrity of her sacred soil!

In Guatemala it was necessary to get a special permit from the President to give a public performance. With the help of friends, I submitted an application, couched in deferential terms, to General Jorge Ubico, then President. I received a gracious reply expressing his satisfaction at my interest in his country's music. I received an even greater presidential appreciation in San Salvador. About half-way through my show, a man in military uniform entered the hall. The entire audience suddenly sprang to their feet and exclaimed, 'El Presidente!' Indeed, it was General Maximiliano Hernández Martínez, President of the Republic of El Salvador. He applauded my performance of piano pieces by three local composers, and came to see me after the show. He told me that he himself was a musician, having played the drums in military bands before entering politics. It was not many days later that I picked up a newspaper which carried huge headlines announcing the expulsion of El Presidente, describing him as a bloody despot.

My last stopover in Latin America was Mexico. I had hoped to meet one of Mexico's most original composers, Silvestre Revueltas, but he had died. He literally drank himself to death. I was told that, after a night of alcoholic stupor, he would collapse into a ditch and be awakened by an Indian urinating on his prostrate body, a method of arousing a drunk freely practised among the natives. Revueltas was a fiery revolutionary. He fought Franco in Spain and wrote music throbbing with the spirit of social revolt.

I was fortunate in being able to see a lot of Carlos Chávez, a world-renowned figure among Latin American composers. Like many artists of great talent, he was quite outspoken about his own worth. He took umbrage at my description of him in one of my articles as 'the foremost Mexican composer'. 'How can I be foremost if there are no other Mexican composers worthy of the name?' he asked. 'What about Manuel Ponce?' I asked. Ponce was his teacher and, while Chávez considered him a fine musician, he observed that his works were more a stylization than authentic representations of the genius of Mexico.

I happened to be a travelling companion with Ponce, by plane, autobus, and automobile, from Peru to Mexico. After my talk in Lima, he wrote an amusing piece of doggerel:

> Sin declararle la guerra
> Llegó Slonimsky al Perú
> Y sin magía ni tabú
> Hizo temblar a la tierra.

I did play Cowell's *Amiable Conversation* in Lima, which requires the use of fists and forearms, but I doubt whether it produced a temblor.

It was in Chile that I learned of the attack on Pearl Harbor. Dorothy wrote to me in an unusually patriotic vein:

The great blow to our Pacific defenses has solidified the USA. The Boston Museum has a distribution of sandbags in all the galleries; the most valuable objects are being withdrawn to safety. The Japanese exhibition rooms are locked up to the public. Germany has declared war on us. We are now in the con-flagration full blast for better or for worse. The other day when I was scheduled to speak in a private home in Newton, there was an alarm over the radio that ten planes were sighted within half an hour of Boston! The schools closed and there was much running about and some mild panic. The meeting was called off and I was being driven to the railroad station where we heard on the radio that it was a false alarm. Back we drove to the lecture which I gave on the subject of Madonna in Art, full of the Xmas spirit. The women said they were so grateful to me for relieving their minds with the discussion of beauty. When I returned home, Electra told me they had taken the children down into the playroom at school. That is to be their procedure if there is an air raid alarm.

The fruit of my exotic journey was a book, *Music of Latin America*, which was published in 1945. I made a great effort to present information about all the twenty Latin America nations, including the islands. I divided the book evenly into ponderous musicological matters and lightweight anecdotes. I also tabulated the density of composers per area and per population for each country, a summation that aroused delighted or, as the case may be, indignant response from specialists. I appended a concise dictionary of indigenous songs and dances, and, for visual effect, drew a map with their names strategically placed within each country. The national dance of Chile was zamacueca which fitted into the long spine of the map most perfectly. Whatever its virtues or faults, the book was the first attempt to give an adequate account of musical culture south of the border.

For better or worse, I became among certain circles somewhat of an authority on Latin American music. In 1965 I received a letter from Stokowski, asking my advice for a programme of Cuban music he planned to give with his American Symphony Orchestra in New York. I recommended a piece by Amadeo Roldán which included the *quijada del burro*, the jawbone of an ass to be played by making glissando on its molars. Stokowski responded promptly, adding that in regard to the *quijada del burro* he would have no trouble obtaining a specimen. 'We have plenty of asses,' he wrote, 'and they all have jawbones which they manipulate at length, saying very little.'

CHAPTER 16

INTERPOLATION:
GROSSMUTTERAKKORD

Parallel to my exploration of musical exotica, an idea began to form in my restless mind whether an entirely new taxonomy of scales and melodic patterns could not be formed outside major and minor modalities. In my usual extravagant way of thinking, I boldly compared my neo-musical elucubrations to non-Euclidean geometries, in which strange things happen in space, and the shortest distance between two points turns out to be a stereo-metrical curve. I viewed the entire evolution of musical composition before the present as a constricting course limited to the arbitrary compass of seven diatonic degrees, with occasional chromatics growing inside and outside a given mode. The antiphonal strength of modulatory processes and fugal imitation had its source in the unequal division of the octave into two parts, from the tonic to the dominant and from the dominant to the tonic, leading to non-symmetric procedures. But why not try a democratic division of the octave in two equal parts, with the tritone rather than the perfect fifth as the line of demarcation? Yet the tritone was the 'diabolus in musica' of medieval theorists, a cardinal sin for teachers of counterpoint.

What fascinated me in the division of the octave into two tritones was not the aura of diabolism, but the possibility of generating new scales. The tritone contains six semitones. Why not form a scale made up of two sections, each containing the succession of three, two and one semitones? The resulting scale is most provocative. For one thing, it is binary; for another, it contains three different intervals. Experimenting further, I discovered that it could be harmonized euphoniously by a sustained dominant seventh chord with its fifth omitted, provided the chord is made up of the tones contained in the scale itself. Either the entire scale, or any part thereof, can be harmonized by such a chord, creating beguiling sonorities of the dominant ninth with a trilling, thrilling, lowered fifth in the upper octave. The scale could be shuffled and permutated at will. It could be arranged melodically in a most attractive impressionistic manner by convergence (playing the first note, then the last note, the second note, then the penultimate note, the third note, and then the ante-penultimate note), or by divergence (playing the convergent version in reverse), or in permutations, in any order of the tones whatsoever, with the same fifthless dominant seventh chord sonorously supporting the resulting pattern. By skipping every other note of this scale beginning with the first, and repeating the same operation beginning with the second, one obtains two mutually exclusive major triads at the distance of a tritone. When struck together, these triads form the 'Parisian' bitonal complex so dearly beloved by modern composers of the first quarter of the twentieth century. When these triads are spaced in open harmony in the bass register and in close harmony in the treble, the result is positively enchanting. Under such circumstances, the medieval 'devil in music' becomes an inspiring 'daemon' in the Socratic sense.

The formula for this bitter-sweet bitonal scale, reckoned in semitones, is 3, 2, 1, 3, 2, 1. By starting on the second interval, we obtain the progression 2, 1, 3, 2, 1, 3. By starting on the third interval, we get 1, 3, 2, 1, 3, 2. Each modal displacement of this scale yields the same succulent bitonality of two major triads distanced by a tritone.

Another unexpected connection: if we arrange a series of intervals in a descending arithmetic progression, from nine semitones to three, we obtain a wonderfully euphonious bitonal chord in diminishing intervals; starting on C we have C, A, F, C, F-sharp, B, D-sharp, F-sharp.

The notes of scale 3, 2, 1 (in semitones) can be permutated in any desired order and arranged in a canon of 2, 3, 4, or 6 voices. The whole complex can then be projected against the background of the dominant seventh chord, minus a fifth, with the resulting spectrum of coruscating harmonic colours, while the canonic progression itself yields delectable melodic excrescences and acrid secundal protuberances. By manipulating the rhythmic patterns of these elements, including the device of repetition of the same note, it is possible to improvise a whole impressionistic musical landscape, using both piano pedals (since the harmonies are euphonious), assigning to it some oxymoronic title such as *Le Soleil sombre*.

The basic design of the division of an octave into two equal parts can be further variegated by multiple interpolation (as in the case of the scale 3, 2, 1, 3, 2, 1), ultrapolation (by inserting a note, or several notes, above the tritone), and infrapolation (by adding a note, or several notes, below the initial note of the basic design). An attractive example of interpolation of the tritone division is C, D, E, F, F-sharp, G-sharp, A-sharp, B, C, a truly bitonal scale combining the tetrachords of the two polar major tonalities, C major and F-sharp major. The whole scale, or any section of the scale, can be harmonized by a fifthless dominant seventh chord, such as B-flat, D, A-flat, or E, G-sharp, D, with euphonious effects.

The octave has twelve semitones. This is fortunate, for it is divisible into two, three, four and six. By dividing an octave in three parts, we produce an augmented triad, which is amenable to ornamentation by interpolation, ultrapolation and infrapolation. The next step is obvious. We divide the octave into four equal parts, resulting in an arpeggiated diminished seventh chord. Interpolation here will produce a scale of alternating whole tones and semitones, beloved by Rimsky-Korsakov. By ultrapolation of one, two, or three notes and a symmetrically arranged infrapolation we obtain melodic patterns encountered in Wagner's *Tristan und Isolde*.

Division of the octave into six equal parts produces the familiar whole-tone scale. There is no sense in applying interpolation to this scale, which would result in the formation of the chromatic scale. But ultrapolation and infrapolation of the whole-tone scale will provide interesting melodic patterns evoking technical passages used by Liszt.

The division of an octave into twelve equal parts yields the chromatic scale. By using devices of ultrapolation and infrapolation, we obtain arabesques of fascinating technical brilliance. Yet even thorough exploration of scales of equal division within a single octave will not exhaust our newly discovered melodic resources. We can now proceed to divide a double octave into three parts, forming an expanded augmented triad. By inserting a pentachord on each node of this division, we will obtain a most interesting formation of a continuous scale of three different major or minor keys, with their respective pentachords flowing into one another with the utmost naturalness. Beginning with C, we obtain a most alluring triple scale, C, D, E, F, G, A-flat, B-flat, C, D-flat, E-flat, E, F-sharp, G-sharp, A, B, C.

Continuing along these lines, five octaves can be divided into six parts, resulting in a formation of consecutive minor sevenths, which can be filled in by interpolation. The division of five octaves into twelve parts will provide the cycle of perfect fourths. By filling each fourth with a tetrachord, we obtain a conjunct polytetrachord, either major or minor. The cycle of fifths results from the division of seven octaves into twelve parts, familiar from elementary theory books. By filling up the empty spaces we obtain a disjunct polytetrachord, a companion to the conjunct polytetrachord formed by a cycle of perfect fourths.

In the process of compiling a self-consistent system of scales of equal division, I came upon some fascinating phenomena. I found, for instance, that the seemingly atonal melody resulting from the triply ultrapolated tritone division of the octave, C, upper B-flat, lower A, G, F-sharp, upper E, E-flat, D-flat, C, yields, when arranged canonically in three voices, a succession of tonally unrelated major and minor triads. Stumbling upon this quite unexpected development, I felt like the bewildered stargazer of

Keats when 'a new planet swam into his ken'. Even more fantastic was the curious interweaving of twelve different notes with eleven different intervals in a huge dissonant chord.

The problem of arranging twelve different notes in a column using eleven different intervals is analogous to the problem of covering the face of the clock by advancing the hour-hand 1 hour, 2 hours, 3 hours, 4 hours, etc., up to 11 hours, without stopping at the same hour twice. It is useless to try the simple arithmetical progression 1, 2, 3, 4, etc., because at number 5 we will land at 3 o'clock which has already been covered. A solution was discovered by a Hungarian-born theorist, Fritz Heinrich Klein, who made use of it in his orchestral work *Die Maschine*, which he published under the characteristic pseudonym, *Heautontimorumenos*, meaning self- tormentor in Greek. Alban Berg was amused by it; he called this column of notes 'Mutterakkord', for it had as its progeny the entire chromatic scale. Ernst Krenek referred to it in one of his articles as a unique combination which cannot be altered without repeating a note or interval.

Somehow I could not believe that the Mutterakkord was unique. I sensed that there had to be a tritone somewhere in the middle, because the tritone is the only self-inverting interval. Going to bed I imagined that the pillow was a tritone which hurt my medulla oblongata with its protruding F-sharp. Then I woke with a start and shouted, 'Eureka!' The general formula for the construction of mother chords came to me in a flash. I called Krenek who was staying in a Boston hotel nearby and told him the news. There was a pause at the other end of the phone, and Krenek said, 'Unglaublich! Ich komme sofort!' We sat together at the piano figuring out the many possibilities for forming chords of twelve different notes containing eleven different intervals, totally oblivious of the life around us. We could have passed for a couple of medieval monks debating a thorny theological problem.

With my new-found formula, there was such a proliferation of mother chords that I began weeding them out by further specifications, until I hit upon the idea of ultimate symmetry of intervallic invertibility with the self-inverting tritone in the centre. I called this chord Grossmutterakkord. Then it dawned on me how obvious the generating formula was (all great discoveries are obvious after the fact). The Grossmutterakkord could be constructed by the method of the clock. Setting the clock at 12 o'clock, you advance it 1 hour, then go back 2 hours, advance 3, go back 4, advance 5, go back 6, advance 7, go back 8, advance 9, go back 10, advance 11, in a marvellously symmetric pendulum motion: 12 o'clock, 1 o'clock, 11 o'clock, 2 o'clock, 10 o'clock, 3 o'clock, etc., covering every hour spot on the face of the clock. And the numbers can be read backwards too! In musical notation, the result would be as follows : C, B, D-flat, B-flat, D, A, E-flat, A-flat, E, G, F, F-sharp. The Grandmother could be stood on her head with equal ease! Krenek was impressed, and signalized his approbation in our guest book. Not so Prokofiev, who wrote: 'To the devil with grandmothers! Let us write music!' Hindemith opined on the same page: 'I wish great prosperity and more progeny to the Grossmutterakkord.' The Swedish composer Karl-Birger Blomdahl used the melodic version of it as the principal motto of his interplanetary opera *Aniara*, and several other composers applied it in their compositions as well.

Fascinated by the suppleness and subtlety of the apparently rigid framework of twelve tones of the chromatic scale, I investigated the possibility of tying it up with triadic structures by arranging twelve different tones in four mutually exclusive triads. I felt intuitively that the tritone was the crucial interval in this arrangement. And so it turned out to be. Two major triads in the relation of a tritone and two minor triads in the relation of the tritone would form a group of four mutually exclusive triads: C major, F-sharp major, D minor, and G-sharp minor. I also found that it is possible to arrange the chromatic scale in four different kinds of mutually exclusive triads: an augmented triad, a major triad, a minor triad, and a diminished triad. Still I had no inkling as to the underlying principle of this crystallographically symmetric division.

I then faced what was perhaps the most formidable problem, concerning the nature of triads within the matrix of the chromatic scale: Is it possible to form a chain of four mutually exclusive triads linked by major or minor thirds? In other words, is it possible to construct a chord of the 23rd? Modern composers have used chords of the 11th and the 13th, arranged in a chain of thirds; the next link would be a chord of the 15th, completing the cycle of fifths. It was by sheer luck that I was able to extend the structure to the minor 23rd, formed by the triads of C major, B-flat major, G-sharp minor, and F-sharp minor, with linkages in thirds. To avoid enharmonic imbroglios, it is expedient to start the chain on F-sharp, as follows: F-sharp major, E major, D minor, C minor. The order of tonalities is readily obtainable by running a descending whole-tone tetrachord from F-sharp to C—the ubiquitous tritone again!—and building two major and two minor thirds on these notes. I asked a friend who had access to a large computer to check whether my chord of the minor 23rd was really unique. He arranged the problem in mathematical terms and fed it into the machine. The motors whirred, the stroboscopic lights flickered, and after a few hours of mighty labour, the computer came to a halt, flashing my solution in red. The chord proved unique! The line of Horace comes to mind: 'Parturient montes, nascetur ridiculus mus.' Well, the nascent mouse may not have been so ridiculous in the computerized parturition and the mountain may not have laboured in vain. The creation had a musical meaning.

In the course of time I organized my scales in an orderly fashion and took the product to the friendly musical director of G. Schirmer Company, Carl Engel. His response was characteristic. 'Dear Mr Slonimsky,' he wrote. 'Anything you do in music is bound to attract attention. Your knowledge, your wide range of interests, your . . .' I did not have to read more to guess what was to follow: G. Schirmer, Inc., was a commercial publishing house and could not very well print something as bizarre as my elucubrations. I swallowed my disappointment and gave the scales to a friendly bassoon player named Herbert Coleman who was just branching out into publishing. He looked over my manuscript and asked me how many people would buy such a book. 'Seventeen,' I replied without hesitation. 'Why seventeen?' he asked. 'Because I have seventeen friends who can afford to plunk down ten dollars, or whatever the price will be, for a book of scales.' Impressed by my wisecracking candour, Coleman decided to take a chance on the book. He found in Boston a retired music engraver with plenty of time on his hands who charged only $2.50 per page and who even brought the proofs to my place for the final layout to avoid awkward page turns. This exceptional co-operation allowed me to organize some sections of the book in a manner that looked like modern-istic paintings.

Finally, in 1947, it was published. The title, *Thesaurus of Scales and Melodic Patterns*, was impressive. The jaw-breaking nomenclature, how-ever, such as sesquitone scales, pandiatonic melodies and harmonies, palindromic canons, etc., was bound to frighten away a tyro and to annoy a music professor. Still, I got nice reviews. Olin Downes devoted a Sunday feature article to my *Thesaurus* in *The New York Times* of 22 June 1947, in which he paid me an ambiguous compliment as 'a modern-spirited musician, with an extremely sensitive ear, and a damnably active mind'. I particularly enjoyed the modifier 'damnably'. Hugo Leichtentritt pub-lished a scholarly evaluation of my opus in the *Christian Science Monitor*, calling it an epochal accomplishment in musical scholarship and compar-ing it to Busoni's essay on new musical aesthetics in significance.

Henry Cowell delivered a fanciful pronouncement on my book in *Music Library Notes* in which he said: 'Musical history may be saved from becoming a palindrome through the progress made possible by Slonimsky's *Thesaurus*.' Honegger wrote: 'Absolument remarquable, une source de documentation inépuisable.' Malipiero said that on the pages of my book he found himself in his own world. The most remark-able response came from Schoenberg, who wrote (in English): 'I looked through your whole book and was very interested to find that you have in all probability organized every possible succession of tones. This is an admirable feat of mental gymnastics. But as a composer, I must believe in inspiration rather than in mechanics.'

There were coincidences between entries in the book and actual compositions. The theme of Schoenberg's *Ode to Napoleon*, which he wrote about the time I completed my scales, corresponded note for note to pattern number 231 in the section 'Infrapolation of One Note, Ditone Progression, Equal Division of One Octave into 3 parts'. I arranged a four-part canon on this theme and sent it to Schoenberg for his seventy-fifth birthday in 1949. He responded graciously with a handwritten postcard in which he commended me on my cleverness, and, characteristically, asked whether the manuscript was in my own hand. It was, and he thought it calligraphically excellent. I appreciated the compliment.

In the summer of 1947, when the *Thesaurus* was published, Aaron Copland had a choral piece performed at Harvard University. To my surprise, I recognized in it a passage of twenty-two notes which corresponded, note for note, to the ultra-interpolated sesquitone scale in my book. Copland told me that he had received the *Thesaurus* just after finishing this piece, and remarked, with his typical gentle humour: 'Now if I am stuck for an idea, all I have to do is consult your book.'

Virgil Thomson favoured my mutually exclusive triads in a twelve-tone matrix. I was pleased to recognize a sprinkling of these triadic formations in one of his pictorial symphonic pieces which he conducted with the Boston Symphony Orchestra. I went to see him after the concert, and he winked at me: 'Did you hear your little triads from the *Thesaurus?*' he said, pronouncing Thesaurus with a stress on the first syllable which made it sound quaint.

I was deeply moved when Eugene Goossens wrote to me, shortly before his death, to ask permission to use a fragment from the *Thesaurus* in a work he was composing. I had always admired Goossens, and his appreciation of my work meant a great deal to me.

Alas, all the tributes and endorsements lacked the kinetic power to move copies of the *Thesaurus* from the basement of Coleman's house in Boston which served as his editorial office, treasury department, publicity division, and shipping room. During the summer months no copies were sold. Then something unexpected happened. Jazz players began to buy the *Thesaurus* for use in their improvisations and cadenzas. They could not say Thesaurus, and they certainly could not pronounce my name, but, when they asked for 'Resaurius by Slumsky', sales followed.

The *Thesaurus* was eventually taken over by Scribners, and several printings of a thousand copies each were issued. It did not make me rich, but I felt smugly pleased that the most esoteric of my productions proved to be a success among the musical masses.

CHAPTER 17

BACK IN THE FAMILY FOLD

I was born in St Petersburg in 1894. I left Petrograd in 1918. I revisited
Leningrad in 1935. Throughout my wanderings abroad I maintained
active correspondence with my older brother Alexander who continued to
live in my twice-renamed birthplace. He even stayed there during the
terrible siege of the city in 1941 and 1942; eventually he moved to
Moscow. My younger brother Michael remained in Leningrad. My
mother joined me in Paris and later in the United States. My sister Julia
also followed the wave of emigration. There had been an agonizing break
in communication with my brothers during the last years of the Russian
Civil War in 1919 and 1920, when I left Russia; I could not even find out
whether they were still alive.

   For me, Russia was rapidly becoming a land of distant memories. I
maintained a lively correspondence with my older brother Alexander, but
communication with my younger brother Michael was chiefly through
literary channels, as his works became available abroad. His first important novel was *The Lavrovs*, in which he described the gradual decline of an
intellectual Russian family during the Revolution. Its main character was
Clara Andreyevna, an impetuous and selfish woman who dominated her
household; it was clearly a portrait of our own mother. Michael's details
were photographic: her impatience, her loud voice, her flaunting of
illnesses, the characteristic anacoluthons in her speech, her habit of losing
her pince-nez which was actually dangling on a string around her neck.
Even her fictitious name had an isometric arrangement of vocables not
unlike that of my mother's, Faina Afanasievna. Michael denied that he
meant to blacken mother's image, but his denials were rather unconvinc-
ing. My mother never forgave him for his literary pasquinade.

   Michael portrayed himself in the novel as a socially conscious young
man trying to liberate himself from the psychological shackles of middle-
class mentality. He goes to the front, and his fiancée is befriended by
Clara Andreyevna, who admonishes her, 'You must give me a girl as a
present!' 'What girl?' 'A girl! I do not want a boy. Boys go to war and leave
their mothers behind. Trust my experience! Give me a girl!' 'But I am not
married,' the bewildered young woman replies. 'All the more reason for

it,' Clara argues heatedly. 'You are going to marry my son, aren't you? You must tell him that I want a girl. He would not disobey his mother's wish.'

The episode reflects Michael's childhood. He was born third in the *troika* of boys—I in 1894, Vladimir in 1895, and Michael in 1897. My mother was disappointed when her last child turned out to be another boy. She wanted a girl, and so she dressed Michael in girl's clothes and braided his long hair in girlish fashion. When Michael went to grade school, his long braid (then about 16 inches) had to be cut. I kept it in a confectionary box for many years. When I visited Russia in 1935, the subject came up. 'It was a case of child abuse,' Michael remarked grimly.

Maxim Gorky praised Michael's portrayal of Clara Andreyevna. 'This is an original and vivid character,' he wrote. 'She overshadows all others in the book. Two or three colourful strokes and she would have become a truly tragic figure, for the most tragic loneliness is the loneliness of a mother.' Michael never told my mother about Gorky's letter, which was not published until long after her death. How she would have gloried in this praise by a famous Russian writer! How she would have prized Gorky's words that a mother's loneliness is the most tragic of all lonely lives! This was her own constant refrain. 'When you mock your mother,' she used to say, 'You spit in your own face.' My mother saw Michael for the last time in Paris in 1927, when he visited there with his young wife.

In 1935, armed with my newly acquired American passport, I was able to visit Russia as a tourist. I found Russia little changed from what it had been before the Revolution. Urban transportation in Leningrad and Moscow was still provided by horse-drawn carriages presided over by bearded coachmen wielding reinforced knouts over their bedraggled beasts. Taxicabs were few and difficult to get. There were no private automobiles. It was impossible to imagine that a couple of decades later Russia would make history by launching the first artificial satellite into space, and that Moscow would build the prettiest city metro system. Was the Russian soul really transformed by the Revolution?

After this first journey into my Russian past, I maintained contact with my brothers through correspondence. The elder, Alexander, was a passionate Pushkinist. By a curious whim of fate, his wife, Lida, was a direct descendant of Pushkin's sister Olga. He wrote to me from Leningrad on 17 May 1939:

Lida is immersed in the history of her ancestors in the Pushkin family, and she fell in love with her great-great grandfather, Sergei Pushkin. She copied all of Sergei Pushkin's correspondence with Olga Pushkina, his daughter, a sister of the poet. In one of her letters, Olga expresses her concern about the pregnancy of her daughter, Nadia (Lida's grandmother). The fruit of this pregnancy was

Elena, Lida's mother. Thus a direct line is established between Pushkin's sister Olga and my own Lida!

Both of my brothers, Alexander and Michael, had sons. Michael's son Sergei was to become a well-known Soviet composer of operas, symphonies and numerous other works. But Alexander's son, Vladimir, became a victim of tuberculosis, and died at the age of 20. Alexander was disconsolate in his loss. He even gave way to superstition. Could it be, he asked himself, that the very name Vladimir, that of our brother who also died of tuberculosis at the age of 20, had doomed his own son? Both were called Vova, rather than the more common Volodia. The young Vladimir was a talented caricaturist; Alexander sent me some of his drawings because, as he said, I was the most secure member of our family and could be counted on to preserve such memorabilia. He also sent me a detailed chronicle of the life and death of Vova, or, as he affectionately called him, Vovotchka. The chronicle comprised six letters. Some of them arrived with cuts made by the Soviet censor: the war was still raging on the Russian front, as it was in the West. Here are the most arresting excerpts:

Monday, 10 July 1944. Moscow:
Our boy is no longer with us. He left us a week ago. The death sentence hung over us for a year and a half; the diagnosis was that of tuberculosis of both kidneys and of the bladder. But in May we were told that only one kidney was affected. A dazzling ray of light! The doctors, the best specialists here, announced the happy verdict: He will live! He will be totally cured! On June 6 he was operated upon to remove the bad kidney. The operation was successful; the remaining kidney worked well.

21 July 1944. Moscow:
It takes six or seven months for postal communication between Russia and America, so I cannot expect your answer earlier than a year and a half from now. There was no telegram from you. Why? I sent a telegram congratulating you on your 50th birthday. That was during the time of hope, when the doctors promised complete recovery. The catastrophe came as a sudden blow. Lida and I live in a strange state. We perform the necessary vital functions, we get the necessary ration cards, we eat, we sleep, but all this is like an exercise in somnambulism. The worst is that our boy, with his voice, with his smile, with his little jokes, recedes farther and farther away into memory.

28 July 1944. Moscow:
My letters take months to arrive. They may turn out to be posthumous. I will try to recall the events by fragments. On 3 December 1941 a bomb fell near our house in Leningrad. It was a time bomb, with a delayed action. Vovotchka was at military exercises. Suddenly there was a tremendous shock. A bomb fell some ten yards behind our house. I went to see. There was a hole in the snow surrounded

by chunks of frozen soil. We were told to leave the house. I had suitcases ready for such an emergency, but we had to wait for Vovotchka. He came in and became very angry at our cowardice in running away. We went to Lida's mother for the night. The bomb exploded around midnight. Greatest damage was done to my workroom; the bookshelves collapsed, with all my books and manuscripts falling into a heap. Still, I decided not to interrupt my course of lectures, in spite of lack of strength on account of malnutrition. I even gave a talk on the advantages of refraining from food for intellectual progress, citing the experience of hunger training by hermits in the desert. Indeed, I rarely felt such an elevation of spirit, such a winged sense of being. Students begged me not to cancel my course even during air raids. And so my lectures continued to the accompaniment of falling bombs.

18 June 1947. Moscow:
Today I went to the cemetery. The memorial plate is ready. We managed to obtain some marble for it, and the cost was moderate, only three and a half thousand rubles. The inscription reads, 'Thy Will Be Done. V.A. Slonimsky—25 III 1923—3 VII 1944. Last of descendants of Olga Pushkina, the poet's sister. Defender of Leningrad during the siege.' A Greek Orthodox cross is engraved between the letters.

In 1940, while the war was going on in Russia and France, Julia succeeded in moving with her young son Mitia to Portugal, where she found some work to do on Portuguese folklore. But she kept sending agonized appeals to Aunt Isabelle and me to get her out of Europe. She was convinced that Spain and Portugal would eventually fall prey to the Nazis, or join Hitler under pressure; she was aware that, no matter how Christian she was according to her passport and her persuasion, the Nazi test of Jewishness was genetic. The situation was perilous in the extreme, and Aunt Isabelle and I did everything in our power to obtain American visas for Julia and her son.

I went to Washington to testify before the Immigration Panel on her behalf. Oddly enough, the committee asked me about her possible Communist associations, in spite of the fact that she was a contributor to an anti-Soviet *émigré* newspaper. Kerensky, who was by that time in the United States, supplied an affidavit attesting to Julia's correct political stand. When I produced Kerensky's affidavit, a member of the panel asked, 'Was not Kerensky a socialist?' He was reassured by the chairman of the panel that Kerensky's government enjoyed official recognition by the United States. I was then asked whether Aunt Isabelle was ever involved in labour activities. 'I'm afraid not,' I replied. 'Why do you say "afraid not"?' the chairman quickly interjected. 'Well,' I said, 'she is a piano teacher, and has never had any connection with labour organizations.' The chairman consulted his dossier, and asked pointedly, 'Then why is it that the Jewish Free Labor Committee of New York interceded in your sister's behalf, at a specific request of your aunt?' The way he pronounced the word Jewish had a curious undertone of distaste. Other questions betrayed a similar anti-Semitic tilt. 'Is your sister Jewish?' I was asked. I explained that our family was ethnically Jewish, but that we had all been baptized in infancy.

Poor Julia! All her life she tried to exorcise the stigma of her Jewish origin, only to find that it stood in the way of her getting a visa from Christian America.

Julia and her son were ultimately granted their American visas. They travelled on a Portuguese boat from Lisbon. Once in New York, she made contact with the Russian *émigré* newspaper published there and became its constant contributor. The pay was miserable, but better than nothing, and she supplemented her income by teaching Russian at $3 an hour. She loved the very process of teaching, which restored her sense of human dignity.

She also had the good fortune to receive a well-paid contract to write a book on Russian literature for the Chekhov Publishing House in New York, an *émigré* organization financed by the State Department for propaganda purposes. She completed only the first part of her task, which was published in two volumes, a remarkable achievement since history of literature was not her speciality. She hoped to get it translated into English to establish herself as an author in America and worked on it with a British professor of Russian. But his Russian was limited, and her English non-existent, and the project was ultimately abandoned.

As was to be expected, my mother found even less happiness in New York than in Paris or Boston. She soon began bombarding me with letters full of imprecations, accusations, and denunciations. She even reported in melodramatic detail the atrocities inflicted upon her by Julia and Aunt Isabelle. Here are some excerpts translated from the original Russian:

I realize [she wrote to me] that your sister, your aunt, and who knows, perhaps even you, too, want to see me dead. But just to spite you all I refuse to croak. . . .

The darling baby whom we called Newtonchik became the celebrated musician Nicolas Slonimsky. And the more his fame grew, the stronger was his hatred of his mother who was the source of his life. If I had enough strength left in me, I would write a 'Message to My Children' in which your wretched mother, doomed to end her life in total physical and spiritual isolation, would give a commentary on her life in the 'promised land', the United States of America. At first, my celebrated son refused to let me come to live with him, and then did everything in his power to make sure that America would become my grave, so that my death would justify his original refusal to let me in. . . .

I sit down at my typewriter with the greatest reluctance in order to stipulate my wishes regarding the disposition of my body. I do not want to be cremated. I want to be laid in my grave in a decent Christian burial. But I fear that your aunt, making quick calculations with pencil and paper, will decide that cremation is less expensive than burial, and will instruct you accordingly. Naturally, you would not dare to oppose her, not because any pennies saved would land in your pockets, for your pockets are full of holes, but because you will still be owing her money for her past disbursements. I can just imagine her sitting at the table at 2 o'clock in the morning, carefully adding up dollars and cents you owe her for occasional meals you had at her apartment. And she makes thousands of dollars a month! That is why I decided to appoint your wife Dorothy to make proper arrangements for the disposal of my mortal remains. At least I can be sure that she will respect the wishes which my still functioning brain is able to express before I enter the realm of eternal peace. In the meantime, let these few lines serve as directions to act upon, when there will be a sudden telephone call at an odd hour of day or night to announce the inevitable. . . .

I could not close my eyes all night. Just how I manage not to croak is beyond my comprehension. My doctor says that I owe my survival to extreme nervous tension, and this despite my chronic diseases, a gynaecological hernia and kidney ailment, not to mention asthma. Doomsday awaits those who are guilty of amoral conduct! The vengeance is mine; I shall repay. (For God's sake, do not take it personally, for how can I wish evil on a part of my own body? No, this relates only to others.) Vengeance awaits the instigator of this campaign against me, your celebrated but heartless aunt, who is so diligently trying to dig a grave for her 85-year-old sister. But she will not succeed in her design with her serpent fangs and her falsehoods. She even accuses me of telling people her real age. She is now 65 years old, but her passport falsifies the year of her birth, to make her appear younger. When somebody asks, I usually say that she was born after my marriage, that is, after 1880. The sin of telling a lie is hers, not mine. When someone asks me how old I am, I say about 90, even though, thanks to the ministrations of my wonderful family, I look much older. . . .

My mother was not a Christian, while I secretly became a Christian when I was 4 years old. I lived then at my grandmother's place, and she used to take me to church and even to communion on Christian holidays. Our family was not typically Jewish. My great-grandfather even received an honorary citizenship for renting a large area to be farmed by members of the Jewish community without fee, with the sole reservation that they would not engage in liquor trade. Unfortunately, the next generation returned to tavern keeping, and had to sell the land. My youngest uncle Mark made such a good sale that even I got two thousand roubles out of it, though I was already a married woman. Both Mark and another uncle, Zinovy, proposed to me, as did many others in Minsk, but I rejected all offers, because I believed that marriage would ruin my spiritual interests. I enrolled in a school of medicine, and planned to go into the country upon graduation to teach peasant women how not to be slaves. What an interesting, happy life I had then! And I was only 18 or 19 years old. I engaged in fervent debates with my young friends, and preached abolition of economic inequality which made it possible for some people to own carriages while others had to walk barefoot. I even rented a room in a house where prostitutes lived, and tried to persuade them to abandon their shameful profession while there was still time to redeem their lives. My mother was horrified by my radical ideas. She introduced me to one young man after another, hoping that I would select a suitable bridegroom, but I was concerned mainly with education. The poet Minsky, who was a lodger in our house at the time, could not make up his mind whether to court me or my older sister Lisa; eventually he married Lisa's daughter and, after her death, your aunt Zinaïda. To save me from this chaotic environment, my mother decided that I had tuberculosis. She called in a council of doctors (each of whom addressed me as 'my esteemed colleague', because I was a medical student) and I was sent away to a private sanitarium in Dresden, where I was placed under the guidance of a renowned professor. His wife taught me how to cook and to make beds, something I had never done before because we had many servants. When I returned to Russia a year later I was much better adapted to life. I became fascinated with chemistry, which I studied under Professor Borodin. He tried to persuade me to be his assistant after graduation. At that time Borodin was better known as a chemist than as a composer; that was before he met Wagner who converted him definitely to music. And now I cannot even remember the chemical formula for air and water! But I recall Borodin very vividly; he was young and handsome, and I can see him clearly in my imagination. I also remember his lectures in the auditorium of the chemistry building in St Petersburg, with shelves filled with retorts, jars, and various chemical appurtenances. But soon fresh social ideas captivated my youthful comrades. I was quite taken by new ideology, and I found that I could be effective as a public speaker. Following this new trend, I decided to abandon natural sciences and enrol in the newly opened private college where women were admitted. Among the professors was Vladimir Solovyov, your future Godfather. There were several foreign exchange students, mostly Czechs, who taught us Latin, and we taught them Russian. One of them proceeded to read poetry to me instead of Latin, and then without further ado, asked me to marry him. But I was repelled by the very idea of marriage, and turned him down.

To this letter, which started with an exudation of visceral hatred, and ended with reminiscences of her romantic past, my mother appended a piece of verse:

> My hand writes words,
> My soul is in pain,
> My suffering is great,
> I want to run away.
>
> But run away to where?
> There is no safe retreat.
> The Beast is everywhere,
> Just look at it, and flee!

No, wait, a star cries out,
Yes, wait, repeats the moon.
My friendly moon, shine on,
But not on me, for I am old.

Shine on those lovers yonder
While their souls are young.

The 'fateful telephone call' of which my mother warned came in the afternoon of 6 January 1944, from Aunt Isabelle. My wife answered the telephone, and for a few seconds spoke slowly and in a very low tone of voice. (Dorothy never raised the tone of her voice, and the contrast between her conversational habits and those of my mother and other members of my family was such that for years I could not get accustomed to her reaction to events, important and unimportant.) She turned to me and said quietly, 'Your mother is dead.' On the following day I received a letter from Julia, which began with the words, 'When you receive this letter, mother will no longer be among the living.' I went to New York and stayed in Aunt Isabelle's apartment. Together we went to the German pension where my mother lived and collected her papers and other memorabilia. I kept her bifocal glasses and other personal belongings for many years.

No, my mother's body was not cremated. She was buried according to the ritual of the Russian Orthodox Church; an elaborate octagonal cross was engraved on her tombstone, at a surburban cemetery in New York.

For months I could not absorb the finality of the event. Oddly enough, what I missed most were her voluminous letters, her repetitious reproaches and demands. I kept her entire correspondence in a large trunk for many years, until I decided to destroy most of them and save only letters that were of psychological interest.

I sobbed disconsolately, until Dorothy remarked in her quiet but decisive manner that my grief over the death of my old mother was an offence to her. She could not anticipate the immensity of my sorrow when she herself died twenty years and five days after my mother. The accursed month of January still held its mortal sting over me.

Faithful to her promises (and her threats), my mother haunted me in my dreams. As a rule, she appeared to me in her better days, busily talking about her 'important' plans. 'But you must be 120 years old!' I exclaimed in a dream of the summer of 1977. (My chronological awareness never abandons me, even when I am asleep.) In another dream, in the early morning of 19 August 1979, my mother came over quite unexpectedly, and said she was living in Tunis where she had business to transact. Why Tunis? Upon awakening, I tried to recall any association I might have had with Tunis, for ordinarily dreams are mosaics of remembered bits of actuality or recollected memories of such remembrances, but could find none. I begged her not to go back to Tunis, but she said she had to go. I said I would drive her to the airport, and she refused. She had money, she said, and would take a cab. It was a very disquieting dream.

Another remembered dream came on 30 August 1980, at 4 o'clock in the morning. It was so vivid, I had to get up to dispel the vision. I was in the street when two men were helping my mother out of a subway station in New York. She was unconscious, her eyes were open, and there was a smile on her lips. Then suddenly I was in an apartment. A woman came in with a pink receipt which I had to sign in connection with my mother's death. I had to press a large enamel button in the kitchen which said 'Leichen'. This is the German word for corpses, in plural, but German even as a subliminal language is rare in my dreams; furthermore, I could not recall my ever coming across the word *Leichen* in any of my recent readings. Yet, the word was shockingly appropriate in the context of my dream, relating to my mother's corpse. It was a horrifying dream. The hypnopompic period between dream and reality lasted several torturous minutes.

In my subliminal consciousness, Aunt Isabelle continues to be a figure of authority, legislating the code of conduct, criticizing, admonishing, exhorting. If my mother appeared in my dreams as a helpless person reproaching me of neglect, Aunt Isabelle was always the mentor of my conduct. A typical dream is this: I am to play a piano programme in a public recital, and have no idea of what I am to play. Aunt Isabelle sits in the front row with an expression of horror on her face, as I desperately try to find my way through the music.

Meanwhile Aunt Isabelle had become a legend as a piano teacher. The very qualities that aroused such bitterness in my mother's heart—her insistence on doctrinal purity in art and life, her seeming relish in exposing the defensive prevarications of a person caught in the web of dissimulation—became the principal asset of her teaching. Her students could be sure that she would not leave off until every minuscule detail, every nuance, every action of the loud and soft pedal (she was chary of the middle sustaining pedal as a modern affectation) was brought to perfection. Her demand for technical accuracy and proper style of performance contrasted eloquently with the commercialized methods used by piano teachers in 'master classes' who guaranteed success to gullible house-wives and amateur pianists. Aunt Isabelle imposed merciless discipline on her students, no matter how talented. Because of that, or in spite of that, the 'Vengerova stamp' became a mark of distinction. One of her students, a professional piano teacher herself, made monthly trips by train from California for a session with Aunt Isabelle.

At the Curtis Institute of Philadelphia she had celebrated students, among them Leonard Bernstein, Lukas Foss, and Samuel Barber. Bernstein lived in mortal terror of his 'beloved Tyranna', and yet stated that 'the Vengerova influence abides in my playing (when I play well), and I am for ever in her debt'. Barber said in an interview that he had learned more about melody writing from Vengerova than from his composition teachers.

Aunt Isabelle's personality and her teaching left a lasting impression on her students, famous and ordinary. Twenty years after her death, a music magazine conducted a survey of opinions among her former students, eliciting interesting response. Here are some samples: 'I feel that discipline was inseparable from Vengerova's musical and/or technical method.' 'Being "Vengerova-ized" resulted in my becoming aware that it was my responsibility to understand and be able to control at will every physical activity related to technical mastery.' 'Intelligent, vital, sensitive, dedicated.' But there were also negative reports. The dissenters were quite brutal in their criticism of Vengerova's teaching methods: 'Autocratic, didactic, uninspiring, unsympathetic, frequently impatient, perhaps destructive.' 'Poor psychologist, limited in teaching ability, unscientific.' 'Tyrannical, dominant, relentless, awesome, authoritarian, uncompromising, demanding, overpowering.' 'Intimidating, egotistical, sadistic, cold and cruel, Russian paranoid.'

In his 1981 autobiography, *I Really Should Be Practicing*, the American pianist Gary Graffman has a few revealing words to say about Vengerova, his teacher from the age of 9: 'Like most pedagogues of the Russian persuasion, she assigned her students rather heavily edited music.' Graffman was of a new generation that doted on authentic editions free from the arbitrary interpretations of the nineteenth-century editors which were my aunt's main sources. When he brought a copy of such an authentic edition for his lesson, my aunt was disgusted. 'A plague of green locusts on her living room rug could not have upset Vengerova more,' Graffman recalls. She also berated him for indulging in unnecessary body movements while playing. Graffman quotes with obvious relish the remarks she inscribed on the inside cover of his copy of Chopin's *E minor Concerto*, in her 'bold, firm handwriting': 'Watch, your left foot beating time. Your left arm you throw kicking it up. Your posture is too erratic . . .' Graffman adds: 'Vengerova was extremely articulate in several languages, including English, so her regression to this garbled syntax can only mean that she must have been very annoyed indeed.'

In the summer of 1956 Aunt Isabelle made her customary European trip, but had to interrupt it for an urgent operation to correct the occlusion of the bile duct. The diagnosis was ominous: a cancer of the pancreas. The food went through her organism undigested; she rapidly lost weight. When she returned to New York, there was a dark mask of disease on her face. I was horrified when I saw Aunt Isabelle sitting on the bed and caught a glimpse of her legs that were all bone. 'All my life,' she remarked to me, 'I wanted to lose weight [she weighed nearly 200 pounds before her illness], and now I am desperately trying to gain weight.' But determinedly she continued to teach, even when she had to instruct her students from a semi-recumbent position on an armchair. She was never told of her true condition, but everybody else knew. Fortunately for her, cancer of the pancreas was never painful. She expressed her gratitude at the attention that her friends and students paid her. Leonard Bernstein came and cooked a meal for her; Samuel Barber arrived to entertain her with pleasant chit-chat; and so did Lukas Foss and many others. She was strong enough to accompany me to a film, but inevitably her vitality ebbed. I asked her doctor to tell me frankly how long she had left to live. He said three or four months.

Aunt Isabelle had a harmless superstition about the significance of number 7 in her life. She was born on 17 February 1877, according to the Russian calendar, and number 7 also played a role in her remembered meetings with important men in her life. She died in New York on 7 February 1956. As the nearest relative, I had to view her body. Her unseeing eyes were focused on infinity. I could not summon enough courage to close them.

Her funeral was solemnized in New York in a secular ceremony. The Curtis Institute Quartet performed Barber's funereal *Adagio*; Barber himself cried openly. Her obituaries extolled her as a master teacher; the one in the *New York Herald Tribune* used the word 'genius' in its headline.

CHAPTER 18

AMERICA LOVES RUSSIA

A new source of income was opened for me in the post-war years—teaching Russian. The meeting on the Elbe between Russian and American soldiers was the beginning of great friendship between the two victorious allies. Russian boys and girls were busy studying English, and American war veterans were trying to learn Russian. My good friend Professor Samuel Cross spoke Russian like a native and was head of the Slavonic Department at Harvard University. He engaged me to teach a class in advanced Russian, combined with Soviet songs and ballads. I was thrilled. Here at last was an opportunity to do something useful and to get away from the hopeless task of trying to make pianists and composers out of musically retarded individuals. I plunged eagerly into the comparative philology of Russian grammar and syntax, reviving my long dormant passion for linguistics.

The Russian manual I was given as a guide for my class was full of the sort of stilted unidiomatic phraseology and idiotic and ungrammatical concoctions that had stultified language students for years. Disgusted, I decided to compile a manual of my own. I began inventing all kinds of gimmicks, puns, and curiosities to introduce the student into the very heart of the language. For instance, in a session with male students at Harvard, I ventured to tell an off-colour joke about Catherine the Great. The names of her lovers among the palace guardsmen were Longinov, Godunov, Stroganov, and Putiatin. She summoned all of them one night and declared: 'You are long-enough, you are good-enough, you are strong-enough, so put-it-in!' Among other things, I strove to establish the semantic values of verbal prefixes. I discovered that some Russian prefixes closely corresponded to those in Latin, French and English. Thus the prefix 'pro' attached to a Russian root changes the meaning of the verb similarly to those in English and French. For instance, the 'pro' of prophet bespeaks divination. In Russian, the same prefix appears in the work 'prorok', meaning prophet, the second syllable being an ancient Russian root signifying speech. I found that 'ob' implies circumscription, or any circular motion, and that 'pri' denotes adhesion and performs the same function as a Latin-derived word having the prefix 'ad'. 'Pred' means 'before' and corresponds to the Latin-derived 'pre'. Thus, 'pred-log' means preposition, the Russian 'log' connoting the action of laying down, or placing in position.

I perceived a didactic value in giving students the roots of nouns or verbs and letting them form new words constructivistically with the aid of prefixes that function as modifiers. Thus, taking the word 'pisat' which means 'write', a student can derive from it a number of words of related meanings. For translations into English, the Latin-derived root 'scribe' should be used. Thus, 'o-pisat' means 'de-scribe'; 'perepisat' means 'again-scribe' (copy); 'predpisat' means 'pre-scribe'; 'pripisat' means 'a-scribe', etc. I was fascinated by the precision with which this scheme seemed to work. And, given the extraordinary wealth of Russian verbal tenses and such grammatical moods as frequentative, intermittent, and tentative, an interested student could form dozens of verbal forms without memorizing by rote.

On the eve of my first semester at Harvard, Samuel Cross, who had just divorced his wife and was about to marry his librarian–secretary, went to the campus doctor for a check-up and collapsed of a fatal heart attack. As a result, his assistants, myself included, had to take over his classes. I mourned Cross, but my mind brimmed with novel ideas concerning Russian grammar and syntax. Much of my philological euphoria stemmed from my own ignorance of the science of languages, but I was convinced that I could teach Russian, or Latin, or French, or Spanish for that matter, more effectively than a specialist. Adding to my euphoria was a salary the like of which I had not commanded since my Rochester years.

For tests in translation, I used the Russian transcripts of the Nuremberg trials, then in progress. My enthusiasm was soon deflated, however, when I found that most of my students were woefully lacking in any kind of linguistic sense. The greatest shock came when it dawned on me that they were not even sure about English. One of my students, translating from Russian, read: 'Then the Nazi criminals received their impunity.' 'But they were hanged!' I exclaimed. 'That's what I mean,' the student countered. 'They got their impunity!' 'Wait a minute!' I cried. 'What is impunity?' 'Why, punishment!' was his answer. Another time a student asked me to translate a tricky Russian word. 'Cryptic,' I said. A pause ensued. 'What is cryptic?' 'Cryptic? Why, it's enigmatic.' 'What is en. . . enmatic?' 'Enigmatic,' I corrected professorially, 'means arcane, recondite.' A general outburst of laughter relieved the tension.

Translators from Russian into English were much in demand in the early post-war years. Practically anyone who took a quickie course in Russian at Columbia or Harvard could get a government job translating for visiting

Soviet dignitaries. Many of these translators were plainly incompetent, but on the Soviet side, too, there was a dearth of qualified translators. *Traduttore, traditore*! When Khrushchev came on his first visit to the United States, he used the services of Oleg Troyanovsky, the son of the Soviet ambassador, and himself the future Soviet ambassador to the United Nations, who studied at an American college and spoke English fluently. He lamentably lacked the capacity of correlating the two languages, however, especially in subtler shadings of meaning. At a news conference, Khrushchev was asked when the Russians planned to send a man to the moon. Troyanovsky translated, using the verb 'zabrosit' which means roughly 'to toss over'. Khrushchev went into a self-righteous tantrum. 'We do not toss men over!' he screamed. 'When our scientists tell us that we are ready to send a man to the moon, we will do so.' Then pointing a finger at the chairman of the conference, he imperiously instructed Troyanovsky: 'Tell him not to use a word like *zabrosit*. Tell him to say *poslat*, send!' When *The New York Times* published a verbatim transcript of the conference, it failed to point out that it was the translator's use of the wrong word that had triggered Khrushchev's explosion.

Americans did no better. When a group of Soviet composers, among them Shostakovich, Kabalevsky, and Khrennikov, came to the United States in 1959, the State Department, which was in charge of providing translators, chose an authentic Russian prince for the job. At a reception given by officials of Broadcast Music Inc., Shostakovich was asked by one of those present if he would accept an invitation to a private party that night. Shostakovich said he was sorry, but he was going to see *Madama Butterfly*. The prince translated: 'Mr Shostakovich regrets but he has an appointment with Mrs Butterfly tonight.' At that point I had to intervene. The prince, whose breath betrayed a liberal consumption of alcohol, apologized and explained that he did not know much about music.

I was recruited to serve as a simultaneous translator for the network broadcast of a meeting between American and Russian composers, and received an accolade from *The New York Times* for my expertise. I also did some professional translating jobs; among these was a three-volume edition of Russian songs, from Glinka to Shostakovich, for which I provided English texts. I made it a point not to allow a single deviation from the number of notes of the original, so that the original rhythm was preserved.

Among other Russian jobs I undertook was a translation of the memoirs of Gretchaninoff, the venerable Russian composer who emigrated to America and died in New York in 1956 at the age of 91. Ordinarily, I would have declined such a chore, but Gretchaninoff wrote me a poignant letter asking me to grant his last wish to see his autobiography published in English. This was a powerful appeal, for Gretchaninoff was, along with Tchaikovsky and Rimsky-Korsakov, a part of my musical consciousness. In New York he was like a phantom from a vanished world. When he went to see Schirmer about publication of his songs, Schirmer exclaimed, 'My God! I thought you were dead!' Psychologically, Gretchaninoff was still in old Russia. 'They are all foreigners here,' he complained about New York. He was perplexed by the English language. On the margin of the proofs of his memoirs he wrote: 'Nichevo nye ponimayu!' 'Nothing no understand!'

The memoirs were originally published by the Russian *émigré* press in Paris. In order to check on my translation, Gretchaninoff took a ruler and measured the length of his introductory note in the Russian edition and the corresponding section of my translation. 'You cut it down!' he observed reproachfully. 'No, I didn't,' I said. 'English words are generally much shorter than their Russian equivalents. For instance, you say in your foreword that you were always *zastyenchivyi*; in English it is *shy*. Or take the word *chelovyekonyenavistnichestvo*; in English it is *hate*. That is why it comes out shorter in translation.' Gretchaninoff sighed. 'Well, if you had to cut it, there is nothing to be done about it.'

International mistranslations have become part of the language into which they were fed. Many are from the Bible. The camel that has a better chance of passing through the eye of the needle (than a rich man of entering Heaven) is not a dromedary but the brand name of a thick rope of Biblical times. When the Soviet Cosmonaut Titov orbited the earth, and announced his code word 'Ya oryol' ('I am Eagle'), American editorial writers interpreted this identification as a case of soaring conceit and drew invidious comparisons between the modest American astronauts and the cocky Russians. But 'Eagle' was the name of Titov's spacecraft, 'oryol', containing the sonorous liquid consonants 'r' and 'l', and the diphthong 'Yo', phonetic elements that make the identification sound very clear. The practice is not dissimilar to the American use of the confirming word 'Roger', the two r's of the word making it aurally unmistakable.

My friendly association with various Russian interests during the war got me into trouble with the pervasive patriots of the McCarthy stripe. My treasonable conduct was well substantiated. I contributed several articles on Russian music to the *Christian Science Monitor*, and my report on the 'Leningrad' Symphony of Shostakovich was reprinted by the *New Masses*, a publication which was on the subversive list of the Attorney General. I found myself the focus of attention of the self-styled 'Communist for the FBI', one Matt Cvetic. In a speech given before the Optimist Club of Pittsburgh on 26 August 1952, he boasted of having helped to uproot 'the infected tree of Communism in Western Pennsylvania, nourished by pinkos, sympathizers, fellow travellers and apologists for Communism'. To bolster evidence of my own subversive activities, Cvetic adduced a quotation from the 5 May 1938 issue of the *Daily Worker*, 'an official publication of the Communist Party of the United States', which announced that I was to speak on Soviet music at the Progressive Labor School in Boston. As if that were not enough, I was also to be a speaker on 8 February 1941 at a symposium on the Dean of Canterbury's book, *Soviet Power*, to be held under the auspices of the Progressive Bookshop in Boston. And what was that Progressive Bookshop? Why, 'a distribution point for Communist literature', Cvetic informed his audience. As to the Dean of Canterbury, he was the notorious Rev. Hewlett Johnson, the so-called 'Red Dean of Canterbury', who openly preached kindness towards the Soviet Union. Actually the Red Dean never made it to the Progressive Bookshop due to the uncertainties of transatlantic travel in wartime, but the occasion was dedicated to him nevertheless, and I played pieces by Prokofiev and Shostakovich in his honour. 'The question may arise as to what music has to do with public affairs,' Cvetic conceded, 'but let us remember that Nero fiddled while Rome burned.' Was I Nero incarnate? No, but 'Slonimsky, for your information, was born in St Petersburg, Russia, came to the United States, and was naturalized'. However, thanks to Cvetic's vigilance, I was to be rendered harmless. Cvetic wired the US Senator Pat McCarran, chairman of the Senate Judiciary Committee on Internal Security, urging him to review my pro-Communist record, and, should it be found that I had violated the McCarran Act, to take steps to denaturalize and deport me. The McCarran Committee apparently was not impressed by Cvetic's accusations, and no steps were taken to have me banished.

Ironically, while I was under suspicion of being un-American, my younger brother Michael, on the opposite side of the globe, was assailed by the Soviet reactionary element as being un-Russian. His position was of course immeasurably more dangerous. I could expose my accusers to ridicule, but Michael had no such recourse. At the time of publication of his novel, *The Lavrovs*, which reflected the proper Bolshevik attitude towards the decadence of the intellectual class, he had been attacked by the Soviet literary establishment for failing to mention the name of Stalin in his book. But how could he? His novel described an early period of the Revolution when Stalin was virtually unknown except as a participant in some bank 'expropriations' in his native Caucasus. Just the same, Michael had to make amends; in the second edition of the book he introduced the character of a young revolutionary worker who informed his literary *alter ego* of Stalin's important work in Georgia. But Michael had something else to account for. He was editor-in-chief of a monthly literary magazine, in which he published short stories by the prime Soviet satirist Zoshchenko and some lyric poems by the great Russian poetess Anna Akhmatova. But both Zoshchenko and Akhmatova were at that time declared inimical to the ideals of the State, one for his biting representation of Soviet reality, the other for her 'rootless' poetry. As a consequence, Michael was sharply criticized for giving space to these writers and was removed from his post as editor. The attacks were unfair, for in our conversations Michael said time and again that he was a Communist in every sense except for actual membership of the party. Still his loyalty to friends did not allow him to denounce Zoshchenko, even though Zoshchenko himself urged him to do so in self-defence.

Michael was eventually rehabilitated and was able to resume his literary activities. He died in 1972, at the age of 75, of lung cancer—he was an inveterate cigarette smoker. There were laudatory obituaries in the Soviet press. There was also an obituary notice in *The New York Times*; in fact, that is where I learned of his death. The facts were reported correctly, but undue emphasis was put on Michael's attempts to square himself with the Soviet establishment. Every Soviet writer, every Soviet artist, had to dissimulate in this manner. At least Michael was not forced to write a penitential letter to the Central Committee of the Communist Party, as many others were, among them Shostakovich.

As for Matt Cvetic, his career in hunting subversives came to an inglorious end. He was confined for a time in an alcoholic ward, and then moved to California. He died there of a heart attack in 1962, while taking a driving test in Hollywood.

Despite Cvetic's failure to have me exiled, I did attract the attention of the Federal Bureau of Investigation. One fine morning I received a visit from two well-groomed young men, one blond and one dark-haired, who introduced themselves by turning over the lapels of their coats in perfect synchronization to display shiny buttons with the letters FBI. I could not suppress a chuckle, for the scene forcefully reminded me of a grade-B spy film. My visitors asked my permission to ask me a few questions. Was Nicolas Slonimsky my real name? Only a lunatic would select such an unpronounceable name for a pseudonym, I said, and reeled off some of the variants of my name proffered by postmen, telephone operators, and salesmen. Was I ever recruited into the Communist Party? No, I would never join a political or religious group that required unquestioned obedience to a rigid ideology. Did I believe in the Communist cause? Not in the manner practised by Stalin, I said, but I could imagine being in favour of a commune, modelled after the Christian communes, before Christianity was taken over by fanatics of the Inquisition and pogrom makers of the Russian Czardom. I was about to expatiate further on my social philosophy when the blonde agent asked me when I last spoke at a local chapter of the Committee for American–Soviet Friendship. It must have been shortly after the promulgation of the infamous resolution of the Central Committee of the Communist Party of the USSR in February 1948 which damned Shostakovich, Prokofiev, and others for composing music disliked by party members, I replied. Did I remember exactly the date of my talk? In April, I volunteered, 'Yes, 8 April,' the blond FBI man concurred, without even consulting the dossier which he held in his hands. He had done his homework well. The dark-haired agent pointed at a drawing on the wall: 'Is that Electra?' Once more I was struck by the thoroughness of their research. I was beginning to enjoy our interchange, and kept my hapless inquisitors for hours until they were relieved to escape. As Electra phrased it, 'You certainly put those Feds to flight!'

Years later I reminisced about the affair with Aaron Copland. 'It is very funny now,' he said, 'but it wasn't funny then.' Copland had had a really serious confrontation with the witch-hunters and was even called into the presence of Joe McCarthy himself. McCarthy did not seem particularly interested in Copland's own subversive activities. He wanted the names of State Department officials who had arranged Copland's South American trip in 1946. Copland refused to talk, and, after consultation, Joe McCarthy decided not to cite him for contempt. But when the National Symphony in Washington programmed Copland's *Lincoln Portrait* as part of a concert on Eisenhower's first presidential inauguration, a Congressman stood up and declared that there were many 'patriotic composers' free of Copland's 'dubious associations' who could contribute a work for the occasion. *Lincoln Portrait* was taken off the programme.

It was during these times that Wallingford Riegger was brought before the New York branch of the House Committee for Un-American Activities on a charge that he was a recruiter for the Communist Party for the sector between 23rd and 60th Streets in Manhattan; the specific topography of his alleged activities suggested the work of an informer. Riegger refused to dignify his accusers with an answer. Instead, he launched upon an impassioned speech that deserves inclusion in the anthologies of patriotic orations. His forebears came to America and toiled on the soil in the prairies of Kansas territory, he declared, when the fathers of the members of the Committee that interrogated him were still obedient subjects of the Austro-Hungarian Empire. Indeed, the roster of the Committee bristled with names of Czech and Croatian origin.

Another composer who stood up for his rights as an American was Roy Harris. In 1951 the Pittsburgh Symphony Orchestra scheduled a performance of his Fifth Symphony, dedicated to 'the heroic and freedom-loving people of our great ally, the Union of Soviet Socialist Republics'. This rubbed against the grain of local patriots, and they demanded that Harris rescind the dedication. Harris refused and went before the local chapter of the American Legion in Pittsburgh to tell them that he was born on Lincoln's birthday in Lincoln county in the State of Oklahoma, and that all his works are devoted to American ideals. 'We are not asking the Russians to return the weapons we sent them during the war, and there is no reason why we should take back the music we dedicated to them,' he said. The Fifth Symphony, with dedication, was duly performed on the scheduled date. The frustrated patriots appealed to the audience to 'sit on their hands' and not applaud after the performance. Their advice produced the opposite result: the symphony was roundly applauded, and Roy Harris took several bows.

CHAPTER 19

I, DIASKEUAST!

I picked up the word 'diaskeuast' in a crossword puzzle. Like all scientific-looking words, it is made up of Greek components, dia, meaning through (as in diaper), and -skeuazein, meaning to prepare. A diaskeuast is a person who prepares, a redactor, an editor, a researcher, a dictionary maker, a lexicographer.

My travails in diaskeutic lore began with the discovery of the rich archives of Philip Hale preserved in the Music Division of the Boston Public Library. It was there that I found the apparently authentic account of the origin of the catch-phrase 'Three B's of Music', picked up from a German magazine in the 1890s. Hans von Bülow, the famous German conductor who possessed a caustic wit, was asked which of Beethoven's symphonies he prized most. The *Eroica*, he replied, for it has three B's in the key signature—for Bach, Beethoven, and Brahms. His interlocutor suggested that Haydn could join the three B's by modulating from E-flat major through B-natural (H in German nomenclature), to the key of C minor, which, incidentally, is the tonality of Beethoven's Fifth Symphony.

Scavenging further in the American, British, German, and French music magazines which were available in the Boston Public Library, I felt like a time traveller into the pluperfect of music. All those mustachioed tenors and gorgeously coiffed ample-bosomed divas, all those rose-cheeked violinists and ornamentally coiffured pianists, whose glamorous images graced the covers of commercial music journals—what happened to them? What happened to that smiling young Dutchman named Christian Kriens who made his début in the quadruple capacity of violinist, pianist, conductor, and composer all in the same concert, and for whom *Musical America* predicted a brilliant future? No, it cannot be! An item in the same periodical twenty years later headlined: 'Composer Kills Himself After He Loses Job as Arranger for the Hartford Radio Station.' Yes, it was that selfsame happy Dutchman who could compose, play the piano and conduct, but who could not get a job. And what happened to that individual who returned from a 'highly successful concert tour' and was now willing to 'accept a limited number of especially talented students'? My favourite advertiser was a voice teacher whose dignified picture displayed him with his neatly trimmed sideburns, with just a soupçon of fraud in his eyes. His particular business was to sell siphon bottles of genuine compressed Neapolitan air, which he had collected during his regular summer trips to Naples, and which he offered for a reasonable price of a dollar a piece, complete with a guarantee that inhaling a whiff of this magic Italian air would create an instant *bel canto*.

I collected minutiae of this quaint lore, added some parerga and paralipomena from other sources, and threw the resultant tossed salad into the format of a book. David Ewen, who went into publishing for a brief time, artfully arranged the material into chapters and published it in 1947 under the title *A Thing or Two About Music*. Some librarians grumbled mutedly about the lack of an index, quoting Lord Campbell who boasted that he 'proposed to bring a bill into Parliament to deprive of copyright anyone publishing a book without an index'. But my little book sold reasonably well. My whimsical friend William Lichtenwanger, editor for the *Music Library Notes*, asked me if I would review the book myself. Naturally, I agreed, and subjected my compilation to merciless criticism, citing egregious errors and inconsistencies. Everybody thought my signature was a misprint.

As a schoolboy, I had invariably been impressed by the list of errata appended at the end of important-looking tomes. How did the editors know right from wrong in these lists? I stood in awe before books published in German in Gothic type, which to me personified the last word in science. And I particularly savoured the galley proofs of books before publication; there I entered the inner sanctum of great minds at work. I recall how deeply impressed I was when an editorial assistant in Paris showed me the proofs of a novel which had been submitted to Anatole France for review, in which the great master of French diction changed the word 'base' to 'fondation'. Anatole France always preferred Latin-derived words to those of Greek extraction. I was shocked by a street pamphlet issued by a group of French Futurists after Anatole France died, with a sacrilegious caption under his picture, 'Rien qu'un cadavre de plus.'

I remember how deeply I admired A. Eaglefield Hull's *Dictionary of Modern Music and Musicians* published in London in 1924. But upon close examination I began noticing strange things. Were Vitold Malishefsky and Witold Maliszewski, born in the same Russian town two months apart in 1873 and both students of Rimsky-Korsakov, a pair of bifurcated twins? They were not. They were one and the same person; the presence of two separate entries in that dictionary was the result of sloppy editing; the biography was obviously commissioned to two contributors, a Russian and a Pole, and the text and the spelling were not coordinated. On the other hand, two different French composers, Omer Letorey and Pierre Henri Ernest Letorey, became coalesced into one. I noticed also that, while Gustav Mahler married Alma Mahler in 1904, she married him in an adjoining entry in 1902. Instances of prenatal musical activities abounded; the entry on David Popper, born in 1876, contained a reference to his tour as a cello virtuoso from 1868 to 1873.

I was shocked to find out that Eaglefield Hull committed suicide after the publication of his book *Music: Classical, Romantic and Modern*, which turned out to be an assemblage of bits and scraps pilfered without acknowledgment from various other books. Percy A. Scholes took credit for driving Hull to self-destruction: 'Hull's suicide was a result of my exposure of his thefts in his book,' Scholes wrote to me. 'He threw himself under a train.'

Scholes was one of the greatest artists of the musical pen. He was also stubborn. In his *Oxford Companion to Music* he deplored the separation in the two English-speaking nations as far as American music terminology was concerned. He claimed, for instance, that Americans used the word 'cancel' for a natural. I told him that no American musician ever used the word cancel. To convince him I queried a number of American composers and teachers, among them Arthur Shepherd and Walter Piston. None was familiar with the term. But then a postcard came from Warren Storey Smith, who taught music theory at the New England Conservatory, amending his previous disavowal of 'cancel'. 'Doggone it,' he wrote. 'I remembered that in high school we did use the word cancel, even though the teacher always said that natural was the proper term.' I forwarded Smith's postcard to Scholes. His response was characteristic. 'What's doggone?' he asked.

Another bone of contention between Scholes and American writers on music was the term 'bar' vs. 'measure'. Scholes asserted that Americans do not use the word 'bar', while conceding that the alleged American usage is more logical, since a bar is a vertical line, while a measure is horizontal. To disabuse him of this notion, I sent him a copy of the American boogie-woogie classic, 'Beat me, Daddy, Eight to the Bar'. He finally yielded to my persuasion, and changed the entry in subsequent editions of his *Oxford Companion* to read that Americans, too, occasionally used the word 'bar' for 'measure'. Still another controversy resolved around the word record. Scholes complained that Americans used exclusively 'disc' for 'record'. I sent him an entire section of *The New York Times* on phonograph records, not on phonograph 'discs', and he accepted the equivalence of the two designations.

In 1939 I became a contributor and associate editor of Oscar Thompson's *International Cyclopedia of Music and Musicians*. I entered Oscar Thompson's bestiary at the time when he was preparing the first edition of his tome. In his office I beheld a prolixity of young men and women busily copying bits of misinformation from such tainted sources as Hull's *Dictionary of Modern Music and Musicians*, the obsolete 1926 edition of *Grove's Dictionary of Music* and other flawed reference works. The galley proofs of the *Cyclopedia* were already coming in. Somewhat sheepishly, Thompson asked me whether I could conveniently go over the entries for the letter R. How much time did I have? I asked. He looked at the office clock and said that the printer was coming in a couple of hours. I swallowed hard. 'Rybner,' I exclaimed silently. The name was that of a Danish composer who spelled it with a cypher over the u in Denmark, with an umlaut in Germany where most of his works were published, and Ruebner elsewhere. He had changed his name to Rybner when he came to America. Realizing that Thompson's helpers were copying indiscriminately from several conflicting sources, I looked up Ruebner, Rubner and Rybner in the proofs. Sure enough, all three alternatives were there. I killed off Ruebner and Rubner, corrected some errors in the entry on Rybner, and moved on.

Going over the galleys covering other letters of the alphabet in Thompson's tome, I found an interesting remark in the entry on polonaise that Mozart was influenced by Schubert in writing his own polonaises; it should have been Schobert. Philippe de Vitry appeared in triplicate, under Phillipe, under De, and under Vitry, all with different dates depending on which particular dictionary Thompson's apprentices (I almost said accomplices) were copying. Then there was an Australian musician, R. G. Davy, listed in Eaglefield Hull's *Dictionary* with cryptic abbreviations that gave no clue as to the gender of the subject. Thompson's volume added the third person singular 'he' to pinpoint R. G. Davy's sex. But R. G. Davy was a woman!

The most startling phenomenon in Thompson's opus was that of posthumous artificial insemination. If we were to believe that Johan Peder Hartmann, whose dates were 1805–1900, was indeed a son of Johan Ernst Hartmann, who died in 1793, as Thompson's volume indicated, he must have been sired from the grave. This genetic misconception was the result of mindless copying from *Grove's* by Thompson's 'Grove-diggers'. Grove listed musical families under a common heading in chronological order, whereas Thompson rearranged them in alphabetical order. In doing so, his people failed to adjust the references to the antecedents, with surprising results. I wrote to Thompson pointing out that artificial insemination was not perfected in the eighteenth century, and he had a good laugh over it. Accordingly, he changed 'son of the preceding' to 'grandson of the preceding', but unfortunately left in the reference 'a pupil of the preceding', so that it appeared in the next edition that, while the old man did not exactly sire his grandson, he nevertheless taught him music from beyond the grave. It was too late for me to write another letter to Thompson. He had died in his sleep in 1946, leaving me in sole charge of the entire kith and caboodle as Editor-in-Chief.

What Grove-digging could do to the unwary was demonstrated by the mishap befallen to Marion Bauer (Varèse called her 'une pipi crystallisée'). In her book, *How Music Grew*, she wrote with a fine display of tangential wit: 'Bach, who must have been a prodigious walker, walked three hundred miles to hear Johann Buxtehude (1600–1675) play the organ.' Indeed he must have been a prodigious walker to walk eleven years before he was born. The supernatural walk was a result of Marion Bauer's copying the dates of Buxtehude *père* instead of Buxtehude *fils* in *Grove's* which lists both Buxtehudes under the same heading.

In 1950 Eric Blom commissioned me to write articles on American composers for the fifth edition of the monumental *Grove's Dictionary*. I gladly accepted, but through my tendency of supererogation began finding all sorts of things that were wrong with the basic *Grove's*. Blom had a reputation for being a cantankerous person who stuck to his ingrained prejudices, but in our prolonged correspondence he revealed himself as a man of infinite charm. In view of his obsession with precise biographical data, I was surprised to discover that the place of his own birth was not given in *Grove's*. I asked him about it, and he answered my query with unexpected candour. 'I wish you had never asked me where I was born,' he wrote in a most serious vein. He was born in Bern, he explained, but it was a mere accident, owing to his mother's unintentionally prolonged stay in Switzerland. He had not a drop of Swiss blood in his veins. If there had been any admixture of non-English blood in him, it came from remote Danish ancestors.

Inadvertently I became the cause of considerable trouble to Blom. His edition of *Grove's Dictionary* carried the death date of the English violinist Marie Hall; yet I was unable to find her obituary in the agony columns of the London *Times*. I addressed an inquiry to the editor of the British violin magazine the *Strad*; my letter was duly published, and in its wake I received no fewer than eleven communications from various members of the family of Marie Hall assuring me that not only was she very much alive but that she was also active professionally as a concert violinist and teacher in London. What I did not realize was that publication of damaging information, even without malice aforethought, is a legal offence in Great Britain. Hall's solicitors filed a suit against Blom and his publishers for the loss of her trade among organizations which did not care to use the services of a cadaver. I have no idea how it was settled, but I felt terrible about the whole affair. Blom himself could not remember where he had got this premature date on Hall, but thought it was from the venerable British musicologist Fellowes. 'And Fellowes is certainly dead,' Blom asserted. 'I attended his funeral.' Marie Hall died shortly after the notification of her death in *Grove's*, and Blom himself died a couple years after her.

Busy as he was, Blom was capable of maintaining active correspondence on such inconsequential matters as the place of birth of Kaikhosru Sorabji, a remarkable composer of Parsi heritage who described his own formidable *Opus Clavicembalisticum* in a letter to me as the 'greatest and most important work for piano since *Art of the Fugue*'. Blom wrote to me on 23 March 1952:

'I have something to add about Sorabji—an afterthought that has occurred to me, in the middle of the night, as such things do. I suddenly remembered that years ago he told me he was born either at Chelmsford or at Chingford (both in Essex). I am afraid I had forgotten which, and when it came to putting his birthplace in my Everyman's Dictionary, I must have even forgotten that I had forgotten and put Chelmsford without giving the matter another thought. So it now occurs to me that it was I who started that error, and that I thus misled you (which I regret), Scholes (which I don't particularly) and who knows how many other people. . . . This is good enough for *Grove's*, where it shall be Chingford. But is it good enough for you? I hope so, for I am so busy that I hesitate taking further steps to get just one place-name right in *Grove's*, especially when I am so sure that it is right if I make it Chingford. I could, I suppose, go to Epping and find out whether it is true that the registry for Chingford was (and perhaps is) there. The place is really in 'greater' London and now has a station on one of the extensions of the tube trains. But they go a terrifically long way out nowadays, some of them some twenty miles in either direction, so that it would take me at least half a day to get there, make my inquiry and come back. Perhaps you will understand why I am not jumping at the journey. But do tell me if you think it is really desirable.

A charming letter, which I enjoyed no end.

Rather than undertake a journey to Epping or some other putative birthplace of the ineffable Sorabji, I wrote to London for his birth certificate, and received official notice that he was indeed born in Chingford, confirming Blom's surmise. I also learned, to my surprise, that he was born Leon Dudley and not Kaikhosru. I immediately communicated my findings to Blom. He wrote back that he had known all along about Leon Dudley, but advised me strongly against putting this information into print. Were I to do so, Blom warned, Sorabji would take the first plane to America and personally assassinate me. I took the chance.

Paradoxically, Blom combined in his mind a pedantic attention to

unimportant minutiae and singular inattention to facts in his own dictionary. When I pointed out to him that his dates for the Polish pianist Schulz-
Evler were all incorrect, he dismissed the complaint by saying that he
would never deliberately give Schulz-Evler and his ilk a niche in *Grove's*.
But in the very next letter he wrote: 'Believe it or not, Schulz-Evler is
actually allowed to defile one of those pages in *Grove's*, but as we are going
to have something over 8,000, perhaps that blot on one of them will not
look too glaring.'

Then there was the case of Helen Traubel, the singer who preferred to
be born quite a few years after the actual event. She was careless enough
to select St Louis as her birthplace, the city which preserved the
Napoleonic Code long after the sale of the Louisiana Territory to the
United States, with registers of births and deaths still open to anyone.
This enabled me to establish her real year of birth, 1899. I sent a copy of
her birth certificate to Blom. He wrote back:

The appearance in London of Helen Traubel (*must* I go hear her?) reminds me
that she is one of the people who would not give their birthdate. Geiringer did an
article on her and he was unsuccessful about this. I rather suspect he was
intimidated by her. I expect you have dug up this date long ago, and I don't see
why she should get away with it, and I don't mind a bit facing the music if she does
complain.

Blom urged me to continue sending corrections, 'whatever heart-
burnings you may fear they will cause me. I am getting hardened to that
sort of thing; indeed, I must now steel myself to some cruel trials, which
are sure to start the moment our 9 volumes come out.'

For some reason, Stokowski, who was born in London in 1882 of
Polish descent on his father's side and of Irish extraction on his mother's
side, wished to be born in Cracow in 1887. I had numerous inquiries as to
Stokowski's shifting state of nativity, including one from the editor of a
Finnish music dictionary, who wrote to me that the Maestro himself,
while passing through Helsinki, corrected his vital statistics. To forestall
further importunities, I invested 15 shillings in Stokowski's birth certificate from Somerset House in London. It confirmed my previously established information. While one could sympathize with Stokowski's desire
for calendaric rejuvenation after his marriage to Gloria Vanderbilt, forty-
two years his junior, his insistence on being born in Poland was puzzling.
When he found out that his official birth certificate had been unearthed in
London, he contrived a fairy tale that must have been incredible even to
himself. According to this fable, he was born in Pomerania, which at the
time was part of Germany. He then moved to London, and, when the
First World War broke out, faced internment as an enemy alien. To

escape this disagreeable prospect, he had his registry of birth in Somerset House altered to certify that he was born in London; he also caused his age to increase by a few years to avoid being drafted into the British Army. Needless to say, such counterfeit was utterly impossible to perpetrate— Somerset House was a fortress of security.

I sent a copy of Stokowski's birth certificate to Blom. He enjoyed it, and added a story of his own:

Stokowski has been at it again, not disputing his birthday, it is true, but his birth place for a change. He asserted to an interviewer at the BBC that he was born at Cracow, not in London. I don't believe it, as I am almost sure it was you who gave me the truth, and that you got it straight from the horse's mouth, i.e. Somerset House.

Blom wrote again on 7 October 1957:

I must return the Stokowski birth certificate to you, but not without telling you that it was with a pleasure not free from malice that I have now added a footnote to our Grove date for the Supplement, making it clear that this date is confirmed by a copy of the birth certificate supplied by Somerset House. This ought to nail him down once and for all, and he can't very well sue Somerset House for defamatory libel, or us, for that matter. I know the Law is an ass, and they say the greater the truth the greater the libel, but not in a case like this. Would it give you the same sort of pleasure if I associated your name with this in that footnote? I should love to do this, but of course not without your sanction.

Another stimulating tussle arose in connection with Stravinsky's birth date. I had it as 17 June 1882, corresponding to 5 June 1882 of the old-style Russian calendar. Stravinsky's British publishers Boosey & Hawkes took exception to the date, claiming that Stravinsky himself and his factotum, Robert Craft, set the date as 18 June. Blom notified the befuddled Messrs Boosey & Hawkes that they were wrong and communicated to them my labyrinthine explications about the difference between the Russian and Western calendars having been twelve days before 1900 and thirteen days after. To this the recusant publishers replied:

We are not sure that we are altogether prepared to accept your conclusion that we have been badly misled. After all, Mr Slonimsky's researches do not seem to have made an indelible impression on the master himself, since he continues to insist that his birthday is on 18 June, his family continues to celebrate it on 18 June (his granddaughter is in London and was asked about this on Saturday). Robert Craft is at pains to explain that the Los Angeles concert is on the eve of his birthday and, according to *Who's Who*, 18 June is the day. Furthermore, the Russian Orthodox Church celebrates the Feast of St Igor, his nameday, on 18 June Western style. It looks to me rather as if the whole regiment were marching out of step except privates Blom and Slonimsky.

Soon Boosey & Hawkes had to eat their words, evidenced by a letter to Blom of 18 July 1957:

The Blom–Slonimsky heresy certainly seems to be gaining adherence and I shall not attempt to dispute the matter further, particularly as Robert Craft was one of the people who insisted most strongly that the right day was the 18th, almost at the very moment when he must have been writing for *The New York Times* that it was the 17th. I am very glad to think that you and I are at any rate in agreement about the date on which the 20th century began!

(The twentieth century certainly began in January 1901, not in 1900, which was the last year of the nineteenth century. I was cognizant of this numerical paradox when I gave the title to my first book, *Music Since 1900* rather than *Music of the Twentieth Century*.)

A Parthian shot was fired at me from the Stravinsky outposts in reply to my letter to the editor of *The New York Times* in which I expounded the astronomical aspects of Stravinsky's date of birth. 'I intend to celebrate my birthdays in the twenty-first century on June 19, if I wish,' Stravinsky wired to *The Times*. But such a celebration would be an act of supererogation, for the year 2000 will be a leap year in both the Russian Orthodox Church and the Catholic Church, so that there will be no increase of the difference between the two calendars in the twenty-first century. I dispatched this bit of calendarical lore to the editors of *The New York Times*, but my communication was not published, and, since Stravinsky's publishers had already yielded on the subject, the controversy could be regarded as closed.

In 1955 Blom was awarded the Order of the Commander of the British Empire. I asked him how I should address him after he was thus honoured. His reply was characteristic.

Don't bother about the problem of how to address me [he wrote]. Just as before, though some people, at the moment at any rate, do go out of the way to add CBE to the normal style, probably those who want something, though I have not really bothered to analyse it. Some also address me as Dr, and I suppose I am one, as Birmingham University thought fit to saddle me with an honorary DLitt., presented to me in person by the Prime Minister who happens to be Chancellor of that University. Well, well, and Her Little Majesty has by now hung the bauble round my neck, so that I am staggering under these appendages. But I hope people will now forget about them, as they have been thrust upon me, not achieved by me.

I felt an acute sense of loss when I read in *The New York Times* that Blom had died. Only a few days before I had received a letter from him, so courtly, so civilized, and so warm:

Your latest consignment came while I was battling with influenza and bronchitis (in counterpoint). It therefore had to join a vast pile of accumulating work and correspondence; but it was so tempting that it was one of the first things I tackled when I emerged from bed and at that it was perhaps the least urgent. It only shows, doesn't it? On the other hand I ought to have written to thank you days ago; however, I do it now, most fervently.

Irony of ironies! At Blom's funeral, the organist of the Golders Green Crematorium of London asked Blom's widow what music he ought to play. 'A Bach chorale,' she suggested. The organist, who must have been hard of hearing, thought she said Barcarolle, and he confidently embarked on the famous Barcarolle from *The Tales of Hoffmann*, which Blom abominated.

My correspondence with Alfred Einstein was as dear to me as any intellectual exchange might be. He wrote in German, I answered in English. His letters were models of human kindness, but he breathed the fire of hell when it came to Germans who played footsie with the Nazis. When I asked him for information about Hermann Zilcher, who had just died, Einstein confirmed that he had joined the 'most rabid Nazis' in Valhalla, where he was received by Richard Strauss and Hans Pfitzner whom he hated and who in turn hated each other. He called a former Intendant of the Berlin State Opera 'ein Schwein'. When I asked him whether he was in correspondence with the Italian musicologist Fausto Torrefranco, Einstein answered, 'Yes, like a cat with a mouse,' and proceeded to denounce Torrefranco for shuffling the dates of Renaissance composers in order to prove the priority in new techniques of the musicians whom he favoured. 'He is a fool,' Einstein concluded. 'Even as a Fascist he was such a pathetic creature that he might well have been put to death just as Conte Ciano, husband of Edda Mussolini, and her papa were.'

Einstein reserved his most bitter contempt for the German music historian Hans Joachim Moser, an unregenerate Nazi who went so far as to remove the name of Mendelssohn from his history of German music. Einstein warned me not to yield to the false spirit of charity in sending 'Care' packages to Moser and his family in the famine-stricken post-war Berlin. Moser did appeal to me for help. Interestingly enough, he took the precaution to ask if I had by any chance seen the wartime edition of his *Musik-Lexikon* in which he proudly announced that German music was finally free from the infestation of Jews. 'This is what we had to say under Hitler!' Moser added disingenuously. I sent him a 'Care' package, but it was delivered to the daughter of the German musicologist Karl Krebs in Berlin whose address Moser had given me for postal reference. She wrote me a letter of profuse thanks, wondering if I had sent the precious package to her in appreciation of her father's contribution to music history. She and her family ate the contents of the package, and when Moser made his way to her apartment in bombed-out Berlin, he was understandably disappointed. He voiced his despair to me in a letter, and I sent him another package. It reached him safely, and was gratefully consumed by him and his many children by several marriages.

Einstein was editor of the eleventh edition of Riemann's *Musik-Lexikon* before Germany went Nazi, and he did not care for even his non-Nazi successors. The article on him in Riemann's post-Einstein edition stated that he was first cousin of the great scientist Albert Einstein. I faithfully reproduced this bit of information in my various lexicographical publications. It was not until 1979 that I learned from Einstein's daughter that, although Alfred and Albert both lived for many years in Berlin and became quite friendly, they were not related. A search of their respective genealogies failed to reveal a single common ancestor. Yet, there is a letter in the Alfred Einstein archive from Albert Einstein, addressed 'Lieber Vetter'. This must have been a deliberate misrepresentation on the part of the great scientist, safely ensconced in America, to his non-cousin still in Germany, in order to facilitate his getting an American visa.

The more I delved into musical biography, the more inconsistencies, improbabilities, and impossibilities I found. What struck me as remarkable was that many a biographical legend could be exploded by elementary inquiry. My proudest achievement along these lines was the cancellation of a snowstorm that raged during Mozart's funeral and made it impossible for his friends to follow his coffin to the cemetery. I simply wrote to the Vienna Weather Bureau, which kept meteorological data for over two hundred years, for a record of the weather on the day of Mozart's funeral, 7 December 1791. Well, there couldn't have been any snowstorm on that day, for the temperature was well above freezing, and a gentle zephir wind blew. There was some precipitation in the morning, but the weather cleared up in the afternoon when Mozart's body was carried from St Stephen's Cathedral to the cemetery.

While I reported my findings in an article, 'The Weather at Mozart's Funeral', published in the April 1960 issue of the *Musical Quarterly*, it was unfortunately too late to forestall a real blizzard of melodramatic accounts for Mozart's bicentennial in 1956. The great Mozartologist Erich Schenk even specified the size of snowballs falling on Mozart's coffin: they were as large as tennis balls. Who started the story that snowballed into the Mozartian blizzard? I traced its source to the classical Mozart biography by Otto Jahn. Where did Jahn get his story? From an article in a Vienna newspaper published on the occasion of Mozart's centennial in 1856.

Who wrote that article? Nobody. It was signed simply 'a man of the people'. Some commentators speculated that the author must have been the bartender at a Vienna tavern which Mozart attended shortly before his death. How old was the bartender in 1856 to write that article? Putting his age at 30 at the time he tended the bar in 1791, the year of Mozart's death, he had to be about 95 at the time of Mozart's centennial when the article in question was first published. Apart from dubious geriatrics, on purely stylistic grounds it is difficult to imagine that a person lacking journalistic skill could have written the piece, for it abounded in learned references to the history and topology of the city of Vienna. The best guess is that the thing was put together by one of the editors of the paper who assumed a cloak of anonymity as 'a man of the people'.

I derived egotistic pleasure from finding errors in other people's books; it was a throwback to my childhood when, encouraged by my mother, I thought, 'What a smart boy I am.' Now strangers began telling me how smart I was. In his preface to the 1949 edition of *Baker's Biographical Dictionary of Musicians*, Carl Engel called me 'that lexicographic beagle of keen scent and sight'. Eric Blom paid me a similar compliment in his preface to the 1954 edition of *Grove's*. Catherine Drinker Bowen, author of several biographies of musicians, said that my 'hawk-like, lie-detecting eye brings terror to all writers on musical subjects'. In the list of personal acknowledgements in his monumental *Oxford Companion to Music*, Percy A. Scholes called me 'the world's most ingenious and pertinacious musicological detective'.

Climbing to the top of the lexicographical ladder, I achieved the great honour of being appointed Editor-in-Chief of the Fifth Edition of the prestigious *Baker's Biographical Dictionary of Musicians*, published in 1958 by the topmost music publishing empire of G. Schirmer, Inc. In my ambition to achieve comprehensiveness, biographical ubiquity, and, above all, infallibility, I ran into trouble with the publishers who began to fear that uncontrolled expansion of the biographical material would create acute indigestion in a one-volume dictionary. We held a conference in G. Schirmer's office on the top floor of the old Schirmer Building on 43rd Street and 5th Avenue in New York to discuss the situation. Old Gustave Schirmer, a man of impressive bulk, looking over the galley proofs, grumbled, 'Do we really need all these people here? We need Menotti, and we need Beethoven, and we need Malotte, but who is Raymo? He takes a lot of space.' It took me a couple of seconds to realize that Raymo was Jean-Phillipe Rameau, and I explained to Schirmer that Rameau was indeed quite as important as Malotte, an American organist who wrote the enormously popular setting of the Lord's Prayer published by G. Schirmer, Inc., which sold untold thousands of copies each year. When a women's club, somewhere in the sticks, put the song on the programme of their meeting, the chairwoman wrote to Schirmer asking for permission to reproduce the words of Mr Malotte's song. Permission was graciously granted.

I adopted the rule of rewriting most of the articles in the previous editions of *Baker's* dealing with modern composers, but leaving the classics largely intact, after checking on the accuracy of their dates of birth and death. However, when the dictionary went into second galley proofs, I began noticing some strange phenomena in such articles. Of Rossini, for instance, it was written that he found himself in Paris with only £15 in his pocket. What was he doing with all that British currency in France? I also noticed that words like 'honour' and 'favour' in the same article sprouted the intercalatory 'u' which was proper British, but not American usage. I went to bed without giving it a second thought, but woke up with a start, struck with the suspicion that the Rossini article, and possibly some others, were lifted bodily from an early edition of *Grove's*, a practice which would account for the British spelling. I had in my library a copy of the original edition of *Grove's*, published in 1883, and I looked up Rossini. Sure enough, there he was in Paris with all that British money in his pocket. Then I remembered that there was something peculiar in the article on Spohr, which also betrayed a British orientation. I compared the Baker article with that in Grove. The similarity was damning. Apparently, Theodore Baker, the founding father of *Baker's Biographical Dictionary of Musicians*, simply copied the basic entries from the 1883 edition of *Grove's*, without even bothering to remove the *corpus delicti*, to wit, the British spelling. The subsequent editors of *Baker's* had failed to notice the pilferage since the factual information was satisfactory. But once the original perpetrator revealed himself as the horse thief that he was, I could not very well condone his cattle rustling. I called long-distance the director of publications at Schirmer's and related to him my ghastly findings. We arranged for a conference to discuss the matter.

I took an early train from Boston to New York. My feverish imagination conjured up an item in the 'Funny Coincidence' department in the *New Yorker* magazine quoting *Grove's* and my edition of *Baker's* in parallel columns. It so happened that a new edition of *Grove's* had come out in 1954, and it retained virtually all original articles on Rossini, Spohr, and others, so that a suspicious librarian could compare the two and discover the awful truth. In vain would I then have pleaded extenuating circumstances; at best I would have been guilty as an accomplice after the fact, trading in stolen goods.

At the editorial conference at Schirmer's I stressed the necessity of rewriting at least the most flagrantly plagiarized paragraphs, lest the publishers of *Grove's* should sue Schirmer for infringement of the copyright. Schirmer shrugged off the idea. 'They did not sue us for 40 years, and they won't sue us now,' he said. A compromise was reached and I was allowed to rewrite part of the articles.

In spite of my apprehensions, the 1958 edition of *Baker's* was greeted with enthusiastic reviews. The New York radio station WQXR broadcast a special hour on the new *Baker's* under the heading, 'Slonimsky's Discoveries in His New Dictionary'. The *Washington Star* published a feature article entitled, 'Slonimsky introduces new methods of musical lexicography'. *Time* magazine sent a photographer to take my picture for a feature article. The article did appear under the caption 'Musical Super-Sleuth', but instead of my picture there was one of a Russian ballerina. Harold C. Schonberg offered an amusing description of me in *The New York Times*:

Slonimsky is one of those lexicographers with a fixation about accuracy. He would swim the Atlantic under water to gaze upon the birth certificate of an obscure Portuguese composer; he would tunnel the Andes with his bare hands to find when the first performance of *Fidelio* was given in Peru. He takes nobody's word for anything; he wants to see the documents.

Then the morning-after came. I began discovering all kinds of humiliating errors in the thing, many of them of my own making. And my faults were exactly the kind that I derided in other dictionaries. Charles de Bériot (1802–70) could not have sired a son in 1883 (the date should have been 1833). Did 'der alte Ries' really become a father at the early age of 9? No, he was 29, and the sexual precocity implied in his entry resulted from my error in setting his date of birth as 1775, instead of 1755. Reinken, who was born in 1623, could not have studied with Sweelinck who died in 1621, but may have studied with Sweelinck's son. It was presumptuous of me to bestow upon the English pianist Harriet Cohen the title of Dame. She was a mere Commander of the British Empire; it was in Spain that she was a Dame. And if I had only checked the provenance of Pablo Sarasate's Stradivarius in the bibliography adduced in my own entry on him, I would have discovered that he purchased the fiddle with his own hard-earned pesetas, and did not get it from the Queen of Spain as a gift, as the article claimed. I had no business to describe the pianist Glenn Gould as a jazz addict; I apparently confused him with the Austrian pianist Friedrich Gulda, who indeed dabbled in jazz. And to top the list, there was a gross libel on Gustave Schirmer, the head of the firm that published *Baker's Dictionary*, making him a bastard. The entry on him said that he was born in 1890 (he was), but that his father had not married his mother until 1916! Scandal in the house of Schirmer!

How could I atone for all these transgressions? I recall a scene from Electra's childhood. A friend of Electra's named Arlene and another adolescent girl were engaged in an earnest exchange about sin: 'All you have to do is make an act of contrition,' Arlene advised her friend. (Both Arlene and her little friend were Catholics.) I made my own acts of contrition by publishing two supplements to my 1958 edition of *Baker's*. But in my impetuous determination to get as many last-minute obits as possible into the 1971 supplement, I committed a crime that could not be redeemed by any act of contrition: I buried a man alive! William John Mitchell, the American musicologist, had died in Binghamton, New York, on 17 August 1971. I added this date to the page proofs at the last moment, but by some fantastic misapprehension inserted it in my manuscript under Donald Mitchell, a man not only alive and flourishing but actually connected with G. Schirmer, Inc.

Would I be found out? Who was going to search through a measly supplement to a superannuated music dictionary looking for a misplaced tombstone? Who? Why, Donald Mitchell, that's who. A couple of weeks after the unfortunate supplement came out I got a letter from Hans W. Heinsheimer, publication director at Schirmer's, which even now, years later, makes me tremble:

Dear (or rather today, not so dear) Nicolas: Donald Mitchell just stormed into my office to tell me that on page 163 of the new *Baker's* supplement you murdered him in August of 1971 in Binghamton, New York, where he has never been in his life and never hopes to be particularly. It's really a most embarrassing thing, and I am at a loss at this unbelievable error and *faux pas*.

Trapped, I made a desperate effort to save the situation. I sat at the typewriter and wrote an anguished letter to William Van Gerven, manager of publications:

I am in trouble, deep trouble, and I desperately need your help. This is what happened: the obit. I intended for William John Mitchell got into the entry for Donald Mitchell. There is only one way to correct this terrible error: to paste a strip of gummed paper over the offending line on page 163 immediately after the name Donald Mitchell, and do it in all outstanding copies of the book. I would be only too glad to reimburse the costs of this operation. The job can be staggered, a thousand copies now, another thousand copies next year, depending on sales, etc. If Ford can recall thousands of their faulty Torinos and Mercury Montegos and still continue in business, why can't we fix just one line?

The answer to my plea was, alas, in the negative. The best the publishers would do was to insert a slip of corrections which would exhume Donald Mitchell from his unhallowed grave.

Then, out of the blue, I received a letter from Donald Mitchell himself asking me in his most good-natured and courteous manner (he is an Englishman) if I would do him a favour and resurrect him in the next edition of *Baker's*. He also volunteered information about his latest activities. I immediately wrote back to him, praising him for his magnanimity and, as corroborating evidence of my penance, enclosing a copy of my letter to Van Gerven. Mitchell replied, most graciously, that it was worth it for him to be placed temporarily underground to have the pleasure of receiving such a 'charming letter' from me. Fortunately the 1971 supplement had a limited printing and sold out very quickly, so that I could get to work on the new completely revised edition of *Baker's*, in which, needless to say, I paid my utmost attention and applied my most tender loving care to the entry on Donald Mitchell.

My sympathy with Donald Mitchell was all the more heartfelt since I had myself undergone the discomfort of a premature burial at the hands of the annotator of the Philadelphia Orchestra in the programme book of 3 November 1959, in which I was referred to as 'the late Nicolas Slonimsky'. I received an anguished telephone call from Arthur Cohn. 'Nicolas?!' 'Yes.' 'Nicolas . . . .' he kept repeating. 'It said in yesterday's Philadelphia Orchestra program book that you were dead!' Having reassured Arthur Cohn, I wired the manager of the Philadelphia Orchestra: 'Please correct the statement in your program notes referring to me as late. I am never late except in delivering my manuscripts to publishers.' The programme annotator, Edwin H. Schloss, sent me an anguished apology.

When I was shown your wire [he wrote], it is questionable whether crimson, vermillion, or scarlet best described the color of my face. I thought I remembered having read with keen regret a notice of your demise some months ago. How I could ever have become the victim of such a morbid mirage, I simple don't know. And unfortunately, I thought I remembered it so clearly that I did not bother to check. It was a preposterous gaffe and a stupid one.

The demise Schloss must have read about was probably that of Lazare Saminsky, who died on 30 June 1959. I was often confused with Saminsky by people to whom all names that begin with S and end with 'sky' appeared identical.

In his review of the New York concert of the Philadelphia Orchestra in the *New York Herald Tribune* of 5 November 1959, Paul Henry Lang took cognizance of my resurrection: 'The programme notes quote some nice passages from the pen of the "late Nicolas Slonimsky". I can assure the writer that Mr Slonimsky, whom I saw yesterday, is in excellent health, good for another half dozen fine books to quote from.' Paul Henry Lang exercised the privilege of prosaic licence in saying he had seen me 'yesterday'. He had not. He just checked up on me at Schirmer's and was assured that I was indeed all right.

In August 1972 I received a letter from Stephen W. Ellis of Glenview, Illinois, in which he took me to task for errors in my 1971 supplement to *Baker's Biographical Dictionary of Musicians*. 'The entry on John Becker is grossly incomplete and inaccurate,' he wrote. 'Thorkell Sigurbjornsson's name is mispelled, missing the first r in his last name. Shockingly, you are nearly thirty years behind on Marin Goleminov. This important Bulgarian composer has written much, and somewhat radically changed his style of composition, and you have covered none of this.' Of Camargo Guarnieri: 'You show only one work of his for the last twenty years!' Of Alun Hoddinott: 'Your 1971 Supplement shows only one work since 1957. This is sadly inadequate; he has written much since then.' Victor Legley: 'Among with fellow countryman Chevreuille, he is perhaps the saddest case in your new Supplement, because he is not in it at all.' Marcel Mihalovici: 'The 1971 Supplement lists an opera as its sole updating of the Mihalovici catalogue. This is criminal! In nearly twenty years he has written much, believe me!' Among words of abuse he lavished upon me were 'absurd', 'ridiculous', and 'disgraceful'.

  To say I was dumbfounded by this assault would be an under-statement. My first impulse was to put the man in his place. 'Sirrah! [I would begin]. Do you realize that you are addressing one whom the *Penguin Dictionary of Music* called a "modern prince of musical lexicography", one for whom Percy A. Scholes invoked, in a personal letter, the famous lines of Goldsmith, "and still the wonder grew that one small head could carry all he knew". One, who . . .' But then the wind went out of my laboriously contrived sails, giving way to acute curiosity. Who was this Stephen W. Ellis? How did he manage to gather so much information on obscure musicians from all over the globe? I looked up his name in reference books and indices of articles in music journals, but could find no mention. I decided to extend a hand of friendship.

I picture you a man of about 42, married, with two small children [I wrote]. You must be a college graduate, though not of Harvard or Yale. I am sure you have acquired your extraordinary knowledge not from books or music courses, but from record albums, catalogues, perhaps private correspondence and other primary sources. I imagine you read most European languages intuitively, or by philogical extrapolation. I would be pleased if my portrait of you were less inaccurate than my books.

  Ellis turned out to be 30, not 42, married, but having only one child (another followed in a couple of years). He was employed as a copy reader for a Chicago publishing house. He used to play the French horn. Sure enough, he accumulated a large collection of recordings from all parts of the world. He also subscribed to bibliographical information bulletins issued by European composers' unions. Ellis became indispensable to me in my work on the 1978 and 1984 editions of *Baker's*.

My conviction that the best minds in the lexicographical business of music are not members of the academia but people passionately involved in the pursuit of accuracy for the hell of it was once more corroborated by the appearance on my horizon of one Dennis McIntire, professor of humanities at Indiana University. McIntire, aged 36, wrote to me out of the blue politely inquiring about the source of some dubious statements in my newest edition of *Baker's*. While Ellis supplied me with astounding minutiae of works by composers academia never heard of, Dennis McIntire inundated my card index with specific details of careers of European conductors, singers, violinists, cellists, violists, and other performers. He got his precious information through correspondence with managers of European and American opera houses and orchestras, exposing not only my own errors of facts, but also inaccuracies in the revered tomes of *Grove's* and Riemann. McIntire cannot read music, but his knowledge about minor figures in music exceeds that of every musicologist I have ever known.

Then came Mike Keyton of Dallas. He could read music and even composed some, but his profession was mathematics. His help was decisive in manufacturing the 1984 edition of *Baker's*. Among hundreds of corrections, he rectified the date of death of Euler, who was a musical theorist as well as a great mathematician. I was especially remiss in Euler's case since he died in St Petersburg, the capital of the Russian Empire, where I was born 111 years later. And I must not forget the extraordinary help given by Samuel Sprince of Massachusetts, who tirelessly perused authentic data on musicians about whom I could gather little information.

In my lexicographical endeavour I rejected the method of proving the negative. Accordingly, I did not challenge the unlikely tale of the Italian singer Giulio Rossi who 'had a tenor voice until he was 19 when an unintentional plunge into the Tiber in December induced an illness, after which his voice lowered to the range of basso profondo', and let it stand unaltered in the new *Baker's*, for I had no way of proving that Rossi did not jump into the river, unintentionally or otherwise, nor that he did not become a deep bass after that immersion.

On the other hand, I should have questioned the accuracy of the report that the Italian conductor Gino Marinuzzi was shot by the anti-Fascist partisans on 17 August 1945, a story found not only in *Baker's*, but also in

Grove's, Riemann ('ermordet'), and an Italian encyclopaedia ('mori assassinato'). I should have wondered why the partisans waited until several months after the end of the war to kill Marinuzzi. True, he composed an ode on the occasion of the meeting between Hitler and Mussolini. But many other Italian composers were good Fascists as well. They even dated their letters at the time 'E. F.', for 'era fascista'. Even Alfredo Casella condoned this nonsense. When I asked him in 1928 how he could admire Il Duce after he ordered a purge in Italian music of all French and German expression marks, Casella answered, 'Mussolini is a genius, and men of genius often do silly things.' Anyway, it turned out that Gino Marinuzzi was not murdered, *ermordet* or *assassinato* at all. He died of hepatitis, as stated on his death certificate. I could never find out who concocted the assassination story in the first place.

Whatever torments I experienced during *Baker's* successive parturitions, I tried to preserve my sanity. At least one of my remote predecessors, John Wall Callcott (1766–1821), succumbed to the 'morbus lexicographicus'. The *Baker's* entry on him says, 'His mind gave way from overwork on a projected but unrealized music dictionary.' He had reached the letter Q.

I recorded the tale of my lexicographical travail in an article for *Music Library Notes*, entitled 'Lexicographis secundus post Herculem labor' (a dictum attributed to Joseph Justus Scaliger, a sixteenth-century lexicographer). The Herculean labour alluded to was the cleansing of the manure-filled stables of King Augeus, son of the sun god Helius. Hercules performed the job in twenty-four hours; *Baker's* took longer. I laboured like a herculean homunculus on the fifth edition of 1958, the sixth edition of 1978, and the seventh edition of 1984. But I take solace in the marvellous encouragement I received from that great man of music, Alfred Einstein, who wrote to me wondering whether we would ever ('und natürlich vor allem Sie,' he added generously) be rewarded in Heaven for having removed some inaccuracies while here on earth.

I am often asked about my criterion for inclusion (or exclusion) of names in my various reference works. As far as musical biography goes, certain names obviously command hegemony: three B's (Bach, Beethoven, Brahms), three Sch's (Schubert, Schumann, Schoenberg), three W's (Weber, Wagner, Webern), three M's (Mozart, Mendelssohn, Mahler), a couple of H's, a smattering of S's, and, for the watchers of modern skies, even an X (Xenakis). But for every indisputable great, there is a proliferation of perfectly respectable but dreadfully obscure individuals. And so I devised a formula for lexicographical inclusion: Let the symbol *Lex* stand for such lexicographical eligibility. For composers, an opera would rate highest; a symphony would count second. There would follow chamber music, large piano works, choral music, and, in the last category, songs. Of course, intrinsic value would be an important factor. Popularity, too, would command a high coefficient. And finally, the very quantity of published pieces would be taken into consideration. The formula will then look something like this:

Lex = Operas × 50 + Symphonies × 10 + Chamber Music × 5 + Piano Music × 3 + Choral Music × 2 + songs.

Thus, 100 songs will rate only a square root of their number, that is, 10 points. But if such songs are of the excellence of, say, Schubert, then the value coefficient will greatly add to the total sum. The factor of popularity may skyrocket a musically insignificant production to the point of equalling a boring symphony. So, say, a popular song like 'It was the End of a Perfect Day', the musical value of which is nil, would elevate its composer to the level of acceptability in a supposedly dignified music dictionary such as *Baker's*. I am not sure that my attempt at a mathematical computation of musical values would prove acceptable in the groves of Academe, but I entertain a pious hope that some free-thinking professor of music history would encourage the students to compile such a register of values of great, not so great, mediocre, and poor music.

The formula of excellence for performers is much easier to compute. In most cases, true greatness of a conductor, a pianist, a violinist, a cellist or another instrumentalist, an opera singer or a recitalist, can be assayed through the coefficient of popularity multiplied by the estimated greatness of musical penetration. A prodigy of technical skill who lacks a musical physiognomy will rate less than a player who occasionally gets off pitch on the violin, or an interpretive genius who hits wrong notes on the piano. There were great singers (Caruso was one) who never learned to read music, but they remained in the memory of those who heard them as supreme interpreters. Chaliapin was undoubtedly the greatest dramatic singer of the century, but he was apt to falter in rhythm and even in pitch. Here no elaborate formula is needed to measure their eligibility quotient; the popularity factor alone would elevate them to the height of musical appreciation. There is no way of estimating the vocal beauty of the emasculated singers of Handel's time; but several names have remained in the annals of the castratosphere. And we, as diaskeuasts, must not disdain the practitioners of rock 'n' roll music; they may deafen us, but they obviously possess that *je ne sais quoi* that makes multitudes crash the gates to hear them sing.

It seems that in my unexpectedly rapid ascent to the lexicographical ionosphere, I have become a proper noun, complete with adjectival and proverbial forms, in artful conjugations, graceful declensions, and calisthenic perpendiculations. At least this is how I appear in a lively paragraph in the December 1980 issue of *Music Library Notes*, commenting on 'the ideal of Slonimskinian (Slonimskian? Slonimskonian? Slonimsquesque?) perfection' to be attained in some future editions of musical encyclopaedias.

CHAPTER 20

FAME AND FORTUNE

In December 1956 an event took place that completely changed my status in the world of reality, bringing all at once fame, social recognition, and, most importantly, money. This sudden piece of luck came from the most unexpected source—a television quiz show.

One of Electra's friends was employed at an advertising agency which represented the sponsor of a television quiz show. He asked if I would be willing to appear on the show, called 'The Big Surprise', a spin-off of the popular '$64,000 Question'. As in the main show, the gimmick was to quiz contestants on topics outside their occupations. The preference was for an uneducated person who had a quick memory and an unlimited gift of the gab. One of their most successful aspirants was an Italian–American cobbler who loved opera. The canny producers sent him to Italy where he was received by the American ambassador Claire Booth Luce, and even had an audience with the Pope. Then there was a practically illiterate salesman who could rattle off baseball scores in any given year and could recite the names of the Roman emperors, however mispronounced, in chronological order. He also knew the keys of Beethoven's symphonies, and even won a point against a professor of music who insisted that Beethoven's Fourth Symphony was in B-flat major, whereas it is listed as being in B-flat minor, because it does begin in the homonymous minor key.

I could not pretend to be blessed by ignorance, but the producers were impressed by my volubility, and suggested a novel category, misinformation, as my vehicle for the quiz. I armed myself with books on the subject, the most popular of which was *A Natural History of Nonsense* by Bergen Evans, professor of English at Northwestern University, which debunked all kinds of legends of literature and history.

Shirley Bernstein (Leonard Bernstein's sister) was in charge of the production, and she conducted a preliminary 'brainwashing' session to test my ability at instant response, which I passed to her complete satisfaction. Mike Wallace was the master of ceremonies. The questions and answers were contained in a sealed envelope, and deposited in a safety box. A brass fanfare introduced the contestants. The *modus oper-*

andi was this: $100 for the first question correctly answered; $200 for the second; $300 for the third, then the prizes mounted at an increasing rate: $1,000, $3,000, $10,000, $20,000, $30,000. 'The Big Surprise' itself was a whopping $100,000. The hitch was that you lost everything if you failed to answer any of the questions.

My questions in the first and second shows were straight out of the Bergen Evans book, and I answered them without a moment's hesitation. But on the third show, for $300, I nearly met my Waterloo. Does a galloping horse keep all its legs off the ground at any given moment? What was the name of the photographer who resolved the problem? A synapse crackled between the relevant neurons in my brain, and brought up the memory of a recent article in *Life*, which carried consecutive film clips proving that galloping horses do indeed take all legs off the ground at certain moments. But what was the name of the photographer? I had ten seconds to answer the question. It was almost a case of clairvoyance; a typographical error in the *Life* article appeared before me as in a mist (at least I thought it was a typographical error; I have a peculiar memory for typographical errors). The photographer's first name was spelled Eadweard instead of Edward! The purported misprint triggered the photographer's unusual last name in my cerebral memory box: Muybridge. (It was not until much later that I found out that Eadweard was not a misprint but the original Anglo-Saxon form of Edward, which Muybridge favoured for nationalistic reasons. Also, his real last name was plain Muggeridge, not Muybridge.)

My brainwashing sessions with Shirley Bernstein took place a day before each weekly show. She was very efficient in firing question after question at me. She kept a battery of reference books on her desk, from which she apparently selected her questions. I made a great effort to memorize as many of them as I could immediately after the brainwashing.

During the six weeks in November and December 1956 when I was on television I learned what it was to be famous. At the time I was teaching at the Peabody Conservatory in Baltimore; my classes were completely demoralized. Instead of attending to academic matters at hand, my students wanted to know whether I would try to hit the jackpot. Even children were caught in the agitation of the show. One little girl, whose family lived in the same building as we on Beacon Street in Boston, stopped me as I was entering the elevator and asked, 'Are you going for 20?' Time and again, on the street, on the train, on the plane, I became aware of quick glances in my direction, often followed by a direct approach: 'Aren't you the one . . .' There is no greater glory than making money in public. With each week on the show my notoriety rose in an exponential curve. In Boston a policeman stopped me as I was crossing the street. For a moment I thought he was going to apprehend me for jaywalking. Instead, he asked me for an autograph. In New York I took Electra to a restaurant for lunch, but there were no free tables and we decided to leave, when the maître d' ran after us and said, 'Mr Shlumpsky, I will have a table for you. I will be proud having you as my guest.'

Being a street celebrity has its disadvantages, but I enjoyed written tributes from my friends. I had a charming letter from Paul Horgan, my old friend from early Rochester years.

Dear Colya [he wrote], you are both killing me with suspense and shattering me with admiration. *Pour l'amour de dieu*, how long can this *tema con variazioni* continue? I marvel at the expressivity you display, and bridle with a virtuous smirk at the recollection of my small if primal role in your voracious mastery of the English language.

Bill Lichtenwanger, formerly of the Library of Congress, kept sending me funny postcards:

Whee! I been thinkin' about writing you but I ain't used to dealing with gentlemen of wealth and got too bashful . . . Give 'em hell, and be sure to get a wad of dough in return. Take it easy on the poor MC, though; he obviously ain't sure how to handle you; your mind moves too fast for him.

I expected the questions to become increasingly difficult as the show progressed, but they were curiously uneven. I was particularly apprehensive of the subcategory on misquotations. To bone up on it I went over the footnotes in Bartlett's *Familiar Quotations*, which usually indicated alternative sources in the order of priority. Some common misquotations were familiar to me. I knew that 'To gild a lily' was wrong. Why would anybody want to gild a flower? How much more precise is the authentic Shakespearean line, 'To gild refined gold, to paint the lily'. I also knew that 'cleanliness is next to godliness' was not a biblical maxim, but a pronouncement of John Wesley, the founder of Methodism. And I knew that the correct quotation from Alexander Pope's essay on criticism is 'a little learning [not a little knowledge] is a dangerous thing'. All of these came up on one of my Tuesdays, which advanced me to the 'plateau' of $20,000.

For one show Mike Wallace reversed the format and asked me to give examples of misinformation in music. There was an upright piano on the stage. I played the opening bars of the 'Habanera' from *Carmen*, and asked him who wrote it. Why, Bizet, of course, Mike replied confidently. Wrong, I said. Bizet borrowed the tune from a collection of Spanish and Cuban songs by one Sebastian Yradier and incorporated it in his famous opera. It did not make sense anyway, I continued, to have a song of Havana in an opera portraying the life in Southern Spain. As I was talking away I noticed that somebody in the wings kept signalling to me by rotating his right hand in a rapid movement, which meant to talk more to fill the time. So I continued talking, after apologizing for being 'prolix'. In a minute or so the man in the wings made a cut-throat gesture which was a semiotic signal for me to shut up.

I had reached the penultimate 'plateau' of $30,000, when I successfully refuted the common belief that Rouget de l'Isle, the composer of the *Marseillaise*, was a revolutionary. He was not; he wrote the hymn as a patriotic song during the war with Austria. In fact, he was a royalist in his political beliefs, and was even imprisoned during the revolution.

The following week fell on Christmas, and I faced the decision to be or not to be. There were to be seven questions on my last appearance on the show. I had to answer all of them correctly to win, or else I would lose everything. In fact, as I found out later, there was quite a discussion going on in the inner circles of the agency that sponsored the show whether to encourage me to go on for the top prize of $100,000. Their concensus was that I would have an excellent chance of winning the whole pot because (a) they needed a winner and (b) they liked the way I came over. Unaware of the murmurings behind the scenes, I decided to take my $30,000 and call it quits. Dorothy and Electra attended the show; they took their seats in the front row in the studio. A fanfare was sounded to introduce me. Mike Wallace had a sealed envelope in his hand, which he opened ceremoniously. Would I go for the $100,000? There was an audible gasp in the audience when I answered in the negative. Would I try to answer the questions, just for the hell of it? I would. Mike read the questions. Yes, I knew that the battle of Waterloo was fought not at Waterloo, but at La Haye Sainte, situated some 5 kilometres south of Waterloo. Yes, I knew that the Liberty Bell was cracked tolling for a funeral, not to proclaim liberty. But the next two questions spelled trouble. When an infant is born and does not breathe, a doctor applies artificial respiration. What gas does he exhale in order to instil the breath of life into the infant? Oxygen is a life-giving element, but nobody, not even a medical doctor, exhales oxygen. The correct answer is, of course, carbon dioxide; the point of artificial respiration is to get the lungs to inflate. The last question was about the origin of the name Red Square in Moscow. The common temptation is to say that it is red because Moscow is the red capital. But it was called the Red Square long before the Revolution. Red means beautiful in old Russian; Red Square is Beautiful Square. I had answered all seven questions without fail. I could have won $100,000!

The *Boston Traveler* ran a front-page story with my picture, taken from TV, and the caption, 'Loses $70,000, Has No Regrets' ('With hardly a pause to collect his wits, Slonimsky rattled off his answers to seven parts of the question varying from the Battle of Waterloo to the Red Square in Moscow').

A check for $30,000 was handed to me after the show; an agent from the Internal Revenue Service was waiting backstage, and told me that I would have to shell out $11,000 in taxes. Still, I was $19,000 to the good, and that was much more than I had received from all my public appearances for a dozen previous years.

After my last show, on Christmas Eve, I decided to take a brief vacation. At the airport I became aware of the now familiar sidelong glances on the part of people waiting for the plane. A stately grey-haired gentlemen came up and said, 'Mr Slonimsky? I'm Austin Kiplinger, I edit the *Kiplinger Washington Letter.* I was very much impressed by your appearances on the quiz show. Many things that you clarified by your remarks were unfamiliar to me.' I reciprocated by telling him what an honour it was to speak to the editor of that famous publication. In Miami I found an inexpensive hotel room. I carried only a briefcase, and I asked the clerk whether he wanted me to pay in advance. He stared at me for about five seconds, and said, 'No, it will be okay, Mr Plimsky.'

After a few days in Florida, I returned to Boston. The postman, the laundryman, the druggist, and just about every member of the Boston Symphony Orchestra whom I happened to meet on the street told me how eagerly they watched me on TV. There was some delayed post; a postcard came from Varèse, addressed 'Illustre Millionaire,' and signed 'En toute humilité'.

The glamour of quiz shows suddenly dissolved into a malodorous squabble when several unsuccessful contestants claimed that the show was rigged; the target of such accusations was principally the '$64,000 Question', the parent organization of my show 'The Big Surprise'. Ugly rumours grew and finally exploded into a full-fledged scandal, with some contestants hailed into court to testify. The most bizarre public confession of conspiracy was presented by the prime hero of the '$64,000 Question', Charles Van Doren, assistant professor of Columbia University. His confession was right out of the pages of a Dostoyevsky novel, and the more he confessed the more incredible his story grew. He begged the quiz masters to allow him to fail, he said, but they refused because of the commercial value of his name to the show. But why did they have to give him not only the questions but also the answers in advance? Couldn't a Columbia professor do his own homework to save the appearances? On TV Van Doren had put on such a convincing show of brow-knitting in his isolation booth demonstrating his agonized search for answers, that few suspected any hanky-panky. Even the usually sceptical editors of *Time* magazine put Charles Van Doren on the cover as the wizard of knowledge. Finally the organizers of the quiz show decided that enough was enough, or perhaps his ratings began to fall, and Van Doren was released from his lucrative agony when he was allowed to say that the name of the King of Belgium was Leopold, even though he must have known, just from reading the papers, that Leopold had long since abdicated, and that Baudouin was on the Belgian throne. After his confession, Columbia University fired him. There were others who had to confess, but at least their confessions were credible.

My own show 'The Big Surprise' was apparently free from such shenanigans; it was obvious that Mike Wallace, the master of ceremonies, did not know the answers before he opened the sealed envelopes. As for myself, I was probably an asset to the show, not only because I was glib and unfazed in front of the camera lights, but because I certainly would have tried (and won) the jackpot of $100,000 had I been assured that the final seven questions were not calculated to knock me out.

CHAPTER 21

THE FUTURE OF MY PAST

Considering that my name had been on the black list of 'subversives' of several pseudo-patriotic organizations, it was remarkable that in 1959 I was asked by the US State Department to join the panel of the Office for Cultural Exchange, whose purpose was to send American artists, composers and performers abroad. Missions to Russia were top priority because of their propaganda value, and I was in an advantageous position—I spoke the language, and was regarded as a 'friend of Soviet music' by the Russians.

Membership of the Office of Cultural Exchange varied; some have now died. Harold Spivacke, head of the Music Division of the Library of Congress, was chairman. Composer–conductor Howard Hanson was sent with his Rochester music ensemble to Russia where he scored a tremendous success. Arthur Loesser, the pianist and author, was also a participant; during breaks between meetings he would press me with questions about Russian grammar and syntax. One memorable image is stained with blood in my recollection: Charles Frankel, former Assistant Secretary of the State Department, a scholar and mover of men and ideas who had attended several of our panel meetings, was brutally murdered with his wife by robbers in the spring of 1979 in his own home in a peaceful Westchester town.

In October 1962, at the height of the Cuban missile crisis, the Office of Cultural Exchange sent me on an inclusive journey to Russia, Poland, Austria, Yugoslavia, Greece, Israel, Bulgaria, Rumania, and Czechoslovakia, which would last nine months. The US Information Office provided several hundred published scores and recording of American music, which were shipped by air to the American Embassy in Moscow. I was to distribute these materials to proper institutions in the USSR.

I flew to London, where I boarded a Soviet plane to Moscow on the day after President Kennedy declared the blockade of Cuba. By ironic coincidence, I carried with me a copy of the current bestseller, *Fail-Safe*, which described an accidental nuclear bombing of Moscow. I had a sense of unreality as the plane approached Moscow. It was evening, and I could see the word MOCKBA in electric lights. A group of men and women stood by the gate. The music critic of *Pravda* stepped forward and proceeded to introduce me to a tall young man at his side. 'I want you to meet your nephew, the Soviet composer Sergei Slonimsky,' he said. Turning to Sergei, he remarked, 'I am sure you will be glad to meet your uncle, the American musicologist Nicolas Slonimsky.' Sergei inherited from his father (my brother Michael) and from his grandfather (my father) a certain taciturnity, a warmth without exuberance, a feeling of family kinship free of sentimentality. He lived in Leningrad, and had been given a fortnight's leave of absence from his post at the Leningrad Conservatory to meet me in Moscow. My older brother Alexander, and his wife Lida, lived in Moscow. I had telephoned them in advance of my arrival. It was a tearful reunion after so many eventful years.

To my Americanized ears, the new Soviet language sounded almost theatrical in its emphasis, deliberate articulation and expressive caesuras. I also noticed a proliferation of diminutives. At breakfast in the hotel, a man at the next table ordered some 'little coffee with some little cream and a little bread with a little butter', which sounded like 'coffeekins, creamkins, breadkins, and butterkins'. Such diminutives are common in Russian folk poetry. Can it be that the 'people' in whose name the Soviet Revolution was fought actually influenced urban speech? I noticed also that customers addressed the waitress as 'devushka', a poetic word for 'maiden'. In my time, it would have been 'baryshnia', i.e. 'little mistress', but such forms of address were disfranchised by the Revolution. The old honorific form 'Gospodin' was reserved in addressing a foreigner. Various officials with whom I dealt in Russia called me 'Gospodin Slonimsky'. The alternatives were 'citizen' or 'comrade', and when I was on my own, riding on buses or shopping, I was usually called 'citizen'.

During my first morning in Moscow I presented myself at the American Embassy located in an old building once occupied by a Russian nobleman and his family. Cartons of music and records were awaiting me in the shipping room. I was also given my weekly allowance of roubles, and was informed that I could call upon the services of the American Embassy chauffeur as well as the driver of the Union of Soviet Composers for my transportation. Never in my life had I received such aristocratic perquisites as during this fabulous visit. I was a traveller in the future of my past.

The Russia of my youth had been a backward country, with ill-smelling streets and alleys, and air filled with 'maternal' oaths. By contrast, new Russia was prophylactically clean and remarkably free of brawls in public places. I was impressed by the fabulous Moscow Metro, resplendent in its artistic decor, with individual subway stations suggesting halls of a museum. Busts of Lenin, with his bald pate, beaked nose, and trimmed conical beard, surveyed the scene above and below ground. By 1962 Stalin had been relegated to the dustbin of history, to use a favourite Soviet cliché (first enunciated by Trotsky in reference to the bourgeoisie). Although the monarchy had long been liquidated, Imperial artifacts were carefully preserved in Soviet museums as part of the 'Russian national heritage'. The tombs of the Czars, with the exception of that of Nicholas II who had died without benefit of a burial, were kept reverentially in the Kremlin's cavernous mausoleums.

Pride in national culture among Soviet Russians is high. The strongest term of disapproval in Soviet parlance is 'nyeculturny', or 'uncultured'. During a cab ride in Moscow, the driver turned to me and pointed at a church. 'Did you know that this is where Pushkin was married?' he asked. I was astonished by his detailed knowledge of circumstances in Pushkin's life. I was even more astonished by an experience at the Moscow post office, where I posted back to Boston the full score of Khachaturian's ballet *Spartak*, which he had given to me. As is customary in Soviet post offices, my package was wrapped by an employee. The clerk assigned to me, noticing the title page of the score, suddenly asked: 'Do you really consider *Spartak* superior to *Gayane*?' I expressed my appreciation of her knowledge. She dismissed my compliment. 'Any cultured person knows about such important Soviet works,' she said.

Thoughtful friends elucidated new Soviet words for me. 'This is what we call pepperbacks,' one said, pointing to a row of paperbacks in a bookstore. I also learned such Soviet words as *booldozer*, *bestcellar* and *stooardessa*. Indeed, American words had penetrated the entire Soviet industry and transportation. But strangely enough, the word 'aeroplan', familiar to me since my youth, was replaced by the Russian word 'samolyot', which literally means self-flight.

Passing a large bookstore one evening in Moscow, I saw a long line in front of the door. Queues for exotic fruit or theatre tickets were common, but a line for books? I questioned a person nearby. 'They expect a shipment of collected works of Charles Dickens,' he replied. 'But the store is closed for the night!' I exclaimed. 'It will open early tomorrow,' he said. What a commentary on the Russian thirst for knowledge!

Even more remarkable were the enormous sales of published music, particularly modern compositions. At the Union of Soviet Composers I was presented with a gift of real rarity—a newly published edition of the Fourth Symphony of Shostakovich, which had been condemned as 'formalistic', and confined to limbo for some twenty-five years. The person who gave it to me put it face down on the table and whispered: 'Don't let anybody see this. We have only a few copies left.'

The political stand of a composer, no matter how laudable from the

Soviet point of view, does not give him preferential treatment if he composes 'decadent' music. Luigi Nono, a charter member of the Italian Communist party and composer of dissonant music (and, incidentally, married to Schoenberg's daughter), is still 'no-no' in Soviet Russia. On the other hand, Rachmaninoff, an avowed monarchist who left Russia on the day of the Soviet Revolution, never to return, is hailed by Soviet politicians as an exemplar of true Russian art.

The path of Prokofiev was interesting. He blazoned forth in pre-revolutionary Russia as a modern savage who found inspiration in ancient lore, among bearskin-clad pagan Scythians who roamed the Russian plains in pre-historic times. He wrote a brilliant orchestral work entitled *A Scythian Suite*, with a brassy finale glorifying the life-giving splendour of the primordial sun. As sort of preliminary research, he went around asking people what they thought of the sun. Most people responded in the positive: they liked the sun. Prokofiev's solar questionnaire has been preserved in the Russian archives, complete with the answers of the interviewees. Chaliapin wrote in Prokofiev's notebook: 'The widest pathway is on the sunny side, towards the sun.' Artur Rubinstein declared in French: 'Le Roi Soleil a dit: l'état c'est moi.' Vladimir Mayakovsky quoted from his futuristic poem, 'The Cloud in Trousers': 'From you who are moistened with love, I flee with the sun stuck like a monocle in my distended eye.' The chess champion José Raúl Capablanca inscribed in English: 'Sun is Life. When we see the Sun we are happy. When it is hidden behind the clouds, gloom enters my heart.'

The sun of Prokofiev's youth underwent a rather massive eclipse in revolutionary Russia. He decided to leave the country, and because of the total disruption of travel to western Europe, went to Japan by way of Siberia and on to the United States. He later made his home in Paris. He openly boasted that he had kept his Soviet citizenship and yet held a so-called Nansen passport for stateless Russians and other political flotsam and jetsam. He used his Soviet passport for frequent visits to Russia, and his Nansen document for travel aboard. When he applied for the Soviet exit visa for an American tour in the spring of 1939, however, it was refused, and Prokofiev remained in Russia. In the meantime, he became separated from his wife, a Spanish-born soprano named Lina Llubera, and took up with a young Jewish Komsomol member, Myra Mendelson. Lina tried to leave Russia with her two sons, but landed in a concentration camp for her trouble; she eventually managed to settle abroad.

Prokofiev had plenty of difficulties of his own with the reactionary clique in the Soviet Ministry of Culture. He was damned for an alleged Western deviation in the notorious edict of the Central Committee of the

Communist Party in 1948, along with Shostakovich and a number of other Soviet composers. He issued a tame (and lame) *apologia pro domo sua*, maintaining that he faithfully observed the basic tenets of tonality, without lapsing into the dangerous idiom of total chromaticism. He might have added that he was fond of the ultra-diatonic 'white' piano writing, such as passages without using black keys for pages at a time in his Third Piano Concerto. Prokofiev wrote a salutatory overture for Stalin's sixtieth birthday, but its marching music was too artificially contrived, and Prokofiev did not even get a benevolent nod from the inscrutable 'father of the people'. Perhaps the most determined bid for official recognition was his opera to a patriotic libretto dealing with a heroic Soviet flyer who lost both legs in combat but re-entered the service and led the Soviet Air Force to ultimate victory over Fascism. It was placed in production but damned by the Soviet musical establishment for its alleged dissonant idiom.

Prokofiev died on 5 March 1953, a few hours before Stalin. So overburdened were world communication lines with reports of Stalin's demise that the news of Prokofiev's death was not announced until several days later. Ironically, on the tenth anniversary of the double death, it was Prokofiev who was memorialized in Soviet newspapers and magazines, while the now destalinized dictator was remembered only in his native Caucasus village. Prokofiev's opera was produced again seven years after his death, this time drawing hosannas of praise. The legless Soviet flyer, the hero of the opera, honoured the production by his presence.

In old Russia I had never had a chance to visit the Caucasus, which would have taken several days of travel by slow train from St Petersburg. But in 1962 Soviet planes could negotiate that distance in a few hours. I visited Tbilisi, the capital of Georgia, and gave a talk on modern music at the Conservatory there. It was a most gratifying experience. Taktakishvili, one of the most popular Soviet composers whose piano concerto is performed in Russia almost as frequently as Rachmaninoff's Second Concerto (which it frankly imitates), sat in the front row and studiously took notes of what I had to say. Also in the audience was Balanchivadze, older brother of the famous choreographer Balanchine (who cut down his name when he went abroad). Balanchine had visited Georgia with his ballet troupe a year before me. He intended to give his brother an American car as a present, and was willing to pay the customs fee of 100 per cent in American currency. Balanchivadze, on his part, was ready to pay a similar customs fee in roubles. Balanchivadze recited the rest of the story to me in his melodious Georgian drawl (the lilt of spoken Russian in Georgia as compared to the standard speech of Moscow is analogous to that of the state of Georgia, USA, as compared to that of the North). 'What would I do with an American car?' he asked rhetorically. 'Suppose something happens to the carburetor or some other essential part. It would take months to get it replaced. And where would I keep it?' But Tbilisi was not New York, I said, and he could park his car right in front of his house. 'You mean overnight?' he said in utter astonishment. 'The car would be dismantled, and every detachable piece of metal would be stolen.' 'But this is a socialist country!' I exclaimed. 'You mean to say people would vandalize your property even though they could not use it?' 'Metal, particularly aluminum, is in great demand, and can be easily sold,' he replied. He thereupon proceeded to give me an easy lesson in socialist economy. 'Does it ever happen in the United States,' he asked, 'that a shipment of shoes arrives after a long waiting period, but they would all be left shoes?' I said that it would be most unlikely. 'Well, this is what happened in Tbilisi last year. After several vigorous protests, an order was issued to take the left-foot shoes back to the factory, and have them matched with right-foot shoes. A new shipment finally arrived, but they were all right-foot shoes! Until this day we have not received paired shoes!'

My flight from Tbilisi to Erevan over the snow-covered Caucasian mountain chain was spectacular. Just before landing, an image arose which was magical to behold—a pyramid-shaped mountain resting on a layer of cumulus clouds. I asked the stewardess what mountain it was. She replied casually, 'Ararat'. The sound of the name struck a bell-like chord in my psyche. So this was the fabled mountain where Noah's Ark rested after forty days and nights of rain! The city of Erevan lay at the foot of Mount Ararat, but the mountain itself was across the border in Turkey.

My presentation on modern music in Erevan was the longest of all I ever imposed on my Soviet hosts. I talked non-stop for two hours, and the question period that followed took another hour. At the end of the session, I was asked whether I had any particular wishes to express. 'I have one ardent wish,' I said. 'I wish I could transfer this audience in its entirety to New York City!' I hasten to add that the unexampled alertness of my audience in Erevan was due not to the brilliance of my oratory, but to the insatiable curiosity of my Armenian listeners for anything new.

My next destination was Baku, on the Caspian Sea. I was entertained by local musicians under the auspices of the Union of Composers of Azerbaijan, the Tatar Soviet Republic of which Baku was capital. I had already met one of their composers, Fikret Amirov, during his American visit. In his operas and ballets, Socialist Realism reigns supreme. Revolutionary heroes and heroines emerge victorious over the brutality of implacable foes and the dark treachery of false confederates. Amirov and his family arranged a magnificent banquet for me. His Tatar wife prepared a sumptuous meal, with an individual large bowl of Caspian black caviar served as an *hors d'œuvre*. As we began our dinner, Mrs Amirov mysteriously disappeared. I asked my host where she had gone, for I wanted to compliment her on her splendid culinary expertise. 'Oh, she's having dinner in her quarters,' Amirov explained. I was thus reminded that the subordination of women was still very much in force in this Muslim part of the Soviet Union.

In Baku I met a Tatar professor of English whose speciality was Shakespeare. He insisted on speaking English with me; his idiomatic usage was impeccable, even though he had never been to England, America, or any other English-speaking country. We plunged into a discussion of translating Shakespeare. My favourite example was the line, 'A poor thing but mine own,' from *As You Like It*, which the Russian translator rendered as 'I may be poor, but my mien is cheerful,' obviously mistaking the word 'mine' for the French word of the same spelling. A major mystery in Russian Shakespeare lore was the spontaneous generation of the line, 'I fear for mankind itself,' in the standard Russian translation of *Hamlet*, which appears nowhere in Shakespeare, but which has become one of the most frequently quoted lines in Russian usage. I had a regular intellectual feast discussing such things with the Tatar professor.

During my few days in Baku I visited several Mosques. I admit I was dumbfounded by the spectacle of grown men kneeling and banging their foreheads on the marble floors with an audible thud. A number of worshippers must have been members of the Tatar Communist Party. How could they reconcile their socialist convictions with this barbarous ritual? Or was I a religious bigot? Would I have recoiled from the similarly barbarous kneeling of the Greek Orthodox worshippers familiar to me from my Russian childhood?

I heard a lot of Tatar music in Baku before I returned to Moscow. There I had a chance of seeing Alexander and Lida for the last time, but our visit was darkened by tragedy. Both Alexander and Lida had been incapacited by cerebral haemorrhages. Alexander suffered a stroke during a visit of the editor of the State Publishing House, who came to discuss with him a new edition of his book on Pushkin. Suddenly his right arm dropped by his side, and his right leg dragged helplessly on the floor. At the same time he realized that he could not articulate his speech. He soon regained his ability to speak, but when walking he could only drag his right foot along as a useless appendage. But Lida, poor Lida! She used to be a woman of great energy, active as translator of American literature. The stroke paralysed her right arm and right leg, and permanently deprived her of her power of speech. She could understand everything said to her, but she could respond with only two syllables, 'nyet' and 'pooh'. Her speech retained a musical, rhythmic flow. 'Pooh!' she would exclaim. 'Pooh-pooh-pooh-pooh-*pooh*-pooh?' She tried desperately to communicate. I explained to her that all she was articulating was the same syllable, repeated several times. 'Nyet!' she exclaimed in painful desperation. 'Pooh-pooh!' Seeing that I still could not follow her, she exploded in a roulade of expressive sentences. 'Pooh! Pooh-pooh-pooh? Pooh-pooh-pooh-pooh-pooh? Pooh, *pooh*, *pooh*!' Her interrogative inflection was so expressive that it was almost possible to guess what she wanted to say. She made an effort to learn to write with her functioning left hand. But the stroke had also resulted in her inability to read what she had written.

My next destination was Warsaw. A secretary of the Union of Soviet Composers accompanied me to the airport only to find that my flight had been delayed on account of bad weather. Every hour on the hour a woman announcer notified the passengers in her melodious contralto voice that the weather in Warsaw was still inclement, never mentioning that Moscow, too, was snowbound. The litany of these hourly announcements continued until 6 o'clock in the evening, at which point my guide took me back to my hotel. The same sequence of hours was recited by the announcer the next day—and the next, and yet again on the next. I admired the imperturbability of my guide. He sat on the cold bench in the waiting room at the airport with his eyes focused at the point of infinity, never moving a facial muscle. Maybe Stalin had succeeded after all in his vaunted engineering job on the souls of his people.

On the fourth day, my plane was finally cleared for departure, and in a couple of hours we were in snow-covered Warsaw. Immediately upon landing, I noticed a tall, balding, nervous man in a winter overcoat waving at me. It was my cousin Antoni. I had not seen him since his brief visit to the United States in 1949. He took me to his house on a street poetically named Alley of Roses; in Polish, the genitive plural of roses is pronounced 'rouge', which bothered me for awhile. Antoni spoke Russian with a pronounced Polish accent. He was very much family-orientated, and there was warmth in his affection towards me. It did not take me long to find out that the Poles did not care much for the Russians; the enmity between the two neighbouring Slavic nations traces a red ribbon through history. Nor did they love the Germans. When someone asked a Polish politician where he would like to have Poland relocated on the world map, he replied, 'In Chile'.

Antoni arranged a wonderful party for me, with all kinds of notables present. It so happened that the programme director of the Polish State Radio was a graduate of the University of Zhitomir, my father's native city. He spoke French to me. 'But why do we have to speak French since you graduated from a Russian university?' I asked. 'Je préfère de ne pas parler russe,' he replied curtly. Antoni was in a lively mood after several glasses of Polish wine, and allowed himself quite a few political darts which would have been unthinkable in the much more rigidly policed Union of Soviet Socialist Republics. I pointed at the electric plug in the wall and suggested it might conceal a microphone, whereupon Antoni proceeded to spout political blasphemies at the imaginary listening post. Everybody laughed.

From Poland I went by railroad directly to Vienna, on my way to Yugoslavia. The moment I arrived in Vienna, I rushed to the news stand. *Time, Life,* the Paris edition of the *New York Herald Tribune*! I grabbed them all, without looking at the dates, and spent the rest of the day in my hotel devouring the uncensored news.

I took time off to attend the Vienna Opera, and the National-Bibliothek, where I met the librarian in charge of the music division (who, I was pleased to find, knew my name). I enjoyed the unmatched Vienna pastries and Schlagobers, and then reluctantly took my plane to Belgrade.

Yugoslavia, like Poland, was very modern musically, and I enjoyed meeting local composers whose names had already been dutifully incorporated in the 1958 edition of *Baker's Dictionary*. I gave my usual talks, in Belgrade, Ljubljana, and Zagreb, speaking interchangeably in Russian, German, and French. I could understand and read Serbian in the Cyrillic alphabet and Croatian in the Latin alphabet, but I was baffled by Slovenian; it sounded like some kind of perversely mangled Russian. I did not try to master any of these curiously intermingled Slavic tongues, and was content with partial understanding of their locutions.

From Yugoslavia I went to Greece, which I had not visited since 1949. The flight from Belgrade to Athens was replete with mythological thrills. That mountain covered with snow on the horizon, was it really Mount Olympus? In Athens I was met by a representative of the United States Information Service who introduced me to Greek intellectuals and musicians. The Union of Greek Composers co-operated fully with my task of collecting information for future editions of my dictionary. My talk, which I delivered in English, was well attended.

From Athens I was taken on a fantastic automobile ride through Peloponnesus. We actually passed a railroad station of Sparta! We drove through Laconia, where, contrary to the legend, the inhabitants were not laconic at all, but talked very fast and gesticulated wildly. I tried my rudimentary Greek on the lady tourist guide who was assigned to me by the Greek Ministry of Culture, and, hearing me utter her native nouns and verbs, she decided to switch from English to Greek. My *amour propre* would not let me admit that most of it was Greek to me. Later I was taken to the North and spent an entire day in Delphi. I gasped at the familiar names of towns and regions. Travelling through Greece was like taking a refresher course in history and mythology.

A separate trip took me to Crete. During my few days there a remarkable bronze statue was dragged out of the Aegean Sea and brought ashore. The director of the Museum at Iraklion allowed me to see it before it was cleaned for public exhibition. It represented a *kouros*, a young man, and I marvelled at the perfection if its sculptured detail and the amazing state of preservation of the bronze.

The most remarkable encounter I had in Greece was with Jani Christou, a composer whom I did not hesitate to call a genius in my article on Greek music published in the *Musical Quarterly*. Christou used Greek titles in most of his works but these titles referred to the structure rather than to the ethnic origin of the music itself. He invited me to be his guest at his home on the island of Chios, where his father was a rich plantation owner, but I had no time for this tempting trip. Christou was an impetuous driver, and lost his life tragically on his forty-fourth birthday in an automobile accident near Athens.

In Athens I was literally stopped in my tracks when I saw a streetcar marked 'Platon'. Indeed, its terminal was the presumed site of Plato's Academy. I went to a movie, which bore the sign KINO on the marquee, and watched a newsreel reporting the launching of a Soviet missile to Venus; naturally, the announcer called the planet Aphrodite. I was greatly amused to learn that the modern Greek word for menu was katalog, and that a bill was called logarithm! If I wanted mineral water, I had to ask for metallic hydra. I could not get over the fantastic perversion of the meaning of the word idiot, which in modern Greek means private. The Greek Ministry of Culture generously placed a private car at my disposal, and the chauffeur introduced himself by saying 'Idiota'! It was only natural that the telephone would be telefono (spelled with the Greek letter phi for ph), and that the plural of telegram was telegrammata. An automobile is most appropriately named autokinetikon; the English and French word automobile is a hybrid of Greek and Latin. I wondered whether the name Mussorgsky came from musurgia, which means music-making in both ancient and modern Greek. And polemics is not just a literary exchange; it is war. I spotted a van with the sign 'Metaphor'; it was a furniture mover! And a love affair is 'erotic hypothesis'! I think what amused me most was when a customer in a restaurant, where I was having lunch with the Greek poet George Seferis, who was to win the Nobel Prize later that year, ordered a 'trapeze for two atoms'. I knew, of course, that trapeze came from the Greek word for table, but it took me some time to figure out that the word atom is no more strange to a Greek than the word individual to an Englishman; both mean personal indivisibility.

From Greece I flew to Israel. At my lectures in Tel Aviv and Jerusalem I was introduced as a scion of the illustrious Jewish family of scholars; there was a street in Tel Aviv named after my grandfather. I did not dare confess that I was technically a *goy*, but had to admit that I could not read Hebrew. I knew most of the names of the composers whom I met in Israel. One of them, Odoen Partos, told me he played the violin in the orchestra at my concert in Budapest in 1932.

My next stop was Sofia, capital of Bulgaria. The sight of the familiar streets again evoked memories of long ago when I was a Russian refugee there. I renewed my acquaintance with Pantcho Vladigerov, the leading composer of Bulgaria, who remembered our meeting of forty years before, and greeted me as an old friend. Madame Ambassador Eugenie Anderson, an appointee and friend of President Kennedy, arranged a reception for me in her palatial home along with a number of native artists and other luminaries. Ordinarily they would not have risked to socialize with Americans, but, since I was a guest of the Union of Bulgarian Composers as well as an emissary of the US State Department, they apparently felt it was safe to attend. Madame Ambassador and her husband had a Bulgarian servant, who was also acting as their chauffeur and majordomo. He spoke careful grammatical English; he was tall and his face was expressionless; he cut a perfect figure for a domestic spy, and probably was one. Why was he hired? Madame Ambassador explained to me that his presence was a surrogate for such overt acts as perlustration of correspondence or photographing visitors by hidden cameras.

Mrs Anderson was helpful in supplying me with manufactured goods not readily available in Bulgaria. I ran out of toothpaste, and my attempt to purchase a tube at a pharmacy was unsuccessful. 'This is *the* toothpaste,' the salesgirl told me, emphasizing the definite article (in contrast with the Russian language, Bulgarian does possess a definite article in the form of a demonstrative pronoun, but it is placed on the end of the word, as it is in Rumanian), and offered me a little round cardboard box. It felt like cement and made a loud thud when she put it down on the counter. I told this anecdote to Madame Ambassador, and she said she would send me a tube of Viennese toothpaste. Sure enough, a few hours later, her inscrutable Bulgarian factotum delivered a tube of toothpaste to my hotel.

On to Rumania, a country I had never visited before. Its capital city of Bucharest used to be called the Paris of the Balkans, and indeed the avenues radiating from its centre were landscaped like those of Paris around the Place de l'Étoile. The name of Georges Enesco dominated the Rumanian musical scene, despite the fact that Enesco emigrated to Paris and died there. His native village was renamed after him; biennial Enesco Festivals were established in Bucharest. Several profusely illustrated monographs on him have been published, with parallel texts in Rumanian, Russian, English, German, Italian, and French. I gave a talk on modern music, speaking in French with a careful introduction in Rumanian.

Next stop was Prague. The Czech language is the most difficult to crack on account of the prevalence of consonants: I learned a popular Czech tongue-twister and jaw-breaker, 'Strc prst skrz krk', a nonsense phrase without a single vowel which means 'Put your finger on your throat'. I used this phrase as the supposed title of a choral work by the mythical Czech composer Krsto Zyžík, whom I invented and whose name I was tempted (I ultimately desisted) to include as the last entry in my edition of *Baker's Dictionary*.

Prague, Cologne, Bonn—the ancient cities of my past. Then London, and a flight home to Boston. My fabulous trip was over, leaving me in a sort of linguistic confusion of my native Russian and related Slavic languages, manufactured Greek, ersatz Rumanian, and finally the familiar German and French.

Dorothy met me at the Boston Airport, and soon we were back at 295 Beacon Street. During that summer of 1963 Dorothy and I filled several dual engagements, speaking on modern art and modern music respectively. In August we drove to New Hampshire to watch the scheduled total eclipse of the sun, but clouds hid the sun just at the moment of totality, while the spectacle was observed in full splendour just a few miles away. I was disappointed, but Dorothy took the bad luck philosophically; in fact, she was a little concerned about the possible damage to the retina of the eye in watching the eclipse, a hazard that was trumpeted loudly in the press.

The eclipse that soon enveloped my life could not have been predicted, imagined, or believed. Dorothy, no longer able to carry the burden of her life, had a heart attack. She seemed to recover well after several weeks in the hospital, and was ready to resume her customary gallery trotting. On Thursday, 9 January 1964, we went together to two or three art galleries to gather material for her usual daily articles in the *Christian Science Monitor*. On Friday night she complained of pain in her left arm. If only I had had even the most elementary knowledge of symptoms of heart disease, I would have roused the entire city of Boston for ambulances and intensive care. I asked Dorothy to wake me if she felt any discomfort during the night. On Saturday, 11 January, early in the morning, I awoke with a start. Dorothy, breathing laboriously, was lying on her back with her eyes wide open (unseeing eyes that could penetrate the subtlest shades in a work of art), the palms of her hands contracting and relaxing in a strangely regular rhythm. I jumped out of bed, rushed to the telephone, dialled our doctor's number, and screamed, 'Dorothy is dying!' He ordered a police ambulance, but it arrived too late. I had barely enough strength to call Electra and tell her to take the next flight to Boston.

This was the only time in my life when I did not contemplate my own state of mind. And least of all did I entertain any notion of repeating my pseudo-suicide of 1913. It would have been nothing short of sacrilege to propel my distress in such a way at such a time. I was a wounded animal, and whatever sounds were coming out of my mouth were inarticulate. Dorothy's brother, Judge Elijah Adlow, made arrangements for the burial in the family plot in a suburban cemetery. A place was also reserved for me, next to Dorothy. There was a service at the funeral house; a rabbi read an eulogy. The *Christian Science Monitor* ran an editorial, entitled simply 'Dorothy Adlow'. Electra returned to New York after a few days' stay in Boston, and I was left alone in a meaningless apartment. Strangely enough, I was willing, almost eager, to listen to Dorothy's Christian Science colleagues who were smilingly assuring me of an early reunion with Dorothy. Dorothy's articles continued to appear on the art page of the *Christian Science Monitor*, as she always prepared her copy well in advance. What a contrast with my procrastinating, irresponsible ways! I collected these articles religiously, in duplicate for Dorothy's scrapbook and for Electra. Cheques for these articles also continued to arrive, as if nothing had happened. My problem was to contain the torrents of tears when someone called on the phone, or whenever I met a friend on the street. The owner of an art gallery where Dorothy was a daily visitor wept with me.

The dominating thought of my existence was to get out of Boston, which had become for me the City of Death. By an extraordinary concurrence of events, I received a telephone call from my old friend Roy Harris asking me if I would not accept a teaching position at the University of California in Los Angeles, where he was a member of the faculty. For years I had tried to get a college job, and now it came, but under what circumstances! Los Angeles had a great advantage for me, for no one there, with the exception of a couple of friends, knew what had happened. This anonymity was my only salvation, if salvation could be found.

I have since returned to Boston only once, for a few hours, in April 1965, to attend the presentation of a scroll to the *Christian Science Monitor* honouring Dorothy as an art critic by the American Federation of Arts at its Biennial Convention. A brief excerpt from one of the television programmes that Dorothy did for the Boston Museum of Fine Art was featured. The tribute on the scroll honoured Dorothy's 'sturdy and honest art criticism', which 'brought national renown to her and her paper'. The editor of the *Christian Science Monitor*, in his response to the presentation, praised the 'incomparable, indeed imperishable work of Miss Adlow'.

CHAPTER 22

CALIFORNIA, HERE I COME

America is my home now, and yet its very name still evokes the mystery of my Russian boyhood. My romantically inclined older brother Alexander wrote to me in 1957 when the first Soviet Sputnik was launched into orbit: 'How close America is now! Our Sputnik can make the trip in half an hour. Why can't I board it and pay you a visit?' My nephew Sergei echoed this romantic notion in one of his letters: 'Oh, how I wish I could visit your legendary land!'

Why do I stay in California? My daughter and two grandchildren live in New York. My publishers are in the East. The great advantage of California, and particularly Westwood where I took my residence, is that it contains a pullulation of young secretaries without whom I cannot function as a dictionary-maker. I used to call my secretaries, rather playfully, odalisques, evoking the harem beauties familiarized in so many French paintings. One of them caught me using that word and exclaimed: 'I know what an odalisque is! There is one in Central Park!' And I had trouble with names of composers. One of my odalisques could not pronounce Skriabin, and she insisted on calling him Skarabian. I was so taken by this transcription that I began referring to him as Skarabian with my publisher who was to bring out my translation from Russian of a Skriabin biography. Oh, my wonderful 'obelisks'! I still have warm affection for them, and most have remained my good friends.

My prime business in California was to teach music classes at the University of California in Los Angeles. I am a great believer in educational mnemonics as a tool for memorization, and I devised jingles for students in my music appreciation classes. Here is a sample:

Frescobaldi and Monteverdi
Were Baroque men wise and sturdy.
Monteverdi excelled in vocal art,
Frescobaldi was an organist at heart
And both could play the hurdy-gurdy.

Fine. But I did not reckon with students who thought Monte was the first name of Verdi. Here is another:

> Domenico Scarlatti
> Was sometimes pretty catty.
> His Cat's Fugue in G minor
> Makes kitties sound finer
> Than Adelina Patti.

This limerick at least connects Scarlatti with the Cat's Fugue, but not one of my students knew of Adelina Patti, so half of the fun was lost. Two more limericks:

> Arcangelo Corelli
> Wrote rarely for the celli.
> In his concerti grossi
> The violins were glossy,
> And he taught Locatelli.

Locatelli was thrown in for the rhyme, but only cello players would recognize the name. The following limerick represented my desperate attempt to instil the names of Schütz, Schein, and Scheidt into the minds of my students:

> Schütz, Schein and Scheidt
> Are pillars of Baroque might.
> Schütz shoots polyphonious darts,
> Schein shines in harmonious parts,
> And Scheidt sheds songful sweetness and light.

I hoped that alliteration would help, but it didn't. Misspellings were rampant.

One must not underestimate the educational value of ignorance. Some definitions I read in students' assignments were unintentionally inventive: 'Well-Tempered Clavier included 24 preludes and fugues, because W is the twenty-fourth letter of the alphabet.' Unfortunately, W is the twenty-third letter in both the English and German alphabets, not the twenty-fourth. 'Felix Meddlesom wrote wedding marches for marriages.' 'Fis-dur is a town in Germany.' 'The greatest composers were Opus and Anon.' 'Italian operas are very dramatic as when the hero dies a natural death in ill Trovatore.' Then there was this fascinating definition: 'Musical forms are sonatas, cantatas, and traviatas.'

Humour in class is dangerous. Commenting on nonsensical opera librettos, I mentioned *La Traviata*, in which the heroine, dying of consumption, still has enough lung power left to sing out in a lusty high voice. I got this from one of my students: *La Traviata* is a comic opera because she has TB but keeps singing just the same.'

I got a laugh out of a story about Paderewski attending a party at which a famous polo player was also a guest. The hostess mistook Paderewski for the polo player; he quickly disabused her of the confusion by saying, 'He is a rich soul who plays polo, but I am a poor Pole who plays solo.' In one test paper, it came out: 'Pa de Rusky played polo at parties.'

The following scholium gave me trouble: 'Schubert was born in Poland and died of TB in Paris. He wrote the Unfinished Symphony sometimes known as Finlandia.' A confusion between Chopin and Schubert was understandable—both names begin with a sibilant. But why was the Unfinished Symphony also known as Finlandia? 'You talked a lot about Finnish music,' was the explanation, 'and I was not sure whether it was Finnish or unfinished, so I put both of them in.'

To help my students learn the spelling of the name Schubert, I cautioned them not to confuse him with Shubert, the owner of the theatre chain whose name did not have a 'c' between 's' and 'h'. My mnemonic device boomeranged when two students wrote in their exams that Schubert (correctly spelled) wrote songs and also managed a chain of movie theatres. But what nearly drove me nuts was the repeated failure on the part of several of my students to spell Schoenberg correctly, even though our classes were held in Schoenberg Hall!

My students always welcomed my piano playing, which provided them with needed moments of relaxation. I won hearty applause for my rendition of Liszt's *Liebestraum*, even though I muffled the cadenzas. Their enjoyment of the piece, however, did not prevent one of them from identifying *Liebestraum* as 'the name of a German composer'. Another test question elicited the definition that 'Lieder are leading German composers'. Alliteration's artful aid!

Among my all-time favourites are the following: 'Modest Moorsky wrote the opera Boris, good enough.' 'Boris Godunov was a modern composer who wrote the opera *Faust*.' '*Three Places in New England* by Charles Ives are New Haven, New Hampshire, and New Jersey.' 'A piano quintet is a piece for five pianos.' '*The Planets* is a work by Shosty Kovich.' 'Ein' feste Burg (A Gay Mountain) is by Martin Luther King.' 'The crab movement was an early art movement.' 'The Mannheim School was noted for the use of crescendos and innuendos.' 'The original name of the piano was pianissimo.' 'Arpeggio is slower than Andante.' 'The real name of the Moonlight Sonata is Beethoven's Ninth.' 'The Eroica Symphony is called erotica because it is all about love.' 'Sibelius was a national composer. He was Polish through and through.'

I lasted as a 'lecturer on music' at UCLA for two seasons, at which time the powers that be discovered that I had passed the biblical age of three score and ten. The dean and chairman of the music department sent letters to the vice-president asking that exception be made in my case, contending that I was not a superannuated, decrepit, dilapidated, and otherwise obsolete person, but rather possessed such a reservoir of vital energy that my students showed signs of mental fatigue long before I began to falter in class. Indeed, the 1967 publication of UCLA's Associated Students evaluated my services in the most flattering terms: 'He is a terrific piano player and a character who puts on quite a show during almost every lecture.' But rules are rules, and I joined the ranks of the unemployed. Happily, there is no age limit in compiling dictionaries, composing music, or giving guest lectures, and in these capacities I could be employed to the gills. In fact, my standard reply to solicitous inquiries on the part of people who wish to engage me for a lecture and who wonder whether I can talk for a whole hour is, 'No, I cannot talk for an hour—but I can talk for two!' Meanwhile I staged an unexpected resurrection when appointed Regents' Lecturer at UCLA in the academic year 1985–1986, for a fat fee. I simply refuse to act my age.

The memorial gallery of composers, famous and infamous, whom I knew well is vast and perturbing. I became a wailing wall for many of them; my left shoulder was irrigated, figuratively speaking, with their tears, and saturated with the salt, and sometimes sulphur, of their indignation against an unfeeling world.

Who knows the name of Joseph Wagner? Stubbornly, perseveringly he wrote symphonies, oratorios, chamber music, and organ pieces. On his desk was a card file of rejection slips from conductors in alphabetical order, from Abravanel to Zipper. He was grateful for every word of encouragement. When I said, quite sincerely, that one of his passages for trumpet solo with harp accompaniment was a fine inspiration, he brightened and said, 'Believe me, I saw angels in the sky when I wrote this!' Poor Joe! He was found dead in front of his television set, a victim of a burst aneurism.

John Vincent became one of my closest friends. He would come to see me in Los Angeles regularly on Tuesdays, Thursdays, and Saturdays, sit in my rocking chair, and recite tales of misfortune. 'If my music is so bad that nobody wants to play it, then let it perish!' he would say with melodramatic emphasis.

Yet Vincent had known days of grandeur. He had been chairman of the music department at UCLA, and told me with unconcealed pride that Otto Klemperer came to see him about the possibility of a faculty position. He freely dropped 'first' names of celebrated musicians—it was always Jascha for Heifetz and Grisha for Piatigorsky. He had been on the board of the Hollywood Bowl and had the power to engage guest conductors and soloists. His own symphonies had been performed and recorded. Stravinsky himself had accepted invitations to dinner at his house.

Then, inexorably, his exalted positions fell off. Years passed without a single performance, and his recorded orchestral works all but disappeared from the catalogue. In an effort to recapture his place in society, Vincent conceived an ambitious plan. He approached Stravinsky's major-domo, Robert Craft, expressing dismay at the scant social recognition by Los Angeles society of the great Igor. To amend this injustice, he told Craft, he proposed to arrange a banquet in Stravinsky's honour. He would not have to perform or speak, but only lend his illustrious presence to the occasion.

Stravinsky agreed to Vincent's plan. As the time grew nearer, Vincent put in a telephone call to Stravinsky. Exuberantly, he outlined the attractions of the forthcoming affair, the eager anticipation of the guests, and the significance of such an occasion for the people of Los Angeles, when Stravinsky rudely interrupted his effusions and said abruptly he had changed his mind and decided to cancel the whole affair. 'But you promised!' Vincent protested. 'I do not want it,' Stravinsky said with finality. How Vincent felt can easily be imagined. 'Mr Stravinsky,' he said, 'I admire you as a great composer, but I must say that I cannot have any respect for you as a person of integrity. You deceived the expectations of hundreds of people whose sole desire was to render you homage . . .' Stravinsky, unaccustomed to being addressed in such a manner, blurted out a few words of displeasure and hung up. Vincent brooded for months over this rebuke. He died in January 1977, of respiratory failure and cardiac arrest. His music died with him.

Gardner Read, an American composer who worked hard securing performances, came to see me during my Boston days, carrying a score in his briefcase. 'Nicolas,' he said quietly, 'I have just finished my Fourth Symphony. Can you tell me why?' This rhetorical question epitomized the hopeless frustration of many American composers.

Ernst Toch enjoyed great renown as a composer at the time between the two World Wars, and his works were regularly performed at international music festivals. But he could not sustain a similar position in his American emigration. 'I am the forgotten composer of the century,' he complained to me with undisguised bitterness.

Roy Harris was certainly well known as a composer, but his expectations of universal recognition were too high to be satisfied. Once, upon his return from a session with Koussevitzky, he was visibly eager to report the apparently flattering words that were lavished upon him. 'You know what Koussevitzky said to me?' he asked me rhetorically. 'Yes,' I answered, 'the same that he said to Tansman, Dukelsky, and Philip Lazar.' He looked at me for a moment and said, 'Okay, you win.'

After Koussevitzky's death in 1951, Roy Harris had to shop around for conductors. Ormandy promised to put Harris's Seventh Symphony on his programme with the Philadelphia Orchestra, but later changed his mind. He telephoned Harris and said that his programme coincided with the ninetieth birthday of Sibelius, and that Harris's work would positively slaughter the weaker music of Sibelius. 'We could not do that to the old man!' Ormandy said. Roy Harris readily agreed. It is difficult to judge who was the greater hypocrite in this exchange, Ormandy, who invented this ridiculous excuse to rid himself of Harris, or Harris, who pretended to accept Ormandy's outrageous dissimulation at face value.

Rafael Kubelik became sufficiently interested in the music of Harris to place his Ninth Symphony on the programme of the Bavarian Radio Orchestra which he directed. Harris was greatly flattered, and wrote a special appreciation of Kubelik's greatness in a promotional brochure; in it he said, among other things, that Kubelik was born in the capital of Yugoslavia, Prague. I told Harris that Prague was in Czechoslovakia, not Yugoslavia. 'The same thing,' Harris replied. His notions of geography were peculiar. When he returned from a tour of Russia in 1959, he exalted over the beauty of the Ural Mountains in Georgia, and was annoyed when I told him that it was Caucasus, not Ural. 'I just came from over there,' he argued, 'and everybody told me I was in the Urals!'

My choicest anecdote about Roy Harris came from Virgil Thomson. They had lunch together, and Harris was in a pensive mood. 'I am 50 years old,' he said, 'and I don't think I will make it.' 'Make what?' Thomson asked. Harris looked at him and said, 'Beethoven!' Harris was furious when I reported this story to him. He denounced it as a total fabrication, with a flurry of floral epithets related to Thomson's life-style. Then he added, 'Anyway, why should I have said Beethoven? After all, there is nothing in Beethoven's melody, harmony, or counterpoint that is superior to mine. Had I said Bach, it would at least have made sense.'

When I met Harris, he was married to a Scottish girl named Hilde. She was an art student, and copied his scores even though she could not read music. Then he met a lively young Canadian pianist by the name of Beulah Duffy. He became desperately enamoured of her, and told Hilde he wanted a divorce. 'Do you think I'm a son-of-a-bitch?' he asked me. 'You are,' I replied. He married Beulah Duffy, and changed her name to Johana. Why Johana? In reverence to J. S. Bach, the only composer whom Harris regarded as superior to himself. Harris was an amateur numerologist; his vital number was 5. He drove miles with his fiancée to find a place in which to marry that had 5 letters, and chose Union, Oregon. To make the name of his bride divisible by 5, in alphabetical sequence, he dropped the second n in Johana. He wrote a few piano pieces. Johana, with her unique pianistic talent, ingeniously enhanced them. Roy Harris died in 1979. Three years later Johana married her young piano student, John Heggie. She was 70, he was 21. 'He makes me glow,' she told me.

I met quite a number of composers who were frankly flaky, or furfuraceous, to use a more elegant term. Flaky composers spawn in California, and, being myself a California transplant, I had no trouble to infiltrate their company. I also contributed some pieces to their magazine of musical nonsense called *Source*. One of my flaky friends, Ken Friedman, puzzled me when he said he was writing an oratorio dedicated to László Toth. 'Who the hell is László Toth?' I asked. Friedman gave me a look of incredulity. 'Why, László Toth,' he said, 'is the artist who resculptured the Pietà!' Indeed, Toth was the name of the demented Hungarian who hacked Michelangelo's masterpiece. When Friedman told me that the finale of his Third Symphony was the Los Angeles earthquake of 1971, I became interested in his orchestration. 'You do not understand,' he said, with undisguised disdain. 'The earthquake *was* the finale of my work!'

Charles Amirkhanian is the inventor of a new musical form which he calls 'text-sound'. In one of these works he 'canonized' me, in a manner of speaking, by making a canon out of a fragment from one of my lectures in San Francisco; in the recording I sound like a demented dervish, whirling around verbally and periodically returning to the original vocable. The result is imbecilic, but for that very reason the record achieved a certain currency in the musical underground and was even reviewed in *The New York Times*.

Much more embarrassing was a recording Amirkhanian surreptitiously made of my rather loose dinner talk at the home of Mrs George Antheil, widow of the composer. I was in a talkative mood (my normal state), saying outrageous things about mutual friends and acquaintances, with a generous admixture of assorted sexual gossip. I was horrified to learn that Amirkhanian aired the tape over his Berkeley radio station KPFA, under the beguiling title, 'Nicolas Slonimsky Eats Dinner'. It traversed several courses, from soup to nuts, punctuated by my uninhibited comments. I was told the programme was repeated by popular demand, but I never dared to tune in.

The Grand Vizier of all California composers is undoubtedly John Cage. Can it be that John Cage is really 75 years old? Not so long ago he was an object of derision, but has since attained the status of a guru. The fifteenth edition of the *Encyclopaedia Britannica* describes him as a 'composer whose work and revolutionary ideas profoundly influenced midtwentieth-century music'. *Pravda* has offered an ingenious theory for the rise of John Cage: His music demoralizes the listeners by its neurotic drive, and by doing so depresses the proletarian urge to rise *en masse* against capitalism and imperialism. It is for this reason that Wall Street supports Cage financially. When I reported this bit of sociological analysis to Cowell, who was one of Cage's mentors, he remarked in his well-modulated Irish voice, 'This is strange. If John is financed by Wall Street, why did he borrow three dollars from me last night?'

I enjoyed my sporadic encounters with La Monte Young. When I was in New York, he invited me to dinner, warning me that the hour might be unusual since his biological time did not coincide with the diurnal rotation of the earth, his normal circadian period being twenty-five hours. I observed aloud that Russian astronomers estimated the period of rotation of the planet Venus around its axis as twenty-five hours (I spoke without authority, as it seemed to me the axial rotation of Venus was much longer). A pregnant pause ensued. 'Tell me more,' he said.

Musical women leave nothing to be desired in the wilderness of their imagination. My favourite avant-garde composeress is Annea Lockwood, born in New Zealand and educated in England where she gave lectures on anti-music at an anti-university. In the Bakuninian belief that the art of destruction is as creative as that of construction, she devoted her energies to destroying pianos. She once drowned a piano in a private lake owned by a Texas millionaire. Her example inspired a group of enthusiasts, who dropped an upright piano to destruction from a rented helicopter.

To test her theory that composers advance in their idiom after death, Annea Lockwood summoned Beethoven's spirit at a séance. He played for her his posthumous Piano sonata No. 33, composed c. 1890, which amazed her by its modernity. She recorded it on tape, but, when I asked to hear it, she demurred, explaining that she had given her word to Beethoven not to play it for anyone else.

Progressing parallel with my new Californian identity was a renewed acquaintance with modern Russia in the course of several visits at the invitation of the Union of Soviet Composers. It seem that, unbenownst to myself, I have become a *persona grata* in the Soviet Union. I was proclaimed a 'Friend of Soviet Music'. During one visit I was interviewed in the sleek Moscow monthly *Fatherland* (the title was significant, for the journal was dedicated to the proposition that once a Russian always a Russian, and was directed at former *émigrés* who left physical Russia but kept spiritual Russia in their souls). I was even paid 40 roubles for that interview, something that does not happen in any other country. My late lamented friend Grigori Schneerson wrote a long article on my South American book of 1945, and an even longer article about the 1971 edition of *Music Since 1900*. And I was given the honour of delivering an oration before the opening of the Soviet Music Festival in 1979 in the Hall of

Columns in Moscow, the first non-Russian citizen to be invited to do so. I was astounded when the speaker at the occasion mentioned the fact that I had contributed 114 biographies of Soviet composers to *The International Cyclopaedia of Music and Musicians*. They had actually counted those entries!

During these visits I have established a friendly rapport with Soviet composers, and continued a truly affectionate relationship with my nephew Sergei. I have enjoyed watching his progress as a Soviet composer. By 1985 he had eight symphonies to offer, and free access to conductors. He reported to me that, after the completion of his Fourth Symphony, he called up a top Soviet conductor asking for a meeting. 'Are you free for lunch tomorrow?' the conductor asked. 'If you are, then bring your score along.' The Symphony was accepted on the spot, performed, printed, and recorded. When I told this story in the company of American composers in New York, one of them asked with an air of incredulity, 'You mean a Russian composer can call up a conductor just like that, go to lunch with him, and sell his symphony right there and then? I'm going to emigrate to Moscow!' And it wasn't just symphonies that Sergei was composing in such rapid succession, but also concertos and even operas. For one of his recent operas he selected the subject of Mary Stuart. Imagine a Soviet composer writing an opera about a Catholic queen! It was produced almost immediately upon the acceptance of the score by the Union of Soviet Composers, which is the governing body regarding Soviet performances. He was paid 10,000 roubles as a fee for composing the opera, and 500 roubles for each performance. It received its preview in the small city of Kuibishev on the Volga River (the city was renamed from Samara to honour a Bolshevik hero); it was then produced in Leningrad (where I first saw it). An additional, and perhaps unique honour, was the production in 1986 of *Mary Stuart* in Edinburgh, capital of the unfortunate Queen's domain.

What is remarkable in the extraordinary efflorescence of Soviet music is the total acceptance of modern techniques of composition. Sergei's opera includes a variety of contemporary devices, with a total emancipation of dissonances. Even more involved is Sergei's string quartet entitled *Antiphones*, which opens by placing the players in different parts of the auditorium, and assembling them on the stage for the exposition. The score itself looks bewildering to a classically educated musician. It includes fractional tones, non-tempered scales, percussive effects on the instruments' bodies, playing below the bridge, and aleatory passages. Sergei uses graphic notation, similar to that employed by Western modernists.

Sergei belongs to a brilliant pleiade of Soviet composers of his generation, born in the 1920s and 1930s, whose music exemplifies the spirit of liberation reigning in Soviet culture. The names of Alfred Schnittke, Edison Denisov (who received his first name in honour of Thomas Edison), and Sophia Gubaidulina stand high in the ranks of world composers. They make use of all the resources of the medium, including such formerly unacceptable effects as tone clusters.

A new term, Sonorism, was generated in Soviet musicology to describe a sound for sound's sake, implying the inclusion of electronic music. The Soviet attitude towards American and European extremists has also changed in the direction of liberalism. I was astonished to find what interest exists in Russia for such experimentalists as John Cage. My nephew was enchanted with a photograph I gave him of myself, wearing a very serious mien, next to John Cage, laughing uproariously at whatever I apparently had to say. He said, jokingly of course, that he could sell this picture for 100 roubles.

Among American composers who are fully recognized by the Soviet establishment is Charles Ives. An extensive monograph on his music was published in Russian in Leningrad, and the first printing of 10,000 copies was sold within a matter of weeks. A weighty volume on the operas of Alban Berg has also been published. But Schoenberg and Anton von Webern are still handled with caution. A recent book on the Second Viennese School, containing detailed analyses of works by Schoenberg, Berg, and Webern, was published with a prefatory warning by the Soviet editors that, although these creators of a new idiom were honest anti-Fascists and liberals, they exercised a deadly influence on the art. A similar disclaimer is made in Russia towards the late period of Stravinsky's works, but they are beginning to be published in Soviet editions. Thematic dodecaphony is frequently used by contemporary Soviet composers, although total serialism is rarely practised. Even Shostakovich made use of melodies comprising twelve different notes, but he never developed them in the classical Schoenbergian manner. Khrushchev, as Chairman of the Communist Party of the Soviet Union, delivered himself of an alliterative joke when he said, 'They call it dodecaphony, but to us it's plain cacophony.' Dodecaphony and cacophony rhyme in Russian.

CHAPTER 23

THE AGE OF ABSURDITY

One late Saturday evening in the spring of 1981, I received a telephone call. 'Nicolas Slonimsky?' (correctly pronounced) the caller inquired. 'This is Frank Zappa. I never realized you were in Los Angeles, and I want so much to get in touch with you about your book of scales.' I was startled. Frank Zappa was the last person who, to my mind, could be interested in my theoretico-musical inventions. His name was familiar to me from a promotional record jacket showing him seated on the john with his denuded left thigh in view, and a legend in large letters: PHI KRAPPA ZAPPA.

We arranged to meet on the following Monday at 2.30 in the afternoon, and, at the appointed time on the appointed day, his assistant knocked at my door. I stepped out of my apartment and beheld something that looked like a space shuttle—a black Mercedes taking up almost half a block of Wilshire Boulevard. I could not refrain from asking the driver how much such a machine cost. 'Sixty,' he replied.

It took us nearly an hour to get to Zappa's place in the hills of Hollywood. Zappa met me at the door. He looked like a leading man in the movies—tall, slender, sporting a slight Italian moustache. For starters, I asked him the origin of his last name; he replied it meant 'the plough' in Italian.

Zappa's wife came in, an ample, young woman, and served coffee and tea. Zappa told me he did not drink alcoholic beverages; contrary to the legendary habits of most rock-and-roll musicians, he never partook of drugs. But he smoked cigarettes incessantly, tobacco being his only, and quite venial, sin. Zappa led me to his studio, which housed a huge Bösendorfer piano. I asked him how much he paid for this keyboard monster. 'Seventy,' he replied.

Zappa declared himself an admirer of Varèse and said he had been composing orchestral works according to Varèse's principles of composition, with unrelated themes following in free succession. To substantiate this claim, he brought out three scores, in manuscript and each measuring 13 x 20 inches, beautifully copied and handsomely bound. Indeed, the configurations of notes and contrapuntal combinations looked remarkably Varèsian. Yet he never went to a music school, and had learned the technique of composition from the study of actual editions. He had had a contract with an orchestra in Holland to play one of his works, but they had demanded a piece from his recording royalties on top of the regular fee. 'I offered them a quarter,' Zappa said, 'if they would put up a quarter.' It took me some time to figure out that the fractions he used were those in millions of dollars.

Zappa's teenage daughter flitted in, introduced by Mrs Zappa as Moon Unit. She did not seem to be embarrassed by this esoteric appellation. A year or two later she became a celebrity in her own right by making a record with her father's band in which she carried on a telephone conversation in a California language known as Valley Girl Talk. The Valley in question was the San Fernando, nestled north of Los Angeles and populated by a gaggle of young boys and girls, but mostly girls, who seemed to exude a special *joie de vivre*. Most of their lingo was incomprehensible to common terrestials. Everything they liked was not just 'great', but 'tubular' (a term derived from surfing), and something extra good was 'mega' or 'awesome' . They would say 'fer sher' when signifying assent, and express their aversion with such locutions as 'gag me with a spoon', 'I mean, like, *totally*,' and 'gross me out!' About that time, I acquired a cat, black and white and plenty mischievous, which I christened Grody to the Max, i.e. Gross to the Maximum.

Zappa invited me to try out his Bösendorfer. I sat down at the keyboard and played the coronation scene from *Boris Godunov* which required deep bass sounds. Zappa was impressed by these Russian harmonies. He asked me to play some of my own compositions, and I launched into the last piece in my *Minitudes*, based on an interplay of mutually exclusive triads and covering the entire piano keyboard. 'Why don't you play this piece at my next concert?' Zappa asked. 'When will that be?' I inquired. 'Tomorrow. We can rehearse in the afternoon.' I was somewhat taken aback at the sudden offer, but after all, I had nothing to lose. So I decided to take my chance as a soloist at a rock concert.

The next day I arrived at the large Coliseum in Santa Monica where Zappa's concert was to take place. A huge, towering man led me to Zappa's room. 'Mr Zappa is expecting you,' he said, satisfied with my identity. He was Zappa's bodyguard, hired after Zappa had been attacked during a concert by a besotted admirer and hurt his back.

On the stage I sat at the electric piano and played my piece. For better effect, I added sixteen bars to the coda, ending in repeated alternation of C major and F-sharp major chords in the highest treble and lowest bass registers. Zappa dictated to his players the principal tonalities of my piece, and they picked up the modulations with extraordinary assurance. I had never played the electric piano before, but I adjusted to it without much trouble.

The hall began to fill rapidly. Zappa's bodyguard gave me ear plugs, for, when Zappa's band went into action, the decibels were extremely high. Zappa sang and danced while conducting, with a professional verve that astounded me. A soprano soloist came out and sang a ballad about being a hooker, using a variety of obscenities. Then came my turn. Balancing a cigarette between his lips, Zappa introduced me to the audience as 'our national treasure'. I pulled out the ear plugs, and sat down at the electric piano. With demoniac energy Zappa launched us into my piece. To my surprise I sensed a growing consanguinity with my youthful audience as I played. My fortissimo ending brought out screams and whistles the like of which I had never imagined possible. Dancing Zappa, wild audience, and befuddled me—I felt like an intruder in a mad scene from *Alice in Wonderland*. I had entered my Age of Absurdity.

The popular saying is that there are three ages of man: Youth, Middle Age and You Look Wonderful. I graduated to the third age long ago, but when I tried to buy a senior citizen's film ticket at a reduced price, the cashier asked me for my ID. I was so flattered, I paid the full price.

My wisecracks often fall flat. I met a middle-aged lady at a social gathering, and she asked me solicitously how I was doing. 'Okay,' I answered nonchalantly, 'except for my chronic progeria.' I expected to floor her with the word, but she remarked quietly that I did not look twelve or thirteen. Turned out she was one of the most eminent specialists on premature ageing, and the author of a book on progeria. I was properly squashed.

What are the most expressive adverbial locutions to signify the gradual encroachment of the Third Age of Man? Coaxingly, beguilingly, on velvet tiptoes. Differentially. Logarithmically maybe (for while ordinal numbers increase from one to ten, their decimal logarithms advance only from zero to one). Well, with me the numerical figures of the passing years register in geographical movements (half a globe across in three and a half years, between 1920 and 1923), in emotional family experience, in work done, or rather in work to have been done, or even work undone. But—and here is a base of my incredulity: when I am being observed from a distance in time, my record of promises unkept and intentions unfulfilled is relativistically contracted so that the gaping rifts between tangible accomplishments disappear or are absorbed by the visible solid matters. Consider, for instance, the reference to me as 'that amazing dynamo' in a library journal commenting on the seventh edition of *Baker's Dictionary* under my editorship, published in 1984. But from my observation point that dynamo creaks with jarring noise.

I always regarded my besetting trouble to be the seventh deadly sin, Pigritude–no etymological links with pigs, but a nice archaic word from Latin *pigritia*, meaning sloth. As a schoolboy I secretly drew a chart of my future studies in all branches of knowledge, much in the manner of Renaissance scholars who could become omniscient simply because there was not much to be scient about except Aristotelian logic and barnyard animal observation. My chart tabulated a mastery of world languages, including oriental ones, the total knowledge of history, the profound understanding of all philosophical disciplines, particularly German philosophies, religion, biology, astronomy, chemistry, mathematics, medicine, music, and art. I allowed myself sixty years to become a modern Pico della Mirandola, a Florentine scholiast who attempted to create a synthesis of all arts and sciences. I put my own demise in the year 1967 which was as remote as I could optimistically conjecture in my school days seventy-five years ago.

To say that I have failed dismally in these aspirations would be an understatement. My lament is not that I turned out to be a failed wunderkind; far more important is to know whether acquisition of universal knowledge as programmed in my adolescent plan would have made me happier or contributed anything of value to the general font of human understanding. I could not even accomplish adequate knowledge of my favourite subject, mathematics. In place of solid scientific discipline, I concentrated on nonsensical tricks to impress people. I memorized logarithms of prime numbers to the base 10, from which I could interpolate logs up to 3 or 4 decimal numbers. (I remember these primary logs to this day: log 2 is 0.30103; log 3 is 0.47712; log 4 is 2 log 2; log 9 is 2 log 3, etc.; log 1024, which is 2 to the power of 10, equals 10 log 2.) Even in music, I was attracted by the comical aspects of theory. I read medieval Latin treatises which explained the nature of consonances and dissonances, metres and rhythms in theological terms. Why is the octave the most perfect concord? Because Abraham was circumcised on the eighth (octavo in ablative case) day! Why is ternary metre called perfect in medieval lore? Because of the Trinity, of course!

One of my favourite feats was to name the precise distance between the finger on the violin string and the bridge, even blindfolded, for any note played. Suppose a violinist plays G-sharp on the E string. The interval from the open string would be a major third, and its proportion in frequency of vibrations is 5/4. In order to produce such a sound the finger would have to be placed at $\frac{1}{5}$ of the string's length, leaving 4/5 to vibrate. The length of the violin string is $13\frac{1}{2}$ inches. The vibrating portion of the string between the finger and the bridge must then be $\frac{4}{5}$ of $13\frac{1}{2}$ inches, i.e. $10\frac{4}{5}$ inches. Bring in your tape measure! Want to try again? Play high G on the G string. Elementary. The distance from either the peg or the bridge would obviously be half the length of the string. To enhance the impression of a miracle I let the player play his note behind a closed door. (Not for nothing do I possess perfect pitch!) Did I memorize all those fractional numbers? Unlikely. Could I do the same trick on the viola or cello? Sure. The only thing I have to know is the length of the string on each of these instruments. But even when I explained the nature of the trick to a concert violinist he still could not believe that any person alive could multiply or divide fractional numbers in his head so quickly; he was convinced there was some mysterious system of signals in my arithmetic. And, of course, I can instantly name the day of the week for any date of the last two centuries.

As fate would have it, I have actually overtaken, for better or worse, my passive learning that I outlined so long ago. Could I ever have imagined that I would acquire a mastery (well, at least easy fluency) of English, a language totally strange to me then, and that I would write my reminiscences in that unknown language? I never entertained the hope of being a composer, yet I have become one, and earned a place in a book of American composers. I never envisioned publishing hefty volumes of musical lexicography. I could never have foreseen the audacious proposal to add new scales and chords to the existing vocabulary of music, let alone that my publications of such newfangled melodic and harmonic patterns would be used by composers of popular music. But this, too, has come to pass. In school I dreamed of inventing a word. A brief quarter of a century later I did just that; my word, a polysyllabic one (of course), 'Pandiatonicism', is found in music dictionaries. In the field of performing arts, I accomplished the unthinkable: I became a symphonic conductor! I waved by baton over the full contingent of the great Berlin Philharmonic! Can it be that I have actually accomplished more than I dreamed of in my school days? No, I have remained a procrastinating perpetrator of the seventh deadly sin, the despicable sin of Pigritude!

On my ninetieth birthday, 27 April 1984, Hans Stuckenschmidt, the eminent German musicologist, published in his paper *Frankfurter Allgemeine Zeitung*, an article entitled 'Der Unermüdliche'. The Indefatigable One of the piece was I. The lost hours, the lost days, the lost weeks, the lost months, the lost years, the lost chunks of the century somehow closed in to form a continuous continent of accomplishment as seen by a German writer. The more I assert my pigritude, the less I am believed, so that in the end I have to go easy on my self-deprecation, lest it be judged as a pose, an invitation to contradict my thesis by heaps of praise.

Let me summarize my ambitions, my accomplishments, and my failures, according to subject and chronology:

Ambition No. 1: To be a wunderkind of the piano and outshine all other wunderkinder anywhere in the world. Abandoned at puberty, when I discovered that my octave passages lacked bravura.

Ambition No. 2: To be a composer. Pursued off and on, with painful peristaltic effort. The inspirational sphincter of my musical imagination was so constricted, however, that I could produce only miniatures. I was fortunate, however, to have practically all my creations, mostly written for piano solo, published and performed.

Ambition No. 3 (the saddest of all): To be a great orchestral conductor. My short-lived career came to a jarring halt in the cavernous expanses of the Hollywood Bowl, where I put audiences to flight by a cannonade of modern dissonances. In vain did I circulate elegantly printed publicity brochures in which my charisma was attested by critics in several languages. 'Mr Slonimsky won a sensational success. He might justly be called a phenomenal conductor,' was the opening sentence of the report from Berlin in the *Christian Science Monitor*. 'Slonimsky's concerts excited the musical world of Paris,' reported Boris de Schloezer in *Les Dernières Nouvelles*. 'Non seulement il a le don du chef d'orchestre mais il possède une finesse d'oreille que pourraient lui envier les as consacrés de la baguette en Europe,' said André Cœuroy. 'Músico de gran cultura, profunda musicalidad, magnetismo personal y entusiasmo ilimitado' wrote a Cuban critic. I recited to myself from the ringing praise in the lowly Hollywood paper, the *Citizen News*: 'Such poetry of motion, such suavity, such passion! What a spectacle!' So what happened? What happened? And, for the umpteenth time, I whisper Alfred Einstein's extraordinary judgement, 'Das ist ein Talent ersten Ranges . . .'

Ambition No. 4: To excel in musical lexicography. Actually, I blundered into it by accident. If there was any passion in it at all, it was rooted in my infantile lust to prove that I was the smartest of them all. I almost succeeded. I have been touted as '. . . quite simply the world's foremost musical lexicographer'.

Now I have reached the Age of Absurdity. I refuse to believe I am 93. Have I really outlived Tolstoy and Goethe? I don't even have a white beard or bushy eyebrows to attest my age. My eyes still see, my ears still ring with sounds, and my jaws (yes, especially my jaws) are still sufficiently lubricated on their maxillary supports to sustain a steady flow of garrulity. My arms gesticulate in rhythm with my speech, my nether limbs are ambulatory, and I can still run (well, walk) a 40-minute mile. At my latest check-up, the doctor suddenly pinched my forearm. 'Your anabolic reflex is remarkable,' he said. An average nonagenerian's skin, when pinched, stays up like a piece of cured leather for minutes. Mine doesn't. I was so amused by this bit of personal biology that I appended the title '*Anabolism*' to one of the numbers in my piano album, *51 Minitudes*.

To exorcise the ghostly digits of my age, I have now adopted a personal countdown, modulo 100. I am now 7. Next year, *diabolo volente*, I will be 6. In 1994 I will be zero. On this hopeful note, I conclude my rueful autopsy.

LOS ANGELES,
SEPTEMBER 1987

INDEX